A CHRISTIAN VIEW OF ISLAM

FAITH MEETS FAITH

An Orbis Series in Interreligious Dialogue
William R. Burrows, General Editor
Editorial Advisors
John Berthrong
Diana Eck
Karl-Josef Kuschel
Lamin Sanneh
George E. Tinker
Felix Wilfred

In the contemporary world, the many religions and spiritualities stand in need of greater communication and cooperation. More than ever before, they must speak to, learn from, and work with each other in order to maintain their vital identities and to contribute to fashioning a better world.

The FAITH MEETS FAITH Series seeks to promote interreligious dialogue by providing an open forum for exchange among followers of different religious paths. While the Series wants to encourage creative and bold responses to questions arising from contemporary appreciations of religious plurality, it also recognizes the multiplicity of basic perspectives concerning the methods and content of interreligious dialogue.

Although rooted in a Christian theological perspective, the Series does not limit itself to endorsing any single school of thought or approach. By making available to both the scholarly community and the general public works that represent a variety of religious and methodological viewpoints, FAITH MEETS FAITH seeks to foster an encounter among followers of the religions of the world on matters of common concern.

FAITH MEETS FAITH SERIES

A CHRISTIAN VIEW OF ISLAM

Essays on Dialogue
by Thomas F. Michel, S.J.

Edited by

Irfan A. Omar

ORBIS BOOKS

Maryknoll, New York 10545

Founded in 1970, Orbis Books endeavors to publish works that enlighten the mind, nourish the spirit, and challenge the conscience. The publishing arm of the Maryknoll Fathers and Brothers, Orbis seeks to explore the global dimensions of the Christian faith and mission, to invite dialogue with diverse cultures and religious traditions, and to serve the cause of reconciliation and peace. The books published reflect the views of their authors and do not represent the official position of the Maryknoll Society. To learn more about Maryknoll and Orbis Books, please visit our website at www.maryknollsociety.org.

Manufactured in the United States of America.

Library of Congress Cataloging-in-Publication Data

Michel, Thomas F., 1941-
    A Christian view of Islam : essays on dialogue by Thomas F. Michel / edited by Irfan A. Omar.
        p. cm. — (Faith meets faith series)
    Includes bibliographical references and index.
    ISBN 978-1-57075-860-7 (pbk.)
    1. Islam—Relations—Christianity. 2. Christianity and other religions—Islam.
I. Omar, Irfan A. II. Title.
    BP172.M493 2010
    261.2'7—dc22
                                2009048759

To all who engage the Other in dialogue
with *humility* and *sincerity*—
with or without the label of "interfaith dialogue"

Contents

Foreword

JOHN L. ESPOSITO

Christians and Muslims constitute the two largest religions in the world, making up one half of its population. They are the two fastest growing religions. Despite significant differences, they also have much in common, a reservoir of shared beliefs, concerns, and interests. Muslim-Christian relations, past and present, have too often been marked by mutual ignorance and conflict. Religious triumphalism and emphasis on the "other" as a threat have too often obscured recognition of shared beliefs, values, and interests. September 11, 2001 and the threat of global terrorism as well as Muslim and Christian theologies of exclusivism and hate have reinforced stereotypes and fears. Christians and Muslims are challenged to draw on their theological resources to develop contemporary models of religious pluralism and tolerance grounded in mutual understanding and respect.[1]

Both Islam and Christianity have shared beliefs that provide a basis for mutual recognition and cooperation: God as Creator, Sustainer, and Judge; a shared belief in biblical prophets and in divine revelation to humankind; and belief in moral responsibility and accountability, the last judgment, and eternal reward and punishment. The Qur'an proclaims, "We believe what has been sent down to us, and we believe what has been sent to you. Our God and your God is one, and to Him we submit" (Q 28:46), and "We have sent revelations to you as We sent revelations to Noah and the prophets who came after him; and We sent revelations to Abraham and Ishmael and Isaac and Jacob and their offspring, and to Jesus and Job . . . and to Moses God spoke directly" (Q 4:163-164). Similarly, Peter, preaching in Jerusalem shortly after Jesus' death, declared that, "The God of Abraham and of Isaac and of Jacob, the God of our fathers, glorified His servant Jesus, whom you delivered up and denied in the presence of Pilate" (Acts 3:13-14).

The history of Christian-Muslim encounters and relations has been marked by confrontation, conflict, and even warfare: among the major encounters were Muslim expansion out of the Arabian Peninsula through the Middle East and across North Africa in the seventh century; the Crusades and Reconquista of the Iberian Peninsula; the Ottoman period, and European colonialism and imperialism in the nineteenth and twentieth centuries in Africa, the Middle East, and Asia. Too often, these historic encounters and conflicts overshadow major periods of coexistence and constructive engagement in commerce, society, and interreligious relations in Andalusia, southern Italy, and India (for example, during the reign of Emperor Akbar).

The widespread presence of interreligious dialogues today often eclipses its relatively recent emergence. Few people have been more involved globally than Thomas Michel, a pioneer in Christian, and more specifically Catholic-Muslim, dialogue globally. Appreciating Tom Michel's pioneering role requires an appreciation of the historic hurdles of Christian doctrine.

Until modern times Christians, Roman Catholics and Protestants, believed that they had an exclusive claim to the one and only truth and a divine mandate to preach and convert the world. Christian attitudes toward other religions were shaped by biblical passages interpreted as asserting the unique salvific capacity of Jesus, like Acts 4:12: "There is no salvation through anyone else, nor is there any other name under heaven given to the human race by which we are to be saved"; and John 3:16-18: "For God so loved the world that He gave His only Son, so that everyone who believes in Him might not perish but might have eternal life. For God did not send His Son into the world to condemn the world, but that the world might be saved through Him. Whoever believes in Him will not be condemned, but whoever does not believe has already been condemned, because he has not believed in the name of the only Son of God."

For many Christians, these passages clearly indicated that Christianity was the one and only true religion that superseded and replaced other religions.[2] The particularity and singularity of the community of Jesus Christ—the church—took precedence over the universal love of God in matters of salvation, a position that is still maintained by most fundamentalist and evangelical Christian denominations today.

Until the sixteenth century, the Roman Catholic Church maintained the official doctrine of *Extra ecclesiam nulla salus* ("Outside the Church, no salvation"). After the fifth century, and particularly throughout the Middle Ages, this doctrine was directed especially toward Muslims and Jews, although it was also applied to certain Christian groups considered to be schismatic, such as Nestorians and Jacobites. In 1215, the Fourth Lateran Council amended official doctrine to state, "Outside the church, no salvation *at all*," placing new emphasis on membership in the Roman Catholic Church. This was followed in 1302 by Pope Boniface VIII's papal bull *Unam Sanctam*, which clarified that membership in the One Church and acceptance of papal authority were required to achieve salvation. In 1442, the Council of Florence made a sweeping statement denying any possibility of achieving salvation outside of the Roman Catholic Church: "No persons, whatever almsgiving they have practiced, even if they have shed blood for Christ, can be saved, unless they have remained in the bosom and unity of the Catholic Church."[3]

The first recognition of the possibility of conscience and moral living existing outside of the Roman Catholic context emanated from the Council of Trent (1545-1563), which devised the theology of "baptism by desire." It asserted that a person who followed his or her conscience and lived a moral life had, by action, demonstrated a willingness to listen to the voice of God and, therefore, an implicit desire to join the church, and thereby attain salvation, despite not having been baptized or having formally joined the church. This new theology of "baptism by desire" marked the church's first attempt to reconcile God's universal love with the necessary role of the church by expanding the pool of potentially saved candidates while maintaining a single-minded vision of world history and religion.[4]

This position was expanded in subsequent centuries as important questions about the legitimacy of divisions within Christianity were raised. It remained limited, however, to the personal merit or mystical experience of the individual believer. It did not consider the possibility of alternative religious institutions providing salvation. For example, in 1863, Pope Pius IX stated in *Quanto conficiamur moerore* that it was possible for a non-Roman Catholic to be considered "in a state of grace" and on the path to salvation if the person displayed Christian faith in his/her desire and actions. Although this link to the Roman Catholic Church was unconscious and existed in a "way known only to God," the Roman Catholic Church considered it necessary for salvation.[5] The intent of this declaration was to include in salvation those who led godly lives but were not formally part of the Roman Catholic Church. The declaration met with criticism, however, by those who objected to the apparently equal status being given to non-Roman Catholics in salvation and with questions about the necessity of baptism and membership in the Roman Catholic Church if salvation was available without them.

In response, Pope Pius XII limited membership in the faith community to those who had not deliberately sought to be outside of it. *Mystici corporis* (1943) asserted the necessity of baptism and the profession of the "true faith" for salvation. This position was bolstered in 1949 with his *Letter of the Holy Office to Archbishop Cushing* (1949), in which the Pius XII rejected equal access to salvation in any religion as false doctrine. Asserting the necessity of faith in God and repentance for personal sin for salvation, no substitute for Roman Catholicism was recognized.[6]

Although the Roman Catholic Church had abstained from the ecumenical movement, clinging to its more exclusivist claim to possession of the one and only truth and, therefore, path to salvation, a significant breakthrough occurred in the 1960s, especially at the Second Vatican Council (1962-1965). The council called for a new approach to other religions, referred to as fulfillment, declaring the inherent value of other religions because God is found in them and commanded Christians to dialogue with them.

The Second Vatican Council's 1965 Declaration on the Relationship of the Church to Non-Christian Religions (*Nostra Aetate*) called on Christians to engage in interreligious dialogue and recognized the authenticity of Protestant Christianity for the first time. Recognizing and applauding the "profound religious sense" animating other religions (specifically, Islam, Hinduism, and Buddhism), *Nostra Aetate* affirmed the teachings and practices of these religions as potentially leading to salvation.

> Those who, without blame, do not know Christ or his church, but with
> a sincere heart seek God and His will, as it is known to them through

the dictates of their conscience, and who, with the help of grace, try to fulfill God's will in their actions, can hope for eternal salvation. (§2)

Nostra Aetate also endorsed interfaith dialogue:

> Other religions to be found everywhere strive variously to answer the restless searchings of the human heart by proposing "ways" which consist of teachings, rules of life and sacred ceremonies. The Catholic Church rejects nothing which is true and holy in these religions. She looks with sincere respect upon those ways of conduct and life, those rules and teachings which, though differing in many particulars from what she holds and sets forth, nevertheless often reflect a ray of that Truth which enlightens all men. . . . The Church therefore has this exhortation for her sons: prudently and lovingly, through dialogue and collaboration with the followers of other religions, and in witness of Christian faith and life, acknowledge, preserve, and promote the spiritual and moral goods found among these men, as well as the values in their society and culture. (§2)

Muslims were explicitly recognized in *Lumen Gentium*:

> But the plan of salvation also includes those who acknowledge the Creator. In the first place among these there are the Moslems, who, professing to hold the faith of Abraham, along with us adore the one and merciful God, who on the last day will judge mankind. (§16)

In a number of its documents, the Second Vatican Council recognized the existence of revelation in other religions toward the goal of fostering dialogue, mutual understanding, respect, and cooperation. Nevertheless, these other religions continued to be considered a "preparation for the gospel," rather than alternative or additional paths to salvation. "It is through Christ's Catholic Church alone, which is the all-embracing means of salvation, that the fullness of the means of salvation can be found" (§14).

The greater openness to dialogue established by the Second Vatican Council was concretized and made more substantial by Pope Paul VI's 1964 establishment of the Vatican Secretariat for Non-Christian Religions (renamed and reorganized as the Pontifical Council for Interreligious Dialogue in 1989) to build dialogue with Muslims, Hindus, and Buddhists. The Catholic Church proclaimed its support for bringing the "religious life of every nation to its full development," noting that "mission should not aim at the destruction of other religions but at their continued existence so that all religions could stimulate each other in the unity of the most complete truth."[7] In his first encyclical of the same year, Pope Paul VI expressed esteem and respect for the spiritual values to be found in non-Christian religions, although he reiterated Vatican II's position on other religions serving to prepare non-Christians for the gospel.

The outcome of *Nostra Aetate* included the creation of space and official support for interfaith dialogue, as well as the establishment of formal relations between the Vatican and seventeen Muslim majority countries, including Algeria, Egypt, Indonesia, Iran, Kuwait, Pakistan, Sudan, Syria, and Turkey. Since the 1970s, there have been yearly meetings between Muslims and Christians geared toward increasing dialogue and mutual understanding. Both faiths have also focused on the preservation of the family as a sacred institution and the only legitimate means for the continuation of the human race, highlighting the responsibility of parents for raising their children and of children for respecting their parents.[8]

Pope John Paul II played a particularly important role in expanding Vatican dialogue with other faiths and recognizing their virtue, spirituality, and prayer by introducing a new focus on the Holy Spirit in his ministry of dialogue, understanding, and experience. His 1986 encyclical letter on the Holy Spirit, *Dominum et Vivificantem*, proclaimed the universal action of the Holy Spirit: "For, since Christ died for all, and since the ultimate vocation of man is in fact one, and divine, we ought to believe that the Holy Spirit in a manner known only to God offers to every man the possibility of being associated with this paschal mystery." Similarly, his initiation of the interreligious Day of Prayer for Peace in Assisi in 1986 acknowledged the vital role of the Holy Spirit in prayer: "Every prayer is prompted by the Holy Spirit, who is mysteriously present in every human spirit."[9]

John Paul II's emphasis on the Holy Spirit was based on his conviction that the Spirit is the unity that underlies the differences in the world's religions. Although there are many religions, there is only one Spirit dwelling not only in the hearts of individuals but also in "society and history, peoples, cultures and religions" (*Redemptoris Missio* §14). *Dialogue and Proclamation*—issued jointly by the Commission on Interreligious Dialogue and the Congregation for the Evangelization of Peoples in 1991—explicitly recognized "the active presence of God through His Word" and "the universal presence of the Spirit" in both people and religions outside of the Catholic Church, asserting that it is "in the sincere practice of what is good in their own religious traditions . . . that the members of other religions correspond positively to God's invitation and receive salvation" (§17). It also concluded that the religions of the world play "a providential role in the divine economy of salvation," suggesting that people can truly find and connect with God, and thus with salvation, in and through other religions (§29). In 1996, the Vatican International Theological Commission affirmed the "saving function" of other religions, referring to them as "a means which helps for the salvation of their adherents."[10]

This call to dialogue differed from dialogues of the past in which the purpose was to convince the other side of the truth of one's own message without listening to what the other had to say. Although dialogue was to "remain oriented toward proclamation" and was to be "conducted and implemented with the conviction that the Church is the ordinary means of salvation and that she alone possesses the fullness of the means of salvation,"[11] both *Redemptoris Missio* (§55) and *Dialogue and Proclamation* (§9) asserted "mutual knowledge and enrichment" as the goal of true dialogue. Both sides must be prepared to be "questioned," "purified," "challenged," and "transformed" toward a "deeper conversion of all toward God," even if that means leaving one faith for another (*Dialogue and Proclamation* §§32, 41, 47, 49; *Redemptoris Missio* §56).

Pope John Paul II spoke similar words to thousands of Muslim youths gathered in a sports stadium in 1985 in Casablanca:

> Christians and Muslims: We have many things in common as believers and as human beings. We live in the same world. It is marked by numerous signs of hope, but also by many signs of anguish. Abraham is the model for us all of faith in God, submission to his will and trust in his goodness. We believe in the same God, the one and only God, the living God, the God who creates worlds and brings creatures to their perfection.[12]

Since the last decades of the twentieth century, Catholic-Muslim dialogue has come from a position far behind that of mainstream Protestantism to a robust encounter globally and locally, led by the Vatican through the Pontifical Commission for Interreligious Dialogue, by national conferences of Catholic bishops, and by interested clergy and laity in cities and towns. Thomas Michel, S.J., has been a major force in Catholic-Muslim dialogue across the world, in his capacity globally at every level. Trained in Arabic and Islamic studies in the Middle East and at the University of Chicago, where he earned his Ph.D., he was appointed to the Asia Desk of the Vatican Pontifical Council for Interreligious Dialogue in 1981, and in 1988 became head of the Office for Islam in the same Vatican department. In 1994, he became executive secretary of the Office for Ecumenical and Interreligious Affairs of the Federation of Asian Bishops' Conferences (FABC-OEIA) in Bangkok, and in 1996, director of the Jesuit Secretariat for Interreligious Dialogue in Rome and ecumenical secretary for the Federation of Asian Bishops' Conferences. The long list of those Michel has advised, engaged in dialogue with, or taught has included everyone from Pope John Paul II, cardinals, bishops, grand muftis, and prominent scholars, to students and local communities.

Few can write with more authority, based not only on scholarship but equally on a broad and deep encounter with Muslims and Christians throughout the world. As we face a world of globalization—as well as one in which Muslim-Christian relations have been threatened by the attacks of 9/11, by the voices of preachers of religious exclusivism and chauvinism, by Islamophobia and xenophobia, and by those whose actions provoke fears of a clash of civilizations—Thomas Michel's writings have much to say and offer invaluable lessons for all who seek to reaffirm the religious roots and kinship of the Children of Abraham and seek to build a future more firmly rooted in mutual understanding and respect.

Notes

1. See "Pluralism in Muslim-Christian Relations," in *From Baghdad to Beirut—Arab and Islamic Studies in Honor of John J. Donohue, S.J.,* ed. Leslie Tramontini and Chibli Mallat (Beirut: Ergon Verlag, 2007), 496.

2. Paul F. Knitter, *Introducing Theologies of Religions* (Maryknoll, N.Y.: Orbis Books, 2002), 3.

3. Cited in Knitter, *Introducing Theologies,* 66.

4. Ibid., 67.

5. Francis A. Sullivan, S.J., *Salvation outside the Church? Tracing the History of the Catholic Response* (New York: Paulist Press, 1992), 123, 134.

6. Ibid., 138.

7. Leonard Swidler, "Religious Pluralism and Ecumenism from a Christian Perspective," in *Religious Issues and Interreligious Dialogue: An Analysis and Sourcebook of Developments Since 1945,* ed. Charles Wei-hsin Fu and Gerhard E. Speigler (New York: Greenwood Press, 1989), 336.

8. *Recognize the Spiritual Bonds Which Unite Us: 16 Years of Christian-Muslim Dialogue* (Vatican City: Pontifical Council for Interreligious Dialogue, 1994), 54.

9. Sullivan, *Salvation outside the Church?,* 195.

10. International Theological Commission, "Christianity and the World Religions" (San Francisco: Ignatius Press, 1997), 84, 87.

11. Ibid., 19, 22, 58, 75, 77; and *Redemptoris Missio* §55.

12. The text is cited from *Origins* 15, no. 11 (August 29, 1985): 174ff.

Preface

The idea for this book first came to me during a conversation with my colleague in philosophy, Richard Taylor, as the two of us were making plans to host Father Michel at Marquette University for a public lecture on Islam and peace in the spring of 2007. Later, as I communicated with Father Michel about this idea of putting his essays together in a volume, he forwarded to me a note from Edmund Kee-Fook Chia (Catholic Theological Union) who had just recently inquired about the same possibility. Apparently all three of us, almost concurrently, envisaged having Father Michel's writings in a single book, as we all saw the significance of such a volume for the growing library of literature in Christian-Muslim studies. In his communiqué, which Father Michel sent jointly to all of us, he suggested that I should be the one to edit such a volume in order to bring out the interreligious dimension of the project. Thus I am grateful to both Richard and Edmund for sharing their idea with me, and I thank Father Michel for entrusting me with this task of bringing some of his essays together in this volume. Without his collegiality and support I would not have been able to cope with this reasonably ambitious and yet very useful exercise in interreligious engagement. Father Michel helped me to identify the initial set of essays from among the numerous entries in his bibliography. The essays that are included were chosen because of their importance in Christian-Muslim relations and their relevance for the contemporary reader, while at the same time presenting a reasonable breadth of topics covered.

Many thanks to Susan Perry and Catherine Costello of Orbis for agreeing to work with me once again and for their counsel, patience, and impressive editing. From the previous experience of working with them, I was confident that they would handle the entire process very professionally and with great care despite some unexpected delays on my part in submitting the materials in a timely fashion.

Several other colleagues have been supportive of my work and have helped me in different ways to complete this project; I would especially like to mention John and Bobbie O'Hara Schmitt, Philip J. Rossi, S.J., Jame Schaefer, Phillip Naylor, Terry Crowe, and Shalahudin Kafrawi. Thanks also to John Esposito for writing the foreword. I am delighted and grateful to him for taking the time despite his very busy schedule to honor the work of Father Michel in this way.

I would also like to acknowledge the help given by my former teaching assistant, Thomas Bridges, and other students, Ben Juarez, and Sinan Othman, for doing the initial research and scanning. In particular, I received invaluable help from Tim Cavanaugh and David Luy in discussing various aspects of the project in its initial states, in tracking down missing sources, placing references, and preparing the bibliography.

Note on Transliteration and Style

In general, Arabic words have not been subjected to the double-strike features, such as over-bars and under-dots. However, Islamic terms relevant to the subject matter of the text (both within the body of the text as well as in notes) are italicized and have been rendered with complete diacritical marks, as they facilitate correct pronunciation. Islamic terms commonly used in English such as the Qur'an, hadith, surah, and jihad are not italicized and are free of diacritical marks.

The Arabic letter *'ayn* has been retained in most Islamic words and is represented by an open single quote mark (') while the closing single quote mark (') denotes the *hamza* consonant.

To indicate the feminine, the final *h* (*ta' marbuta*) has been retained in terms such as *shahādah*. The *h* becomes a *t* in *idafa* elisions as in *zakāt al-fiṭrah* (from *zakāh*).

The short vowel mark (') is retained as in words like *'ulamā'* (religious scholars).

In some instances, dates are given in A.H./C.E. format. A.H. refers to *Anno Hegira,* the Islamic Hijri calendar. The year 1 A.H. corresponds to the 622 C.E., which is the year when Prophet Muhammad migrated from Makkah to Madinah.

Biography of Father Thomas F. Michel, S.J.

Thomas Michel was born in 1941 in St. Louis, Missouri. He pursued undergraduate studies in Christian philosophy at Cardinal Glennon College and graduate studies in Christian theology at Kenrick Theological Seminary. In 1967, he was ordained a Catholic priest in the archdiocese of St. Louis. Father Michel entered the Society of Jesus in Yogyakarta, Indonesia, in 1971 and became a member of the Indonesian province of the Jesuits. He studied Arabic/Islamic thought at the Middle East Center for Arabic Studies in Lebanon from 1971 to 1972 and at the American University of Cairo from 1973 to 1974. Father Michel completed his Ph.D. studies at the University of Chicago in 1978 with a dissertation on the fourteenth-century Muslim thinker Ibn Taymiyya; it was subsequently published as *A Muslim Theologian's Response to Christianity: Ibn Taymiyya's Al-Jawab Al-Sahih*.

Father Michel has been involved in interreligious dialogue throughout the course of his professional career. Being a Jesuit living in Muslim-majority Indonesia and studying Islam facilitated the need for raising questions that went beyond a single faith. In 1981, he was appointed to the Asia Desk of the Vatican Pontifical Council for Interreligious Dialogue and later became the head of the Office for Islam in the same Vatican department. Father Michel also served as the executive secretary for the Office for Ecumenical and Interreligious Affairs of the Federation of Asian Bishops' Conferences (FABC-OEIA) in Bangkok, Thailand, from 1994 to 1996. He was, until recently, the secretary for interreligious dialogue of the Society of Jesus.

Father Michel has taught at a number of educational institutions around the world, including Northwestern and Columbia Universities in the United States; Sanata Dharma University and the Driyarkara Institute of Philosophy in Indonesia; St. Paul's Major Seminary, Dansalan College, and Euntes Asian Center in the Philippines; Ankara, Dokuz Eylül, Seljuk, and Harran Universities in Turkey; the Pontifical Institute for Arabic and Islamic Studies in Italy; St. Peter's Major Seminary in Malaysia; St. Paul's Seminary in Albania; and the University of Birmingham in England.

Father Michel is also a member of the Academic Council of the Prince Al-Waleed Center for Muslim-Christian Understanding at Georgetown University and a fellow of the Woodstock Theological Center at the same university. He is a member of the International Advisory Board of the Khalidi Library in Jerusalem; the Editorial Board for the journal *Islam and Christian-Muslim Relations* in Birmingham, England; the International Advisory Panel of the International Movement for a Just World in Kuala Lumpur, Malaysia; the International Advisory Committee of the Center for World Thanksgiving in Dallas, Texas; and the Advisory Board of the Centre for Civilizational Dialogue at the University of Malaya in Kuala Lumpur, Malaysia.

In 2008, he received the International Tschelebi Peace Prize from the Zentralinstitut-Islam-Archiv-Deutschland in Soest, Germany, and in 2009 he received the Ali Shir Navai Award from the International Turkish Olympiad in Ankara, Turkey.

Besides his extensive teaching and research experience, Father Michel has given numerous lectures and presentations on themes ranging from Christian-Muslim relations to ecumenism, and on grassroots empowerment addressing scholars, students, diplomats, political leaders, and a whole host of groups working for justice and peace in their local communities. In 2000, he delivered the prestigious D'Arcy Lectures on theological topics related to Christian-Muslim relations at Oxford University. He has also often been called on to represent the Roman Catholic Church's position in dialogical encounters.

Father Michel is a much sought-out scholar, as he brings a wealth of knowledge and experience to issues of community building, conflict resolution, and communication across religious and cultural divides under the rubric of interreligious dialogue—topics that remain relevant in the world today. In 2009, he joined the Jesuit community in Ankara, Turkey, where he is presently continuing his scholarly and teaching responsibilities.

Building a "Community of Witness"

Father Thomas Michel, S.J., on Islam and Christian-Muslim Relations

IRFAN A. OMAR

In *Makers of Contemporary Islam*, John Esposito and John Voll argued that Muslim history has been a witness to both kinds of visions: those that advocated conflict as well as those that rested on dialogue.[1] This trend continued in the twentieth and twenty-first centuries with the rise of many Islamist groups taking on the world powers and other state actors in the arena of geopolitical violence. Their vision rests on the division of the world between "them" and "us," and it has been more than adequately publicized by them (extremists are very tech savvy indeed) as well as the Western media as a whole.

At the same time and with much greater energy and impetus, the Muslim world has seen numerous prominent peaceful and progressive movements and individuals that have significantly influenced world politics and international relations, local communities, and religious institutions, arguing in favor of religious reform, greater freedom for the masses, and democratization of their societies. These groups and individuals who seek reconciliation and rapprochement, dialogue, and discussion are not granted even a fraction of the space and sound bites given to the extremist groups and the terrorists.

For both the extremists and the Western media in general, the dichotomy applies perfectly: Muslims are on one side, Christians (sometimes equated with the "international community") on the other. Reality, however, both historically and in the present, is quite different. Historically, more Christians and Muslims have fought and killed other Christians and Muslims, respectively, than the violence they have done to each other. In the present, too, intra-Christian and intra-Muslim violence is more common. At the same time, Christians and Muslims have increasingly come together to discover the vast common ground they share—in beliefs, in ethics, in spirituality, in worldly goals and aspirations.

Muslims have often remarked that the Christian practice of service to others (*diakonia*) and their concern for the neighbor reminds them of the hadith of Prophet Muhammad: "Best among you are those who are useful to others."[2] Similarly, Christians are often moved by the deep reverence for Jesus in Islam, and even though this consideration of Jesus is not akin to regarding him as divine, it is nevertheless significant in "how one world religion chose to adopt

1

the central figure of another, coming to recognize him as constitutive of its own identity."[3] As Tarif Khalidi notes, this veneration of Jesus by Muslims gave rise to many stories about Jesus ('Isa) in the Muslim world, found in texts related to ethics, piety, and the hagiographies of prophets and saints. This, he argues, is the "story of a love affair between Islam and Jesus" and constitutes the "ongoing dialogue" between Christians and Muslims in their "long-enduring search for a community of witness."[4] I believe Father Thomas Michel belongs to this community of witness and this volume may be seen as a celebration of his work and his reach into the hearts and minds of many Muslims and Christians across the world.

The Role of Interfaith Dialogue

Father Michel has been involved in efforts to promote interfaith dialogue for over four decades. He first became interested in Christian-Muslim dialogue when he arrived in Indonesia in 1969, a country that would become his home for the next three decades despite his intermittent appointments in Rome and his leadership role at the Pontifical Council for Interreligious Dialogue.

As one comes to know Father Michel through his experiences of encounter with Muslims, one begins to realize, as the reader perusing these pages undoubtedly will, that he often utilizes an encounter with the other as a means to build bridges between him and his interlocutor. This bridge building takes place at multiple levels: as a Catholic and a Christian he represents his faith to non-Christians, but with a deep respect for the faith of others. As an American and a Westerner, he defies the common perception that Western economic superiority implies that all others should conform to the Western model of development (ironically, in his meeting with Western Muslims, he is seen as an embodiment of the "East," so to speak, since he spent a big part of his life living and traveling in Asia).

As a Jesuit he brings to mind the memory of the learned members of the Society of Jesus who were pioneers in their interactions with Muslims, such as those at Akbar's court in the late sixteenth century. As a missionary who is committed to interfaith dialogue, Father Michel softens the image of those missionaries of the past who, at least in the eyes of some people, seemed to have used less than desirable means to achieve their missiological goals. Father Michel believes there is no dichotomy in the teachings of the Roman Catholic Church on dialogue and proclamation as they point to the "sharing of life at all levels,"[5] implying service and peaceful coexistence.

Finally, as a scholar of Islamic religion, he often becomes a valuable resource in providing an accurate understanding of Islam and Muslims in situations that warrant it. In other words, to his colleagues—Muslims, Christians, and others—Father Michel at once belongs to "us" and "them." He appears closer than any of "us" and yet he so much embodies the "other" that one is given a rare window into the life of the other through his experiences.

Father Michel makes the Christian feel less fearful of Islam while he reassures the Muslim not to be threatened by the West. Muslims see a face of the West and of Christianity they rarely encounter; and Western and other Christians see Islam's most positive and authentic image through his eyes. Like many other visionaries for peace, Father Michel has become a member of multiple domains; he is part of many communities and is claimed by Christians and Muslims, Indonesians and Turks, scholars and lay communities, just to name a few of the demographic entities that see him as one of their own. As the essays gathered here also show, this unique quality gives Father Michel access to the hearts and minds of diverse groups of people, which enables him to facilitate honest interactions between Christians and Muslims.

Learning about the Faiths of Others

As the reader will discover in the pages that follow, Father Michel's writings—as a reflection of his encounters in dialogue—seek to highlight the important fact that most Muslims and Christians know very little about each other's faith. They may know the other at the surface level and to a degree, but in the main they perceive each other through the lens of their largely imagined projections of their respective religions. Thus Father Michel reminds us that Muslims in many parts of the world, particularly in the East and the South, tend to see Christians as synonymous with the West or the United States; this causes them to think of the "Christian faith mainly as a justification for power and wealth."[6]

Similarly Christians tend to see Muslims in light of the stereotypical images of Islam prevalent in the media, which convey Islam as oppressive to women and a violent and intolerant religion.[7] In fact, Father Michel argues, both through his life's example and through his writings, that these stereotypes of others' faiths are the main cause of the negative view of each other. Based on false information of their religion, we often construct an image of the others that transcends their humanity, allowing our biased and prejudiced understanding to persist.

This volume seeks to address the continual problem of harboring false images of the other. It seeks to open new pathways for viewing another's faith from inside out. In the previous volume, *A Muslim View of Christianity* (Orbis Books, 2007), I collected and presented the theological views of a Muslim scholar and a person of faith, Professor Mahmoud Ayoub, on the subject of Christianity and its interrelationship with Islam. The end result was a very moving and sympathetic understanding of Christianity that rested on sound theological reasoning and pointed to the compatibility and common ground between the two faiths. Similarly, the present volume attempts to illustrate how a Christian scholar and a person of faith, in this case a Jesuit, sees Islam and finds a remarkable parity between the two religions' teachings of social justice, compassion, and concern for the poor, and a deep spirituality and love for God.

The works selected here have been previously published; however, many of these are not easily accessible even as they remain ever more relevant to our contemporary discussions on Islam and its relationship with Christianity. They are presented here with the hope of providing a unique and fresh perspective and to invite further reflection on the emerging practice within interfaith dialogue of documenting systematic and positive considerations of the other and their religions as a way to build bridges.

As is the case with many original thinkers with a deeper understanding of the subject and whose writings tend to be grounded in experience more so than in intellectual argumentation, several of the essays included here have very few or no references. In some places, as editor I have provided explanation or a reference for the convenience of those who might wish to pursue the thread of research beyond that point. Such comments are marked with an abbreviation, "Ed."

The Importance of Faith and Experience

An important feature of Father Michel's writing is that he is able to explain difficult issues in an easy to understand format by sharing personal stories and providing examples of his own interactions with Muslims. He reminds us that affirmations alone are not enough to build a culture of dialogue. We must move beyond theoretical dialogue to action—interreligious action, that is, as witnessed in the work of many groups Father Michel regards as successful movements working for the common good.

Father Michel's writings are "organic" in that they almost always involve a personal element of faith, life, and encounter with the other, which tells more about the dynamics of interaction than the facts regarding one's faith tradition. In other words what the reader experiences through his writings are the *effects of faith in action* on both sides, operating within the framework of a dialogical model that is built on trust and lasting friendships. It is, as Father Michel points out, living and being with the other that results in a bond that is truly lasting. This, in short, is "applied dialogue," not a mere description or the logistics of dialogue, but rather what emerges out of such interactions when one is engaged with the other in humility.

Very often religious communities seem to be locked in their respective confessional frames of reference—and are not used to move outside of that "box." Globalization has made a significant impact on the way we think today in our gradual recognition of wider ethnic and cultural differences. There is greater effort to understand similarities in the stated goals and aspirations shared by people of all cultural and national backgrounds. But when it comes to religious and confessional aspects, many continue to think in exclusive terms, often not giving the recognition to others that they themselves seek, which is one of the main pillars in interreligious dialogue. This necessitates widening the circle of dialogue to include peoples from all walks of life and from all levels of educational and professional backgrounds. It is important because too often interreligious dialogue focuses excessively on issues of dogma or on debating finer theological points while ignoring the fundamental principles of working to establish justice and freedom for all. This is due to the fact that many who engage in such dialogues are, in the words of Father Michel, "well-fed, well-housed, well-educated, and well-placed in society."[8]

Interfaith dialogue is many things, and to limit it to scholarly or theological concerns would be very unrealistic. At its most basic, it is human interaction, which takes place at many levels and "includes a broad range of relationships and activities among peoples of various faiths."[9] Thus, Father Michel believes that dialogue must never be separated from culture because it is vital to engage in dialogue with sensitivity to others' cultural values. Since interreligious dialogue is often also intercultural and/or inter-civilizational dialogue, it is quite appropriate to view this process, using Father Michel's language, as a "pilgrimage" where each is enriched by the other, not only in sharing a common goal of compassionate understanding but also, and more importantly, in journeying together toward that goal.[10]

Father Michel wants Christians and Muslims to be honest with themselves and with their interlocutors from other faith traditions. It is important that the dialogue partners remain firmly placed at the ground level of what our respective scriptures and traditions demand of us: to seek and serve God and God's creation and to do it in the best way possible. At the same time, each partner in dialogue should be able to discuss opinions, reservations, and concerns regarding practices within their own tradition that are deemed challenging from the perspective of the core principles of that tradition. Thus each member of the dialogue should also be willing to look critically within his/her own religious tradition and history and help others understand and contextualize issues that might be difficult for the dialogue partners.

From the Past to the Present

As my former teacher and mentor, Willem Bijlefeld, once said, Christian-Muslim dialogue is one of the most challenging and at the same time deeply rewarding experiences in interreligious interaction. The challenge, to be more specific, is due to our very histories and our perceptions of each other. Christian-Muslim relations are laden with an unmistakable baggage from the past that is emotional and cultural, religious and political, and sometimes referred to as the "burden of history." In the past Christian and Muslim views of each others' faiths were often marked by fear and misunderstanding and, in some respects, these trends have continued into the present. Thus, as Bijlefeld recently argued, in our contemporary efforts in dialogue, "we cannot deal meaningfully with the present and the future of Christian-Muslim relations without paying careful attention to the past."[11]

At one level, this volume represents both the past and the present in that it includes studies that reflect a diversity of Christian perspectives of Islam from various periods in history. Although written by a single author, Father Thomas Michel, as a responsible scholar, reflects and channels various contemporary voices and opinions in his writings. This collection also addresses the future by way of pointing to an exceptional example of interreligious scholarship that continues to be relevant and is welcomed by members of both traditions.

Many of the essays in this collection are addressed to Catholics, Christians, and Westerners, often extolling the virtues of dialogue[12] and invoking Catholic teachings that call for and emphasize the need for continuing engagement with members of other communities. Father Michel cites scripture, appeals on behalf of the papal authority, quotes from papal encyclicals, and reminds us of the past efforts that have already resulted in much improved relations between Catholics and Muslims. A generation of Christians and Muslims have now come to understand each other's traditions through Father Michel's sympathetic, spiritually enriching, and yet intellectually refreshing (true to their sources) portrayal of these religions. This rendering is not for the sole consumption of scholars; Father Michel has spent decades teaching Christianity to Muslims, and Islam to Christians, as a way for members of each community to deepen their own faith even as they learn to appreciate the faith of the other. This army, if you will, of practitioners, scholars, seminarians, and others is now poised to continue the vision of the compassionate dialogue across the globe.

Notes

1. John L. Esposito and John Voll, *Makers of Contemporary Islam* (New York: Oxford University Press, 2001).

2. A hadith from *Sahih al-Bukhari*.

3. Tarif Khalidi, introduction to *The Muslim Jesus: Sayings and Stories in Islamic Literature*, ed. and trans. Tarif Khalidi (Cambridge, Mass.: Harvard University Press, 2001), 6.

4. Ibid., 5-6.

5. "Creating a Culture of Dialogue: Toward a Pedagogy of Religious Encounter" (see chap. 2, pp. 20, 25 in the present volume).

6. "Toward a Dialogue of Liberation with Muslims" (see chap. 6, p. 72 in the present volume).

7. "Toward a Dialogue of Liberation with Muslims" (see chap. 6, p. 72 in the present volume; see also chap. 12).

8. "Toward a Dialogue of Liberation with Muslims" (see chap. 6, p. 71 in the present volume).

9. "A Variety of Approaches to Interfaith Dialogue" (see chap. 3, p. 29 in the present volume).

10. "Creating a Culture of Dialogue: Toward a Pedagogy of Religious Encounter" (see chap. 2, p. 24 in the present volume).

11. Willem A. Bijlefeld, "Christian-Muslim Relations: A Burdensome Past, a Challenging Future," *Word & World* 16, no. 2 (Spring 1996): 120.

12. "Creating a Culture of Dialogue: Toward a Pedagogy of Religious Encounter" (see chap. 2, pp. 16-20 and 26-27 in the present volume).

PART I

Interreligious Dialogue

Encountering the "Other"

1

Interfaith Dialogue

A Catholic Christian Perspective

There is an old story handed down in the literature of the Jewish rabbis. It concerns two Russian peasants who were sitting at an inn. Ivan turns to his friend Alexei and says, "I love you, Alexei." Alexei says, "What hurts me, Ivan?" Ivan responds, "How would I know what hurts you?" Alexei says, "If you don't know what hurts me, you don't love me." There is a lot of truth in this story, and it applies not only to individuals but also to religious confessions. If we do not know what it is that bothers others, what are their main preoccupations, their areas of sensitivity, and how the world and the problems of life appear to their eyes, we are not yet in a position to achieve any level of fellow-feeling, acceptance, and affection for them. We remain strangers, although we may live in close proximity and even share a common language and culture. Is this not at the heart of why we engage in interfaith dialogue?

Seeing the "Other" with the Eyes of the "Other"

Interfaith dialogue means coming to know each other. This implies much more than a simple exchange of information, for the latter can be obtained from books and articles. It means encountering one another as persons, people whose outlook and behavior have been formed by one or another of the great religious movements that characterize human quest for the divine. We can presume that each of us lives and represents in a personal way a tradition of faith, a way of approaching the ultimate questions of human existence that guides our daily behavior and attitudes toward one another. Our engagement in interfaith dialogue offers us the opportunity to move beyond the world of our respective confessions, to come to see "with the eyes of others" their concerns, their hopes,

Previously published in *Inter-faith Dialogue and World Community*, ed. G. S. S. Sreenivasa Rao (Madras: Christian Literature Society, 1991), 28-35. Reprinted by permission.

their beliefs, and yes, also their complaints. It is an exercise expressing our common humanity and our common desire for peace and harmony in this world.

To return to our two Russian peasants, coming to know what hurts, bothers, and excites another is not an easy process. It means putting ourselves in their place and learning to accept them as people who, despite our differing beliefs and religious practices, are basically not much different from ourselves. They have their strengths and weaknesses, as do each of us: they have their dreams of what life and society should be like and of how we can move toward building that kind of society. It means coming to realize not merely intellectually, but from experience and personal encounter, that those of other faiths are not our enemies, but that they could and should become our natural allies and co-workers in service to the human family. It is in this sense that interfaith dialogue can be an effective force both for national integration and for solidarity among people.

The Second Vatican Council has strongly favored and encouraged such interfaith meetings as important means to live according to God's will on earth and to fulfill our proper destiny as human beings. On January 1 of 1986, Pope John Paul II stated, in his message on the World Day of Peace, the reasons why dialogue is essential for our time:

> Dialogue is a means by which people discover one another and discover the good hopes and peaceful aspirations that too often lie hidden in their hearts. True dialogue goes beyond ideologies. Dialogue breaks down pre-conceived notions and artificial barriers. Dialogue brings human beings into contact with one another as members of one human family, with all the richness of their various cultures and histories. A conversion of heart commits people to promoting universal brotherhood; dialogue helps to effect this goal.[1]

We live, as we know, in an age of great possibilities for humankind. Through advances in science and technology, mankind has unequalled opportunities to eradicate disease and hunger from the world. But we know also that technological advances can be and are being used for destructive purposes. Human beings' capabilities for savagery in wars and even in "limited" terrorist actions exceed in blind and anonymous destruction anything previously imagined. The year 1985 marked the fortieth anniversary of the Age of Nuclear Destruction. Most of the people in the world today born since that time have never known an era free from the threat of atomic annihilation. Advances in science have also accelerated the threat to our physical environment: the seas, the forests, and the atmosphere are all in danger of irreversible elimination as living ecosystems. The great advances in consumer goods, communications, and leisure activities bear a similar ambiguous quality; they can serve to make human life more knowledgeable, enjoyable, and comfortable, or can be misused to render mankind more selfish, passive, and controllable in unjust and dehumanizing systems. The values of the human spirit can be degraded and ignored in the pursuit of material comforts. Even the great advances in medical science have been accompanied by the production of new forms of narcotics, which are being refined and marketed internationally with efficient, computerized methods, to the enslavement of millions on every continent.

Our age is also one of polarization of peoples, as Pope John Paul II said in a speech given in Yaoundé, Cameroon:

> It must be admitted that we live in an "age of polarization." Around the world, racial and ethnic groups, religious bodies, economic and political ideologies are choosing to make their point of view prevail to the exclusion of those who disagree, to defend their rights to the point of ignoring those of others, to refuse offers of cooperation and human fellowship.[2]

What guidance can our religious traditions give us in the face of these new, unprecedented challenges? What wisdom can we bring from our various spiritual heritages to confront constructively the issues of life and death that the human family faces today? As persons who believe that we stand before the divine as responsible agents, how can we work together to build our human societies in accord with our spiritual values?

Each of our religious traditions teaches values that can show us the path toward greater human liberation and integration and how to avoid destruction and despair. My own Christian tradition is based upon the person of Jesus whose whole life was lived in obedience to the will of God, in love and service for mankind, especially those who suffer, and whose central message was the announcement of God's governance over human affairs. Islam understands a human being as the steward of God, His vice-regent on earth, given the responsibility of ordering human life in accord with God's designs. The Hindu tradition, always conscious of God's manifold presence and manifestations, has elaborated an ethic appropriate to each stage of mankind's spiritual development; Buddhists follow the path to enlightenment that confronts directly the problem of human pain and enjoins right living: they have the example of the compassionate Buddha who left the Bo tree to guide and assist suffering humanity.

Religious Ideals and the Human Condition

One could go on and catalogue the values of the other great traditions, but these examples are sufficient to make my point. We are already in possession of the values and teachings needed by our world. They have been handed down to us by our ancestors in faith. This is the fund of convictions and experience from which we must draw in our discussions during the seminar. We know, however, that announcing beliefs and living them are two different things. Nikkyo Niwano, the Japanese founder of a reform movement within the Buddhist tradition, tells the story of the Tang-dynasty poet Po Chu-i who heard of a great Zen master and went to visit him. Po Chu-i asked the master: "What is the Buddha's Law?" The master answered: "Commit no evil. Do only that which is good. Purify your mind. This is the teaching of all the buddhas." "But even a three-year-old child knows that," scoffed Po Chu-i. "Yes," answered the old master, "but what may be understood by a child of three is not easy even for an old man of eighty to practice."[3]

And here lies the root of our confessional conflicts and strife. Our world is one where those who call themselves Christians often do not follow and display in their lives the example and teachings of Christ. Similarly there are Muslims who in practice do not surrender their lives to Allah in the ways that he has asked of them. Hindus do not always act according to the teachings of their sacred literature, Buddhists frequently do not embody the example and teaching of the Buddha, and so on. We know also that there are hypocrites in every religious group, people who use and manipulate religious sentiment and ideals for personal ambition and gain. No religious tradition teaches hatred, suspicion, enmity, and competition toward other sincere believers. Rather, the relationship among believers is probably best expressed by the passage of the Qur'an that states that if God wanted He could have made all people one religious confession. But He has not done so in order that "we might compete with one another in what is good."[4] In this sense, confessional rivalry is legitimate and can be beneficial for humankind. But the human condition is such that we all fall far short of our religious ideals. Every confessional group can make a case against the others, pointing out the occasions in history and the world of today where the other religious communities have failed and continue to do so. Thus, interfaith dialogue, if it is to be an effective force for national integration and human solidarity, must be realistic. We do not encounter idealized partners, but rather erring human individuals and communities whose behavior falls short of their ideals. We must also be humble and frank about admitting our own failings and those of our communities. We are all pilgrims together on this earth, conscious of our shortcomings and living in hope that we can act better in the future.

But we must also be realistic about the future. It would not help interfaith dialogue, I believe, were we to succumb to the myth of a bright new future around the corner in which all the religious confessions live together in peace, harmony, and love. Maybe I can illustrate my point with a bit of personal history. When in 1965, the Second Vatican Council of the Catholic Church produced its document *Nostra Aetate* concerning the relations of the Catholic Church to other religions, I was a young seminary student. When my companions and I studied the document, it was for us the opening of a door. With great enthusiasm we read how Christians must respect and esteem other religions, how the divisions and conflicts of the past must be forgotten, how believers must work together to build peace, social justice, human development, and moral values in today's world. We felt that we were on the threshold of a new age in interreligious relations and threw ourselves into the study of other faiths and into personal encounters with other believers. We came to know well, learn from, and share much with Muslims, Hindus, Buddhists,

Jews, and others. Corresponding activities went on in ecumenical relations among Christians of different churches.

Much has been accomplished in the past few decades, and the Catholic Church has many times confirmed and reaffirmed its strong commitment to interreligious dialogue and cooperation. But at the same time, we are all aware of how many conflicts, riots, and even warfare, often religiously motivated, have occurred. Ireland, the Philippines, Lebanon, Ethiopia, Israel, Sri Lanka, and even India, despite its great and long tradition of tolerance, are only a few of the countries where religious allegiance has played a role in recurrent confessional conflicts. In almost every case, the root causes of conflict are found inextricably entwined with economic, cultural, ethnic, and linguistic factors so that, upon close inspection, one cannot say that religious convictions have in themselves produced such suffering, death, and destruction.

It is important to realize that in the complex world in which we live, advances in interreligious understanding and respect have occurred and still occur simultaneously with new tensions and outbreaks of violence. This sad and humbling fact must not be forgotten in our discussions or in any of our interfaith encounters. Here I am reminded of a well-known short novel that appeared in the United States in the mid 1960s. The central characters were a severely emotionally disturbed teenage girl and her psychologist. The psychologist first met the girl in a near-catatonic state where she had completely withdrawn herself from life. Through months of long discussions, the psychologist helped the girl to understand better the conflicts in her life, the unbearable crisis that had brought about her mental illness and withdrawal. The girl slowly improved, but as her contacts with the "outside world" increased, she began to see that many of the sources of her troubles remained unchanged, principally her relationships with her family and friends. The girl sought to regress into her catatonia. At this point the psychologist spoke sharply but with compassion: "I never promised you a rose garden: the world is often a harsh and unyielding reality. What I have tried to do is to give you the means by which you can live constructively and achieve a degree of happiness in that world."[5]

The phrase that gave the title to the book is one that is a key to all of us who are involved in interfaith dialogue. "I never promised you a rose garden." In our meetings and encounters we cannot provide rapid and facile solutions to conflicts and tensions that have plagued humankind throughout the whole of human history. Such conflicts will probably, sad to say, continue so long as there are differences in race, religion, nation, language, class, and gender. There will always be conflicts of interest between confessional groups. But seeing our interfaith activities in this sober light should not make us lose hope nor give in to a fatalism that presumes that "nothing ever changes." Things have changed considerably in our own lifetimes; it would have been difficult for previous generations to envision the great number and variety of interreligious encounters that are taking place around the world today.

The Buddha asked almost twenty-five hundred years ago why we think that goodness is a less powerful agent of infection than evil. We hear frequently of "bad influences," mutual breakdowns of relations, and almost every culture has proverbs equivalent to that of "the bad apple spoils the lot." While not denying the truth of such statements, I ask whether the forces of tolerance, mercy, acceptance, peace, respect, love, patience, justice, forgiveness, reconciliation, moral uprightness—in short, the godly virtues—are not stronger than those of evil and destruction? As a Christian I would say that our finer qualities and higher ideals are the fruits of God's own Spirit at work among men and women of good will in all of the religious traditions.

We can be heartened in our interfaith endeavors by the conviction that in striving to build mutual understanding and respect we do not rely solely on our own efforts. We are agents of the Transcendent Power with whom humanity is meant to live in harmony, and consequently, in harmony with one another. Although we may define this activity in different categories and use various terms, it is clear that our true destiny is never served by enmity and wrongdoing within the human family and that each of our religious traditions calls us to more positive and beneficial relations. As Pope John Paul II said in his August 1985 address to a mixed gathering of Muslims and Hindus:

> It is never God's will that there should exist hatred within the human family, that we should live in distrust and at enmity with one another. We are all children of the same God, members of the great family of man. Our religions have a special role to fulfil in curbing these evils and in forging bonds of trust and fellowship. God's will is that those who worship Him, even if not united in the same worship, would nevertheless be united in brotherhood and in common service for the good of all.[6]

The efforts of interfaith encounters will have results, but we must not demand to witness their immediate fruit. What is most real is usually difficult to detect with a superficial glance. Moreover, the strongest tree takes years to grow. Nevertheless, we can proceed with firm grounds for hope that the seeds we sow here will bear fruit for our grandchildren and their children in ways that are unforeseen by us. For we will each be changed by what occurs in these encounters. The effects of that slight transformation in our attitudes and approaches to others will have imperceptible effects in our relations with friends, family, and coworkers, in our vision of what national integration and human solidarity can and should mean, and in our projects to attain those goals. Every time a Hindu or Christian parent, for example, teaches a small child that God also loves Muslims, Sikhs, and Buddhists, each time a schoolteacher brings some element of personal experience of other faiths to illustrate the common human quest for the transcendent, every time a guru, *bonze*, *ustādh*, minister, or priest teaches and preaches that people of all confessions must join hands to build a just and human society, the ideals of brotherhood, esteem, and tolerance are moved forward a slight bit. Is this not an understanding of karma that both Christians and Muslims as well as the followers of the Indic religions can accept, that no good act is ever without its effect? In each of these cases, someone else is affected and the godly virtues and values are spread.

In this chapter, I have tried to outline the reasons why I, as a believing Christian and representative of the Vatican, am convinced of the importance of interfaith gatherings. To this end, I conclude with a citation from Pope John Paul II's radio talk to the Christians of Asia, on the occasion of his 1981 visit to that continent:

> The Church of Jesus Christ in this age experiences a profound need to enter into contact and dialogue with all these religions [of Asia]. She pays homage to the many moral values contained in these religions, as well as to the potential for spiritual living which so deeply marks the traditions and the cultures of whole societies. . . . Christians will [therefore] join hands with all men and women of good will who share a belief in the inestimable dignity of each human person. They should work together in order to bring about a more just and peaceful society in which the poor will be the first to be served. Asia is the continent where the spiritual is held in high esteem and where the religious sense is deep and innate. The preservation of this precious heritage must be the common task of all.[7]

Notes

1. John Paul II, "Peace Is a Value with No Frontiers: North-South, East-West: Only One Peace." Available online at www.vatican.va (accessed August 15, 2009).—Ed.

2. On Pope John Paul II's visit to several African countries, see http://www.vatican.va/holy_father/john_paul_ii/travels/sub_index1985/trav_africa_en.htm (accessed August 15, 2009).—Ed.

3. This story is found in Nikkyo Niwano's book *Invisible Eyelashes: Seeing What Is Closest to Us* (Tokyo: Kosei, 1994). For an online version please visit http://rk-world.org/publications/invisible_B1.aspx (accessed August 15, 2009).—Ed.

4. The idea that had God willed, God could have made humankind one single community appears in the Qur'an in several places; see, for example, Q. 11:118-19; 16:93; and 42:8. Reference to the notion that various communities are encouraged to compete with one another in doing "good works" is to be found in Q. 2:148.—Ed.

5. Joanne Greenberg, *I Never Promised You a Rose Garden: A Novel by Hannah Green* (New York: Holt, Rinehart and Winston, 1964).

6. "Address of Pope John Paul II to the Leaders and Representatives of the Islamic and Hindu Communities in Kenya, Nairobi (Kenya) 18 August 1985," available online at www.vatican.va (accessed August 15, 2009).—Ed.

7. "Address of His Holiness John Paul II during His Visit to the Auditorium of Radio Veritas Asia, Manila, 21 February 1981," available online at www.vatican.va (accessed August 15, 2009).—Ed.

2

Creating a Culture of Dialogue

Toward a Pedagogy of Religious Encounter

How do we create a culture of dialogue in our religious institutions? The topic presumes two more fundamental questions: What do we mean by dialogue? and, What do we mean by a culture of dialogue? The idea of interreligious dialogue seems obvious, but it is worth taking the time to see what the church is intending when it says that we should be involved in this dialogue. Too often, people regard dialogue in a very restricted sense, but what the church intends is something much wider.

What Is Dialogue?

People sometimes think of dialogue as situations in which religious leaders and scholars are sitting down together, making pleasant, optimistic statements, choosing their words guardedly, trying to put a positive twist on controverted questions, and carefully avoiding any topic that might cause friction or hard feelings. In short, they are thinking of something akin to an interreligious tea party. If this is the idea we have, it is no wonder that many Christians and followers of other religions are suspicious of the value of such encounters, which they might well consider a waste of time, a luxury that our busy schedules cannot afford, an exercise in public relations, or even a compromise on matters of faith.

If this were what dialogue was really about, it would be hard to understand why the Catholic Church, beginning with the Second Vatican Council, has been so insistent in urging Christians to be committed to interreligious dialogue. For example, we can hear the very powerful statement of Pope John Paul II in his

---

This chapter consists of passages previously published in [1] "Creating a Culture of Dialogue: Methodology of Interreligious Dialogue," in *The Priority of Interreligious Dialogue: A New Commitment for the Consecrated Life* (Rome: 63 Conventus Semestralis Unione Superiori Generali, 2003), 53-65; and [2] "Towards a Pedagogy of Religious Encounter," in *Learning from Other Faiths*, ed. Hermann Häring, Janet Martin Soskice, and Felix Wilfred (London: SCM Press, 2003), 103-11 [used by permission].

1991 encyclical, *Redemptoris Missio* (§§56-57), about interreligious encounter: "Each member of the faithful and all Christian communities are called to practice dialogue, although not always to the same degree or in the same way." "For most," the pope continues, "this will be through what is called the dialogue of life." This is a strong statement. Does the pope really mean that each member of the faithful, and all Christian communities—including all Catholic religious institutes—should in some way be involved in the practice of dialogue?

Obviously, the Holy Father was not speaking of tea parties. Pope John Paul II was proposing that dialogue with the followers of other religions should be a characteristic of the mission in the world that Jesus entrusted to the community of his disciples. Just as our following of Christ should include daily prayer and worship of God, a special concern for the poor and victims of oppression and injustice, care for the sick and aged, theological reflection on the significance of our Christian faith in each cultural context, proclaiming our faith by sharing "the reasons for the hope that is in us" with all those who are seeking truth, and communicating our faith to new generations of Christian disciples, so also one of the basic elements of our Christian mission is the encounter with people of other faiths. These are all aspects of the one mission that Christ has given us.

One might say that dialogue is the other side of the obligation to proclaim our faith in this world. There are millions of people in our world who are seeking God, who are looking for a way to live in accord with God's will, who want to find meaning, a reason for living in their daily situations. We have a duty to share with them the Christian faith that has given direction to our lives, that inspires us and gives us the courage to love, that sustains us and gives us reason for hope in moments of failure and desperation.

But our world also presents us with many other millions of people, who are good and honest and self-sacrificing, who are not searching for God, precisely because they have already found and daily encounter the Divine in and through the religion they already follow. Through the practice of their own religion—be it Judaism, Islam, Buddhism, Hinduism, Taoism, or the traditional religion of various continents—God's Spirit is guiding them, enabling them to pray and worship, teaching them to live in accord with God's moral will, and inspiring them often to reach the heights of self-sacrifice, generosity, and service of others, and enabling many to plumb the depths of spirituality and mystical experience. They love their religion. It means as much to them as the Christian faith means to Christians.

Do we [Christians] have anything to say to such people? Do we have anything to learn from them? Can we be enriched by the testimonies of their lives and their faith? Are there possibilities of working together with them for the good of all? Or do we simply turn our backs and wash our hands of them because they are convinced of the rightness of their religious path and committed to following its teachings and hence are not interested in becoming Christians? The Roman Catholic Church teaches us that we have much to communicate and much to learn. This whole world of positive relations with the followers of other religions is summed up in the word "dialogue." Already in 1979, in his first encyclical, *Redemptor Hominis*, Pope John Paul II had this to say:

> What we have just said must also be applied . . . to activity for coming closer together with the representatives of the non-Christian religions, an activity expressed through dialogue, contacts, prayer in common, investigation of the treasures of human spirituality, in which, as we know well, the members of these religions are not lacking. Does it not sometimes happen that the firm belief of the followers of the non-Christian religions—a belief that is also an effect of the Spirit of truth operating outside the visible confines of the Mystical Body—can make Christians ashamed at being often themselves so disposed to doubt concerning the truths revealed by God and proclaimed by the Church and so prone to relax moral principles and open the way to ethical permissiveness? It is a noble thing to have a predisposition for under-standing every person, analyzing every system and recognizing what is right; this does not at all mean losing certitude about one's own faith or weakening the principles of morality.[1]

This dense paragraph is packed with advice on which we can build in our efforts to create a culture of dialogue. The Holy Father emphasized the importance of common prayer, coming together before the Source and Final Goal of our religious journey. He noted that the benefits of dialogue are not only for the Other, but also for Christians. Cannot the firm belief of the followers of other religions often make us [Christians] ashamed of our own doubts and laxity? He stressed that the belief of others is an effect of the Spirit of truth. He underlined the nobility of the commitment to dialogue, of being open to understand oth-ers, analyze their belief systems, and recognize all that is good in them. None of this, concluded the Pope, involves losing confidence in the beauty and truth of our own Christian faith.

Sharing Life

When one examines the teachings of the church about dialogue, it is clear that we are asked to commit ourselves to something much broader than mere "talk" with the followers of the world's religions. Dialogue includes not only a wide range of activities but, more importantly, demands a fresh existential approach to the followers of other religious traditions. In his encyclical *Redemptoris Mis-sio*, Pope John Paul II indicates just how broad a compass dialogue embraces:

> A vast field lies open to dialogue, which can assume many forms and expressions: from exchanges between experts in religious traditions or official representatives of those traditions, to cooperation for integral development and the safeguarding of religious values; and from a shar-

ing of their respective spiritual experiences to the so-called "dialogue of life," through which believers of different religions bear witness before each other in daily life to their own human and spiritual values, and help each other to live according to those values in order to build a more just and fraternal society.[2]

In the documents produced by Vatican offices, these forms of dialogue have been generally elaborated as four facets of interreligious encounter: the dialogue of life, cooperation in social concerns, theological exchange, and the sharing of religious experience. What is involved are various dimensions of our life as Christians that we share with the followers of other religions. It means a way of living with others as Christians that involves interaction at the levels of being (dialogue of life), doing (cooperation), studying (exchange of views), and reflecting on one's experience of the Divine (sharing religious experience). In the church's vision of life shared by Christians and the followers of other religions, talking or discoursing plays a role, as it does in all forms of human life, but discussion must not dominate, nor must the shared life denoted by the term "dialogue" be limited by or reduced to formal occasions and deliberations.

Once we see the broad extent of what the church means by dialogue, we can move beyond the restrictive notion that dialogue is only for experts or religious leaders. The illiterate farmer or housewife who has been blessed with a strong Christian faith but has not had the opportunity to engage in advanced religious studies is called to approach his or her neighbors of other faiths with a dialogical spirit. Such Christians need not feel that they are constrained to discuss subtle theological points, but they are called to live with respect and openness for their neighbors, to share the joys and crises and sorrows of life with others, and to teach their children that God also has great love for faithful Muslims, Jews, Buddhists, etc. This is what the pope means when he says that each Christian, and every Christian community, should be involved in dialogue, although not all in the same way.

For most Christians that form of shared life to which we are called is often termed the "dialogue of life." Already in 1979, the Asian bishops called this "the most essential aspect of dialogue," and they said that it occurs when:

> each [the Christian and the follower of another religion] gives witness to the other concerning the values they have found in their faith, and through the daily practice of brotherhood, helpfulness, open-heartedness and hospitality, each show themselves to be a God-fearing neighbor. The true Christian and their neighbors of other faiths offer to a busy world values arising from God's message when they revere the elderly, conscientiously rear the young, care for the sick and the poor in their midst, and work together for social justice, welfare, and human rights.[3]

The shift of emphasis that occurred in the teaching of the bishops of Asia is significant. The bishops are moving the accent in dialogue away from being mainly a way of "talking or discussing" to that of "a way of living together," shifting the focus from scholars and religious leaders to ordinary believers, reformulating dialogue from being an activity of the elite to understanding it as the task of grassroots Christians and their neighbors.

It took the magisterial teaching of the universal church more than a decade to catch up with this central insight of the Asian bishops, but the Roman documents can be seen gradually to incorporate the idea, culminating in Pope John Paul's statement cited above that "each member of the faithful and all Christian communities are called to practice dialogue, although not always to the same degree or in the same way." "For most," the pope continued, "this will be through what is called 'the dialogue of life'" (*Redemptoris Missio* §§56-57)

Dialogue versus Proclamation, or Dialogue with Proclamation?

This paradigm shift has important implications for the much-controverted theological debate over "dialogue and evangelization." Since interreligious dialogue is already recognized in church teaching as one of the integral elements of the evangelizing mission of the church, along with "presence and witness; commitment to social development and human liberation; liturgical life, prayer and contemplation; interreligious dialogue; and finally, proclamation and catechesis" (*Mission and Dialogue* §13; *Dialogue and Proclamation* §2), the debate can be more accurately phrased as one of determining the relationship between "dialogue and proclamation" as two authentic and irreplaceable aspects of evangelizing activity.

When dialogue is understood primarily as conversation between Christians and the followers of other faiths, the question inevitably arises: Should Christians devote their efforts to preaching the Gospel, or should they enter into mutual exploration of one another's faiths? Should Christians try to discover basic commonalities in spirituality, morality, and commitment with their partners of other religions, or should they seek opportunities to proclaim those doctrinal elements that characterize and distinguish Christian faith from that of others? The debate has continued, with inconclusive results, for over forty years since the publication of *Nostra Aetate*. However, if dialogue is understood as the sharing of life at all levels among believers of various faiths, the issue is more readily resolvable. Christians are called to share that life, which sometimes means simply living together in harmony or working for reconciliation after conflicts, sometimes coming to the aid of the weakest and neediest in their midst, sometimes working together in defense and solidarity with the poor and victims of injustice, and sometimes sharing their deepest motivation for living the way they do. This motivation is the personal encounter of each with the Divine, whether that be imagined and expressed as responding to God's Word, doing God's will, coming into harmony with the eternal Tao, realizing the Buddha nature in oneself, or discovering one's identity with Brahman who exists beyond all attributes and images.

The dialogue of life implies much more than peaceful coexistence. It means that we live deeply our Christian faith amid believers of other religions and show by the way we act and treat others the values that we have discovered in the course of our pilgrimage as disciples of the Lord. Similarly, our neighbors of other faiths show us, not so much by word as by deed and attitude, the values they seek to follow in their own religious path. This might be called a dialogue of "mutual witness."

In real life, there is no conflict between dialogue and proclaiming the Gospel. Sisters working in clinics in Libya, for example, are proclaiming the Gospel value of care for the sick at the same time they are in dialogue with patients and neighbors. Mother Teresa and many like her give eloquent testimony to what the Gospel is really about when they offer the poor an environment in which they can die with dignity. Yet Mother Teresa often said that she prayed that "Christians become better Christians, Hindus become better Hindus, and Muslims better Muslims."[4]

In this light, the focal question is not whether the church should be proclaiming the Gospel or engaged in dialogue, but rather whether Christians are actually sharing life with their neighbors of other faiths. The basic distinction is not between being a church in dialogue or one that proclaims the Gospel, but rather the option of being a church that is following the Spirit's lead to partake humanly in life with others, and thus constantly engaged in dialogue, witness, and proclamation, or else that of being a church that is closed in on itself and exists in a self-imposed ghetto with little concern for and involvement with people of other faiths with whom Christians share culture, history, citizenship, and common human destiny.

When people of various faiths live together—not simply cohabiting the same town but sharing life *together*—the question of dialogue or proclamation doesn't arise. When they work, study, struggle, celebrate, and mourn together and face the universal crises of injustice, illness, and death as one, they don't spend most of their time talking about doctrine. Their focus is on immediate concerns of survival, on taking care of the sick and needy, on communicating cherished values to new generations, on resolving problems and tensions in productive rather than in destructive ways, on reconciling after conflicts, on seeking to build more just, humane, and dignified societies. When believers are actively cooperating in such activities, at certain rare but privileged moments, they also express what is deepest in their lives and hearts, that is, their respective faiths, which are the source of strength and inspiration that forms the driving force that guides all their activities.

A Culture of Dialogue

What does it mean to create a "culture of dialogue"? I understand the phrase to mean that when a group of believers has dialogue as an intrinsic part of their religious commitment, whereby a person's very participation in such a group includes an openness and willingness to engage in dialogue, a culture of dialogue exists in that group. This is not something merely theoretical, but has effects in one's choice of activities, use of time and funds, and planning and projects for the future. It results in a community of believers where outsiders can presume that such a group will be open to efforts at dialogue, where one can point to concrete evidence of the group's involvement in dialogue. Dialogue becomes one of the characteristics that identify such communities and movements.

Among Christians, I can note as examples two Catholic lay movements that are well known to all of us, the community of Sant'Egidio and the Focolare Movement. Part of the ethos of these movements is their readiness to take initiatives in the area of dialogue and to participate in the initiatives of others. One takes on this susceptibility to dialogue by the very fact of belonging to Sant'Egidio or Focolare. These two groups are not unique in achieving a culture of dialogue; many other groups of Christians throughout the world have succeeded, in their local situations, in creating a similar culture of dialogue.

We should not think that a culture of dialogue is unique to Christian communities, movements, and organizations. In India, the various Gandhian movements were already in the 1940s among the first to commit themselves to an interreligious approach to nation-building and communal harmony. Among Buddhists, the Tokyo-based Rissho Kosei-kai organization has for many years now given an impressive testimony of their willingness to promote, support (also financially), and participate in dialogue among people of various religions. Among Muslims, one can point to the movement associated with the name of the Turkish scholar Fethullah Gülen that consists of Muslims inspired by the late Kurdish scholar, Said Nursi (d. 1960). They have been especially active in promoting "Abrahamic" dialogue between Jews, Christians, and Muslims. Also, the American Muslim Society (the former "Black Muslims"), under the leadership of Imam Warith Deen Muhammad (d. 2008), built a strong record of interreligious involvement to the point where they can be said to have created an irreversible "culture of dialogue."

In the presence of so many Catholic religious institutes, I do not dare to single out the efforts of some that have taken seriously the task of building a culture of dialogue among the members of their institute, for I would inevitably be neglecting other important examples. However, while acknowledging that other institutes have often done more and done it better and earlier, I would like to take the opportunity to note how my own institute, the Society of Jesus, in its 1995 General Congregation, has committed itself to make the culture of dialogue a characteristic of our institute. These are the words of the Congregation's Decree Five on "Our Mission and Interreligious Dialogue":

> The Jesuit heritage of creative response to the call of the Spirit in concrete situations of life is an incentive to develop a culture of dialogue in our approach to believers of other religions. This culture of dialogue should become a distinctive characteristic of our Society, sent into

the whole world to labor for the greater glory of God and the help of human persons.[5]

Patiently Creating a Culture of Dialogue on the Basis of Trust

Such affirmations are important as statements of intention, but one does not build a culture of dialogue by decree. It is a slow process of study, planning, pastoral decisions and choices, communication among members of the institute, and, most of all, a question of changing attitudes; I must confess that my own institute, despite the good intentions expressed in our decree, is still moving slowly but, I hope, steadily on the path toward creating such a culture.

I believe that the first quality needed is a fruit of the Spirit: *patience*. Like any serious and worthwhile activity, dialogue is not forged overnight and cannot be accomplished by dilettantes. There is much distrust to overcome. Christians can make a long list of wrongs that we have suffered at the hands of the followers of other religions. This includes still unforgotten (and perhaps unforgiven) wrongs of the distant past, as well as those that might have occurred even last month. This is especially the case in those parts of the world where Christians are a minority.

Moreover, we must be aware that the followers of other religions, such as Jews, Muslims, Hindus, Buddhists, have their own lists of wrongs perpetrated against them by Christians. Whether they be the medieval Crusades, European pogroms culminating in the Holocaust, the social indignities, land grabbing, and theft of resources that occurred in the Colonial period, or the history of missionary activity, too often Christians have sought to spread the Gospel by distorting and denigrating other religions. None of this has been forgotten by the followers of other religions. I believe that not only is the burden of history the most difficult obstacle to overcome in building dialogue, but moving beyond that burden is one of the most valuable hoped-for fruits of dialogue. Given this sad burden of history that we all bear, we must not be surprised that both Christians, including members of our institutes, and our neighbors of other religions might show an instinctive resistance to dialogue. Christians may feel that dialogue means associating with the enemy, weakening the social position of Christian minorities, compromising with error, or a naive and willful blindness to problems. The followers of other religions might regard dialogue as the new "soft-sell" face of proselytism, a way of insinuating ourselves into other communities to undermine their faith.

Slowly, and through much hard work, trust must be built. We have to be convinced ourselves and to convince our partners that we are not prisoners of the past, that we can live together and work together better than we have done previously, that individuals and communities can change their attitudes and, above all, that God desires love and mutual acceptance and respect among those who come before the Divine in obedience and worship. Is this not what the Second Vatican Council proposed with regard to Muslims in its decree *Nostra Aetate*?

> Since in the course of centuries not a few conflicts and hostilities have arisen between Christians and Muslims, this sacred synod urges all to forget the past and to work sincerely for mutual understanding, to preserve and to promote together *for the benefit of all* social justice and moral values and peace and freedom. (§3)

In other words, while acknowledging the many conflicts of the past, the council urges Christians and Muslims to move beyond this sad history, urging us to undertake a common mission "for the benefit of all" in four key areas of modern life: social justice, moral values, peace, and freedom.

My Pilgrimage in Dialogue

Over the years, as a teacher I have been engaged mainly in trying to introduce Christians to Islam and to introduce Muslims to Christian faith. This I have done mainly in the Southeast Asian countries of Indonesia, Philippines, and Malaysia, and also in Turkey. Very often these efforts take place in the formal educational situations of university and high school courses, but more often in informal or alternative settings of seminars, workshops, discussion groups, and live-in experiences.

For several years, I have had the experience, unusual for a Catholic priest, of living and teaching in cities in Turkey where I was the only Christian, where *all* my students, teaching colleagues, neighbors, and friends have been Muslims. In those places, our encounters have taken place not only in the classroom but in mosques, homes—my own or those of friends—and even in "secular" locales such as the local produce market, post office, and bookshop.

When Turkish colleagues, students, or neighbors stop by to spend the evening, we do not spend most of the time discussing religion. We talk about politics, the economy, sports, carpets, television programs and films, life in Turkey, in North America (where I was born and raised), and in Indonesia (where I lived most of my adult life). They speak of their concerns for their children and their hopes that they obtain adequate education to find a place in the world and live in a peaceful social environment, but also that their children will interiorize and live according to the values and teachings of Islamic faith. These are topics that present themselves naturally from the common life that we are leading.

Almost always, the moment arrives when I find myself sharing what it means to me to be a Christian and when they elaborate what it means for them to follow Islam. We share our common problems, such as the need to find time for prayer and quiet reflection amid the hectic pace of modern life. We wonder together about God, how a good and loving God would permit such wrongdoing and inequality in this world. We share our experiences of suffering and try to see what we have learned from our acquaintance with sickness, death, and failure. We ask each other what forgiveness means to us and how people can arrive at the seemingly impossible task of actually forgiving one another.

Could anyone claim that the hours that my Muslim friends and I have spent discussing the economy and politics were "merely dialogue," whereas those minutes we spent trying to put into words the place of God in our lives were "proclamation," or for them, the Islamic equivalent, "da'wah"? The reality is that dialogue and proclamation can never be neatly detached from each other in actual life. It is all part of one thing, a life lived together. In a shared life, we are all constantly influencing one another and learning from one another, all growing and being enriched by encountering the acts and attitudes that God produces, through our respective faiths, in each.

The Pedagogy of Religious Encounter: Two Stories

Once, in Izmir, a colleague invited me to his home because his grandfather was dying. When I arrived, the grandfather was in bed, very weak, but still conscious. The family was in the other corner of the room, drinking tea and conversing in low tones. Two or three of the family members—the grandmother, one of the sons, a niece or nephew—were always at the bedside repeating over and over with the grandfather the Islamic profession of faith: "There is no god but Allah (The God)." After a while, other family members would replace those at the bedside, but the prayer went on continually, even after the grandfather fell asleep. I learned that the most common Muslim prayer for a happy death states: "O God, when I reach the moment of death I pray that 'There is no god but God' will be on my lips." During the night, the grandfather died in his sleep, with his wife and three grown children at the bedside repeating, in his name, "There is no god but Allah." I learned more that evening about the Islamic attitude toward death than I had during my years of doctoral studies in Islamic thought.

Another example that remains with me is a "dialogue" I had with several Muslim women whom I never met. I was teaching an introduction to Christian theology at the Theology Faculty of Selcuk University in Konya, Turkey, the city of the beloved Sufi saint and poet, "Mevlana," Jalal al-Din Rumi. I had a small apartment in a working-class neighborhood and was known and well accepted as the "rahip," the Qur'anic word (*rāhib*) for a Christian monk. One afternoon shortly after I began my teaching at the university, I returned home to find a man sitting on the steps in front of my apartment waiting for me. He said that his wife had stopped by earlier in the day but found the door locked. I said, yes, I usually lock my door when I am not at home. He said that I needn't bother, because the women of the neighborhood were always around and would know if anyone who didn't belong tried to get in.

I realized that to them locking my door was an indication that I didn't trust my neighbors, so I never locked my door again during my stay in Konya. Often, I would return from the university to find that someone had anonymously left a covered bowl with rice and eggplant, *börek*, or a few kebabs on the counter. After finishing the food, I used to wash the bowl and leave it in the same place and in a few days it would disappear. Some days later, I would receive another gift of food. Other days I would return after work and find that my clothes had been washed, floors swept, bed linens changed, shirts ironed and folded, and so on. I never saw the person or persons who performed this service, although I presume that it was done by women of the neighborhood.

This went on for six months until, at the end of the semester, it was time for me to leave Konya and return to Rome. I told one of the men who had stopped by to wish me a safe journey that I had a final request. I mentioned all that the neighborhood women had done and asked if I could meet them to thank them for their generous help over the course of the previous months. He said, "You don't have to meet them. They didn't do this for you; they did it for God, and God who sees all that we do will reward them. The Qur'an teaches that *rahipler* (monks) are one of the reasons why Christians are the closest community in friendship to Muslims, so it is an act of worship (*'ibādah*) for us to treat you with kindness."

Neither the man who said this nor the unknown (to me) women who worshiped God by their hospitality were highly trained in the religious sciences, and yet they taught me the important connection between worship of God and generous service to "the stranger in your midst." These women, who epitomize for me Jesus' instructions on the Sermon on the Mount to perform one's charity without letting the left hand know what the right is doing, carried on a genuine dialogue with me, teaching me by deed rather than by word a key aspect of the Islamic way of life. A shared life among believers in God can take many forms.

Mutual Enrichment

Have my encounters with believing, practicing Muslims enriched my life? I can testify without hesitation that they certainly have. Has God used these encounters to make me a better Christian? Again, I can say that God has done so; the encounters have been a great grace. This conviction gives me hope, because if God has worked so powerfully in my life through my encounters with Muslims, I can confidently trust that the same Divine Spirit has been effectively at work among my Muslim friends through their encounters with me. Time and again, Muslims have confirmed how much it has meant to them to have a believing Christian living among them. They remain Muslims, as I remain a Christian, but none of us remains unchanged. We are spiritually richer than before the encounter.

The benefits of dialogue as shared life are not limited to mutual enrichment. Only by living together can people overcome the prejudices, caricatures, and stereotypes that are handed down from one generation to the next and are often reinforced by the communications media. Dialogue provides believers with an opportunity to examine together those universal human tendencies toward exclusivity, chauvinism, hatred, and violence that can infect religious identity and behavior. In dialogue it also becomes clear how much closer religious believers of all faiths are to one another than they are to those who promote the dominant market ideology of competitive wealth, consumerism, and materialism. Some Christians would reduce the benefit of dialogue to a better understanding of the other's faith and reject the possibility of any real mutual enrichment, as though that would imply something lacking in Christian faith. This is not the view of Pope John Paul II. The pope repeatedly emphasized that dialogue should lead to the enrichment of all, Christians as well as their neighbors of other faiths. On his first pastoral visit after his election as pope, the pope instructed the Christians of Ankara to "consider every day the profound roots of the faith in God in whom your Muslim fellow citizens also believe, to draw from it the principle of collaboration with a view to human progress, to *emulation* in doing good. . . ."[6]

Even more clearly, speaking to Muslims in Brussels, Pope John Paul exhorted "all believers, Christian and Muslim, to come to know one another better, to engage in dialogue in order to find peaceful ways of living together and *mutually enriching one another*." He went on to say, in the same talk, that "It is this type of *mutual emulation* which can benefit the whole society, especially those who find themselves most in need of justice, consolation and hope—in a word, those in need of reasons for living."[7] Religious encounter enriches both Christians and the followers of other religions when it is carried out unselfconsciously in the context of shared life. This should not be surprising, for when those who are giving their lives to God through the world's various religions extend their daily worship of that God to include being, acting, discussing, and reflecting with followers of other faiths, the most active participant in the encounter is always God's Holy Spirit.

Notes

1. John Paul II, *Redemptor Hominis (Redeemer of Man): Encyclical addressed by the Supreme Pontiff John Paul II to his venerable brothers in the episcopate, the priests, the religious families, the sons and daughters of the Church, and to all men and women of good will at the beginning of his papal ministry, March 4, 1979* (Washington, D.C.: United States Catholic Conference, 1979), 6.

2. John Paul II, *Redemptoris Missio, Encyclical of the Supreme Pontiff John Paul II on the Permanent Validity of the Church's Missionary Mandate* (Boston: St. Paul Books, 1991), 59.

3. Federation of Asian Bishops' Conferences, "The Second Bishops' Institute for Interreligious Affairs (BIRA II)," 1979, in *For All the Peoples of Asia*, ed. G. Rosales and C. Arevalo, vol. 1 (Manila: Claretian Publications, 1991).

4. Mother Teresa, *A Simple Path*, compiled by Lucinda Vardey (New York: Ballantine Books, 1995), 31.

5. The 1995 General Congregation of the Jesuits, *Documents of the Thirty-fourth General Congregation of the Society of Jesus: The Decrees of General Congregation*

Thirty-four, the Fifteenth of the Restored Society and the Accompanying Papal and Jesuit Documents (St. Louis: Institute of Jesuit Sources, 1995), Decree 5, §17.

6. John Paul II, Homily at Mass, Ankara, November 26, 1979.

7. John Paul II, Address to Muslims, Brussels, May 19, 1985. Many other statements of the pope to the same effect could be cited, for example, his address to religious leaders of various faiths in Jakarta, October 10, 1989, and to the Muslim youth in Casablanca on August 19, 1985, and *Redemptoris Missio*, 56.

3

A Variety of Approaches to Interfaith Dialogue

Interfaith dialogue is a term that encompasses a wide variety of human interaction and includes a broad range of relationships and activities among peoples of various faiths. Narrowing the concept of interfaith dialogue to one type of encounter or identifying dialogue with only one of its forms can limit the richness of what can be hoped for and actually achieved in such encounters.

Examples and Approaches to Interfaith Dialogue

I would like to begin by offering four contrasting examples of interfaith dialogue that have been happening in various parts of the world, and then I will present some reflections on the nature of dialogue that can be derived from these examples.

MuCARD

The southern Philippines, consisting of the large island of Mindanao and the Sulu archipelago, has been in recent years a region of ongoing "low intensity" conflict between Christians and Muslims. The predominantly Christian central government has resisted, sometimes brutally, Muslim aspirations for either full independence or, more often, for an autonomous region encompassing Muslim-majority areas. In the early 1970s, tensions between Muslims and Christians erupted in open conflict of violent nature-killings, the burning of churches and mosques, kidnappings, the destruction of whole villages, disruption of social services and widespread dislocation of populations caused by hundreds of thousands of refugees on both sides.

The reasons for the conflict find their roots in history, in social and economic problems, in ethnic differences and cultural prejudices more than in the-

Previously published in *Ecumenical Trends* 31, no. 2 (Fall 2002): 17-22 (first published in *Pro dialogo* 108, no. 3 [2001]: 342-50). Reprinted by permission.

ology of religious practice. The complex nature of social and political realities ensures that interreligious tensions and their underlying causes will not admit of easy solutions and thus will not be resolved quickly. Mutual suspicions, built up over the years and often handed down to children and embedded in their social psyche at a very early age, are an obstacle that prevents peaceful and mutually beneficial solutions.

Almost twenty years ago, in this environment of suspicion and sporadic out-breaks of violence, MuCARD was born. The name is an acronym for Muslim-Christian Agency for Rural Development. It is an umbrella association of more than 120 village organizations composed of Muslims and Christians working together for local village development. The region is the poorest in the modern Philippines and often lacks the economic infrastructure that characterizes other parts of the nation. The people are mainly farmers, with wet rice paddies or stands of coconut palms for copra production, and fisherfolk.

In this situation, the dialogue consists not in the exchange of philosophical or theological ideas, but in a commitment to work to overcome time-honored prejudices and to produce concrete improvements in the lot of people. The projects undertaken by MuCARD are modest and doable, not abstract aims or grandiose schemes. The project sometimes consists in simply collecting money for the purchase of a small truck to transport fishermen's catch to market or agricultural seminars to train farmers to experiment with new varieties of rice or livestock. Elsewhere, the project may be jointly run day-care programs for children or recreational centers for the elderly. In some villages, MuCARD has concentrated on adult literacy programs or preventative health care. These are concrete activities that arise from the needs of the people and whose benefits for all can be readily observed. In the process of planning projects and working together to realize them, old suspicions and resentments between Christians and Muslims are slowly being overcome.

MuCARD is not another secular NGO aimed at material progress. It is an agency made up of believing Muslims and Christians working for better understanding and harmony through cooperative ventures. Praying together, in a way that is acceptable to both Muslims and Christians, is a regular feature of MuCARD activities, as are cultural presentations in song and dance aimed at enabling both groups to appreciate better the cultural heritage of the other.[1]

Study of Media Presentations of Religion

My second example of interfaith dialogue is taken from a different part of the world, that of the Mediterranean basin. In the late 1980s, the Islamic Call Society,[2] based in Tripoli, Libya, and the Vatican's Pontifical Council for Interreligious Dialogue undertook a study of the way religion is presented in the modern communications media. This joint project also was a response to mutual concerns. The Muslim organization expressed concern at the way the religion of Islam is often presented in modern films, television, novels, and even news programs as a xenophobic, violent, reactionary faith whose followers are unable to live with others. This caricature, they felt, is particularly disseminated by the Western commercial media. For its part, the Vatican office felt that Christian faith is not only frequently misrepresented in European and North American articles and films, but that Christianity in some Muslim countries is also presented as a corrupted, superseded form of true religion, a judgment that wounds the sensibilities of local Christians.

The two organizations gathered a mixed group of religious scholars and media people to study the situations together. It was a long-term project, extending over six years, with seminars carried out first in Tripoli, then in Rome, and finally in Vienna. The scholarly presentations analyzed the role of the communications media vis-à-vis religion and religious groups. On the one hand, the media can play a key role in seeking to overcome prejudices, misunderstandings, and tensions among religious groups. The media has great opportunities to change attitudes and foster mutual respect. On the other hand, the media is all too often an aggravating factor that perpetuates religious, national, and ethnic stereotypes. It can sharpen fears and heighten tensions.

In the study seminars, participants were instructed to bring concrete examples of both phenomena, that of well-made media productions that strive to build greater understanding and acceptance of others, as well as those that distort the faith of others, build fears, and reinforce preconceptions. At the end of this study project, participants signed an agreement to protest jointly against media presentations that promote distrust and misunderstanding as well as to commend those that strive sincerely to create a fairer, more accurate image of religions.

In this example, the religious groups involved were not simply stating how they respectively view an issue of common concern but sought to study the problem in depth and to offer jointly a way of facing the problem. The interfaith dialogue, while scholarly and academic, was action-oriented.

Educating Youth for Dialogue

My third example is one in which I was personally involved. In 1995, the Jesuits—the religious order of which I am a member—committed themselves to be actively engaged in interfaith dialogue. Some individual members had already been quite involved in dialogue, but at the last worldwide governing meeting of the Jesuits, interreligious dialogue was understood to be an integral part of Jesuit life. Jesuits around the world were directed to create a "culture of dialogue" in which the commitment to live one's Christian faith in today's world should be carried out in the context of interfaith dialogue.

This, of course, is easier said than done. It requires an attitudinal change and reorientation of thinking to see committed believers of other religions not as rivals or foes but as partners in working for more just, humane, and harmonious societies. The new generation of young Jesuits, those who will take our Christian way of life into the next millennium, were set as the priority for the transformation of attitudes. Between December 1996 and January 1997, we gathered about fifty Jesuits, still in various stages of their studies, in Kuala Lumpur, Malaysia. The young people came from twelve countries of Asia and Oceania. There we spent the time studying the teachings of the Catholic Church and the pope that encourage all Christians to be involved in interfaith dialogue and the decisions of our last worldwide meeting, which aimed at reorienting the Jesuits toward engagement in dialogue.

It became clear to us that theory alone is not sufficient to change attitudes. It needs to be supplemented by personal encounter, by coming to know people of other faiths as friends and prospective co-workers. So we arranged what we called "exposure" programs for the young Jesuits. They visited the places of worship and had long discussions with the followers of the Islamic, Buddhist, Hindu, and Sikh religions. We were happy to see that the Muslims, Buddhists, Sikh, and Hindus whom we encountered were eager to help prepare the exposure sessions and took part with enthusiasm. For example, the young Jesuits visited the headquarters of the Muslim youth organization of Malaysia, where they shared for several hours on matters of faith. After tea, they were invited by the Muslim students to the mosque to observe the Islamic prayer. Similar programs were undertaken at the Sikh gurudwara, the Hindu temple, and the Buddhist vihara.

This opportunity to learn, not merely the facts about the beliefs and practices of people of other religions, but to discuss matters of faith, life, society, and ethics, and to observe the way that other believers come before God in worship, is essential for any real change of attitude. This kind of interfaith dialogue should not be left to the experts, but should include ordinary believers, especially the youth.

Monks in Dialogue

The fourth example I will offer here is that of an ongoing program of exchange between Christian and Buddhist monks. There are obvious similarities in the way of life of Buddhist and Christian monks. Although there is a wide variety in the way that monastic life is practiced, both by Christian and by Buddhist monks, monks of both religions usually take a number of vows, or religious promises, such as not to marry, to hold property in common, and to obey the direction of a religious superior or spiritual master. They commit themselves to a community life in monasteries characterized by prayer and work, and great importance is placed on the values of silence and contemplation.

United by similar ways of life, Buddhist and Christian monks profess very different faiths, defined in quite divergent theologies. The Buddhist religion can sometimes appear to the poorly informed Christian observer as an atheistic or, at least, nontheistic faith, a position very difficult for Christians, whose faith is rooted in the encounter with the One God, to accept. On the other side, to Buddhists, the Christian understanding of God can seem to anthropomorphize the Divine, to regard God as a giant Personality not very different from (even though much better than) the human person. Buddhists understand their faith not so much as a personal encounter with God as a transpersonal approach to Ultimate Reality.

From this dramatic divergence of theological understanding, it is surprising that both Buddhist and Christian monks consider prayer and meditation to be essential procedures for following their path of the spirit. Both perceive communitarian life as a valid and useful way to live out one's religious commitment. Clearly, there is much for these monks to learn from one another, many elements of their respective ways of life that offer matter for discussion, and many ways in which they can challenge one another and profit from encountering one another's way of life.

About twenty years ago, monks from Christian monasteries in Europe and from Buddhist monasteries in Japan began to take turns spending periods of one to three months in each other's monasteries. They were present not as observers, but as participants in the daily schedule. They took part, to the extent they could do so without compromising their respective faiths, in the practices of worship of the host monastery. They learned the methods and practices of meditation of the other and discovered the rhythms of monastic life, which have evolved over the centuries in their monastic traditions.

Perhaps the most important element of this ongoing intermonastic encounter is the time the monks spend, at the end of the visit, in mutual reflection on their experience. The monks of the host monastery gain insight from the observations of the guests, and the guest monks find their approach to their own faith and way of life immensely broadened by the encounter with a monastic life that is at the same time similar but also very different from their own.[3]

Observations on Interfaith Dialogue

Reflecting on these four examples of interfaith dialogue, I would like to make several observations.

1. Interfaith dialogue is sometimes accused of being an activity of the intellectual elite, involving mainly those trained in religious sciences and academicians. Yet, if interfaith dialogue is to affect the way religious believers regard one another and live together, this dialogue must reach the "grass roots," that is, ordinary believers without formal religious or academic training. For this to happen, dialogue must take up issues that respond to people's needs and offer hope that the dialogue will improve the lot of people in society. Moreover, the dialogue must be carried out in ways that are appropriate to the cultural and educational background of people. Hence, the model of academic seminars cannot be the only model for interfaith dialogue.

The case of MuCARD, the first example cited above, presents us with an instance of interfaith dialogue among farmers, fishermen, and rural villagers. This dialogue has been successful because the people themselves set the agenda and carry out the interfaith cooperation on projects that have meaning for them and that offer the hope of a better life together. In the economically and educationally impoverished setting in which they find themselves, these villagers have placed the priority on development projects rather than the exchange of intellectual concepts.

MuCARD is not simply a development agency but an association of believers with religious goals. Cooperation in socioeconomic areas is a means used to achieve the religious aim of moving beyond conflict to establish peace and reconciliation. Interreligious tension is not simply accepted as "given," but the believer, Muslim and Christian, seek together to identify the root causes of tensions and conflicts in careful social analysis. Only when these deep-rooted factors, often of a political or economic nature, are named can cooperative planning be directed at relieving the causes of tension. The farmers and fisherfolk who make up MuCARD are aware that misunderstandings, resentments, and suspicions inherited from the past—the "burden of history" that we all bear—can have violent and destructive results. They way to move beyond the past and to respect the real differences that exist is by coming to know one another, forming friendships, and working together for the good of all. This is only possible if there is increased knowledge and understanding of each other's faiths. Thus, interfaith dialogue is not an end in itself but oriented toward the goal of a more peaceful, harmonious life in common.

I would not like to give the impression that MuCARD is the unique example of grass-roots dialogue that could be presented. Hundreds of examples, from many regions, of small interfaith groups doing sometimes heroic yet unheralded work at local levels could be offered. Without developing further their activities, I will cite two groups I encountered within the past month in widely separated areas of the southern Philippines. One is the United Muslim Christian Urban Poor Association in Zamboanga, working to oppose through the law courts plans to uproot and relocate urban slum dwellers. The second is the Basilan Human Rights Monitoring Groups, with a membership made up of an equal number of Muslims and Christians. The groups try to keep track of persons who have disappeared or been summarily arrested, to follow up their cases with the authorities, and to advocate their release.

2. None of this takes away from the need for a dialogue of experts and scholars, which remains a key area for interfaith dialogue. Religious believers have the obligation to try to understand the vital issues of today's world. If they remain in closed devotional circles, they will become irrelevant to people's real needs. However, the problems that committed religious believers of every faith face in today's world are complex and require the expertise of specialists in many disciplines. Religious scholars alone cannot hope to treat complicated issues for which they have little specialized training. They need the scientific input of competent experts in the field.

These assumptions underlie my second example, the effort to study and take position on the role of the communications media both in building understanding among believers of different religions and in spreading misinformation, suspicion, and fear of the other. It is not effective simply to gather religious leaders to condemn media abuses. People who earn their living in the media and those whose profession is the study of the media have important contributions to make to the discussion. In order to be grounded in reality, concrete examples of positive media undertakings must be presented and analyzed, as well as the ways the media often distort and show disrespect for people's faiths.

The interfaith effort to study a problem does not provide its own justification. It must be action-oriented—in this case, a joint commitment to monitor the media, to praise what is good and condemn what is bad. The kind of follow-up produced by such a seminar is a key element in its evaluation. What did it achieve? Has the expenditure of time, funds, and scholarships resulted in types of interfaith cooperation that would not have been otherwise attained? In other words, did the seminar produce concrete results that justified the time, money, and effort put into it?

3. Turning to my third example, we see that interfaith dialogue has a place in the education of youth. Interfaith dialogue is not only for the "wise and wizened," but also for those still in the process of preparing themselves for their life's work. It is not only for those who are intending to involve themselves in interfaith activities, but for all those believers whose worldly activities will bring them into direct or indirect contact with people of other faiths.

To be effective, education for dialogue cannot remain limited to information that can be obtained from books and classroom presentations. Such formal introductions to the faith of others, while useful in providing background information, remain on the level of concepts and are unable to touch the crucial "human" element. They remain "outside" the religious reality that is lived by people of faith. For changing attitudes and perceptions, there is no substitute for personal encounters. No books or lectures can substitute for the deep faith values communicated through hospitality, smiles, sharing jokes, and recounting personal histories. No amount of reading can take the place of observing directly how people of another faith approach God in worship. Opportunities for encountering people of other faiths must become an integral part of religious education if we hope to build within our own communities a "culture of dialogue."

4. Finally, let me say a word about the dialogue of monks. I am more and more convinced that religious faith stands or falls on religious experience. Dogmas and ritual are a part of every religion, but at the heart of every religion is the desire for an experience of the Divine. Each of our religions explains and defines this experience differently, but there is an unspoken agreement among all believers that without an experiential encounter with the One, the Absolute, religious commitment has not achieved its goal.

However, it is not easy to share our religious experience with others. We need to build a level of trust before we disclose our deepest faith experiences. No one wants to be ridiculed as superficial, dismissed as naïve or deluded, or suspected of self-aggrandizement. Our religious experience is the "hidden treasure" we carry around with us, and we are careful about what we share in this area and with whom we share it.

For this reason, the monks take a long time to get to know one another, one another's ways of life, and the methods and practices that each uses to deepen their religious experience. Similar terms and practices might be based on very different concepts; conversely, despite extremely diverse conceptual and proce- dural frameworks, some very similar religious experiences may occur. It takes much patience and willingness to suspend judgment in order to sort out and work through the subtle and multilevel misunderstandings than can arise. Only after a long period of having experienced one another's life and after having engaged in the contemplative activities that form an essential part of that life do the monks attempt a common reflection on what they learned or, more precisely, on what they think they have learned, in the process.

I do not believe that as a form of interfaith dialogue the sharing of religious experience needs to be limited to monks. Every sincere religious believer has something to say of his or her experience, but it is difficult to overcome our natu- ral reluctance and caution. It cannot be hoped that people will feel comfortable in doing this unless they know their partners well. This takes time and much good will. But the rewards of being able to put into words some of the deepest values of our personal life of faith and the discovery of comparable honesty and openness on the part of another believer can make the sharing of religious expe- riences one of the richest and most rewarding forms of interfaith dialogue

I conclude by repeating my opening statement. Interfaith dialogue is not one thing. It encompasses a wide variety of human interaction and includes a broad range or relationships and activities among peoples of various faiths. All of these can be beneficial for the individual believer, for one's community of faith, and for society as a whole.

Notes

1. MuCARD continues to play a role in peace-building and NGO activities from within the Philippines and from abroad. For more information, see the following Web site: http://mucaard-uk.org/Whoweare.aspx (accessed August 15, 2009).—Ed.

2. To see the scope of its activities, including Christian-Muslim dialogue, visit http://islamic-call.net/english/ (accessed August 15, 2009).—Ed.

3. A recent effort to expand the monastic dialogue came to fruition in 1994 with the establishment of Monastic Interreligious Dialogue (MID); its Web site is a good resource for the history and rationale for dialogue among monastics from various faiths. See http:// monasticdialog.com/mid.php?id=14 (accessed August 15, 2009).—Ed.

4

Muslim Approaches to Dialogue

A Christian Appraisal

In this chapter, I will try to offer a survey of the views toward dialogue with Christians expressed by Muslims in published articles as well as in addresses, speeches, and interventions delivered at various encounters with Christians. The main purpose is to try to bring together the views of Muslims in recent years concerning relations with Christians in an attempt to listen to them outlining in their own terms the meaning, purpose, problems, and prospects of dialogue with Christians today. A secondary purpose is to offer material for our own reflections on what this might mean for our lives as Christians in situations of daily life among Muslims.

Some limitations of my approach will be immediately apparent. Those who publish articles and attend interreligious conferences in the Islamic community are in positions of academic, religious, and political preeminence, as are their counterparts in the Christian churches. To what extent do they represent and reflect the views, feelings, fears, and aspirations of the "silent majority" of Muslims who have little opportunity to express themselves in the public forum? Moreover, the authors often come from those sectors of Islamic society that are most sensitized to the necessity of living today in a pluralistic world, of coming to terms with the position of Islam as one of a number of world faiths that cannot escape contact—amicable, cooperative, or confrontative—with one another in modern life. I do not mean to imply a priori that the views expressed in this article are always more irenic and optimistic than the opinions of rank-and-file Muslims in the *ummah*. As we know also from our experience in the Christian churches, academic, religious, and political leaders are often more rigidly bound by ideological and theological considerations than the average person. The basic tolerance and cooperation required by survival and well-being in most societies is frequently challenged by those whose education or position removes them from the daily struggles of work, family, and urban or village life.

Previously published as "Muslim Approaches to Dialogue with Christians," in *Islam and the Modern Age* 15 (February 1984): 37-50. Reprinted by permission.

A final preliminary caution is that a topic of this nature, along with our own natural bias, can distort the actual place given to Christian-Muslim relations in the minds and basic concerns of Muslims. Just as the relation with Islam is still a quite marginal issue in the life and thought of the vast majority of Christians, so also most Muslims, in the ambit of their daily problems, do not give highest priority to their relations with Christians. Even for most Muslim leaders, the relation between Islam and Christianity is a very secondary topic indeed. I do not want to form the impression from this article that Muslim-Christian relations is a topic that generates burning interest in the Islamic *ummah* as a whole.

The approaches of Muslims toward interreligious questions could be broadly divided into those that treat theological issues and those whose concern is primarily ethical. Let us briefly look at the issues raised by their proponents in each of these categories.

Theological Issues

The most basic theological question for a Muslim vis-à-vis those of other religions finds a close parallel among Christians and sets the tone for what his attitude toward the other religion will be. It is the question of, according to Islam, the salvation of non-Muslims. If, according to Islamic teaching, the Christian is a *kāfir* destined for hell-fire unless he/she accepts Islam, certainly the Muslim cannot "dialogue" with the Christian with any goal other than of convincing him to change his religion. Mushir-ul Haq states the problem clearly for the Islamic community:

> Analogous to recent Roman Catholic admissions, the question we must ask is this: can Muslims frankly admit that people even outside the fold of Islam will be saved? One of the greatest causes of conflict between various faiths will disappear if all the other religions also admit this possibility.[1]

In working out how this can be possible, Mohamed Talbi refers to earlier theological attempts, such as that of Abu Hamid al-Ghazali (d. 1111) in medieval times and of twentieth-century thinkers such as Muhammad Abduh, Ahmad Amin, and Yusuf Ali.[2] In arguing the possibility of salvation for non-Muslims, Talbi relies on Qur'anic verses such as 2:62; 5:62, 69; and 4:150. Fazlur Rahman underlines the importance of such verses for an Islamic attitude toward those of other religions:

> In both these verses (2:62; 5:69), the vast majority of Muslim commentators exercise themselves fruitlessly to avoid having to admit the obvious meaning: that those—from any section of humankind—who believe in God and the Last Day and do good deeds are saved. They either say that by Jews, Christians, and Sabaeans here are meant those

who have actually become "Muslims"—which interpretation is clearly belied by the fact that "Muslims" constitute only the first of the four groups of "those who believe"—or that they were those good Jews, Christians and Sabaeans who lived before the advent of the Prophet Muhammad—which is an even worse *tour de force*.[3]

Haji Fadlullah Wilmot has approached the question through a careful analysis of the Islamic concept of the *dīn al-fiṭrah*. I will summarize his argument in his words:

> Muslims believe that God has not granted any special status to any person or group. His love, providence, care for and judgment of all men is one. All people—Muslims and non-Muslims—stand to God in identically the same relationship, i.e. they are judged objectively by the same law. The Divine will is knowable directly through revelation or indirectly through science.
>
> The Muslim does not look on the non-Muslim as a fallen, hopeless creature, but as a perfect creature capable by himself of achieving the highest righteousness. Muslims believe that non-Muslims possess what Islam calls *dīn al-fiṭrah*, or natural religion. This is original religion which Muslims define as Islam. The historical religions are outgrowths of *dīn al-fiṭrah*, containing within them different amounts or degrees of it.
>
> Christianity, Hinduism, or Buddhism are to the Muslim *de jure,* legitimate religions despite their divergence from traditional Islam. It is possible for an adherent of one religion to tell an adherent of another: "We are both equal members of a universal religious brotherhood. Both our traditional religions are *de jure* for they have both issued from and are based on a common source, the religion of God which He has implanted in both of us equally.[4]

Islam is the unadulterated, uncorrupted *dīn al-fiṭrah*, but other religions reflect it to a greater or lesser extent. Salvation is the reward of good works, and all those who produce good works will attain that reward:

> Islam not only acclaims the good works wherever and by whomever they are done, it regards them as the only justification in the eyes of God and warns that not an iota of good work or mischief will be lost on the Day of Reckoning. The non-Muslim has the public record of works he has done to justify him in Muslim eyes: to establish him as a man of great piety and saintliness. In Islam, good deeds earn merit with God regardless of the religious adherence of their authors. Salvation consists of nothing more than such merit as the good works earn. The act of faith is a work which is added and whose inclusion affects the whole.[5]

Other authors stress that Muslims must affirm the uniqueness of Islam as the only valid way to salvation, which precludes any positive assertions about the salvific value of previous religions. Muhammad Hamidullah holds that if any religion were to admit any of its predecessors as entirely sufficient for the eternal salvation of mankind, it would put itself in a self-contradictory position.[6] Isma'il al-Faruqi elaborates on the same theme:

> In Islam as well as in Christianity, and probably all other religions, the man of religion does not, in his religious claim, assert a tentative hypothesis, nor *a* truth among other truths, or *a* version of the truth among other possible versions, but *the* truth. This is so much part of religious experience and of the claim resting on such experience that to deny it is to caricature the religion as a whole. Neither Islam nor Christianity can or will ever give it up. . . . If the religion in question lays claim to *the* truth, contrary or diverse claims are intellectual problems which cannot be ignored. In the absence of evidence to the contrary, the exclusivist claim is as much *de jure* as it is *de facto*.[7]

The tension existing in a Christian theology of religions between an absolute claim to truth enclosed within a single revelatory tradition and an existential awareness of divine salvific activity outside that tradition finds a parallel in Muslim attitudes toward Christianity. Some Muslims have attempted to resolve the issue by emphasizing the common elements found in various religions and the action of the one God animating all.

> All religions teach the reality of God and obedience to the will of God which translate as good will and peace among men. . . . Peace and justice are indivisible. Who can understand this better than the true votaries of the great religions which keep the love of God and the love of man in their hearts?[8]

A rather limited, but highly articulate circle of modern Muslim thinkers, including a prominent number of European converts to Islam, resolves the tension between universality of truth and the absoluteness of each religious tradition through esoteric/exoteric dichotomy. At the deepest, esoteric level, the Truth underlying all religion (*dīn*) is one; however, at the exoteric level of scriptures, laws, and rites, the religions are many. Considered eccentric and even unorthodox by many Muslims, but reflecting a long tradition of Sufi thought, the proponents of this view[9] stress the need for a believer to follow strictly and integrally his own religious tradition as the absolute way to salvation, realizing at the same time that Truth/Reality (*al-ḥaqq*) is one and universal. This is put succinctly by an Italian Muslim:

> The ways are different and must stay different, and instead of asking God why He gave us so many ways, we must both face the reality of

the fact that there are many providential and presently valid ways, but we cannot but accept and follow only one of them in its original, traditional, and orthodox formulation.[10]

Approaching the question of the status of Christians vis-à-vis Islam, an Indian *ʿālim* (Muslim religious scholar) has held that someone who meditates on the Qur'an will be led by God to reflect on the closeness of Christians to Muslims and on their many good qualities.[11] On the most basic issue to the two religions, that of the majestic transcendent unity of God, Christians and Muslims are in agreement. These words of M. Hayath Khan are echoed in the viewpoint of many Muslims who consider Christians as people with whom they can speak and live and share because of their common faith in one God.

At the same time, in dialogue situations Muslims often do not hesitate to repeat the Qur'anic accusations of *shirk* against Christians. Individuals like Isma'il al-Faruqi are convinced that Christians were called to the absolute monotheism of Islamic prophethood, but have strayed through a *taqlīd*, a blind following of the errors of their fathers. Possibly the most prolific and challenging of Muslim writers on Christianity and Muslim-Christian dialogue,[12] he sees the goal of dialogue as a conversion to the truth. In a neo-Wahhabi approach to tradition, Isma'il al-Faruqi holds that Christians and Muslims both, through their mutual confrontations, will be led by God to abandon the accumulated errors of past centuries to return to the original, unadulterated message of the prophets.[13]

The idea that relations between Muslims and Christians should lead to a mutual benefit is expressed in various ways by a number of writers. Ali Merad considers the goal to be that of mutual enrichment[14]—Christians and Muslims need each other to stimulate and deepen their appreciation of what each has. His life of Charles de Foucauld was an attempt to see what the life of a Christian saint could mean for a Muslim. Other Muslims in recent years have explored the life of Francis of Assisi for the same purpose.[15] Khaled Bentounes, the *shaykh* of the *Alawiyya tarīqah*, expressed a desire for a meeting with Mother Teresa because "she and I live the same faith in God."

> She is a Christian and lives her faith in Christianity. I am Muslim; Islam is my way. However, we find ourselves at one in the love of God and that of humans who have love for one another. There is, therefore, a convergence in our goal; only the ways of achieving it diverge. How can one find God, if not in His creation?[16]

In the context of constructing interreligious reconciliation, K. G. Saiyadain has called for a frank admission of wrongs committed by Muslims and Christians against each other.

> I am not offering any defense of misguided or irreligious Muslim rulers or others who may have strayed away from the path and defied Islam's

insistence on peace as the only right way to live. While we should condemn unreservedly persons who have fallen from grace—whatever their
religious labels—it would be unfair to place the responsibility for their
ungodly and inhuman acts on their respective religions. In judging a
religion, we should do so as it is at its best and in the context of its
genuine teachings, for what matters in the global context are the elements of rationality, decency, peace, and liberality of mind enshrined in
a religion and not all the faults that one can always find in its individual
followers.[17]

Some writers propose that this is the only attitude that the followers of
Islam are permitted to have toward others. Any approach to others based on
enmity, competition ("except in what is best"), or aggression is inconsistent
with Qur'anic teaching. Fazlur Rahman stresses that the ultimate Qur'anic
statement on the diversity of religions is that God has willed the plurality in
order that the various faith communities "compete with each other in doing
good." Despite continuing conflicts and tensions he is optimistic that this goal is
achievable, "provided the Muslims hearken more to the Qur'an than to the historic formulations of Islam and provided that recent pioneering efforts continue
to yield a Christian doctrine more compatible with universal monotheism and
egalitarianism."[18]

Mohamed Talbi holds that Islam accepts and respects the diversity of
religions. "The most illustrious model is to be sought in the Constitution of
Madinah promulgated by the Prophet himself. This Constitution associates, in
a perfect spirit of harmony, Jews and Muslims."[19] Other Muslims point as well
to the Constitution of Madinah as the basis on which Muslims can construct life
in a modern pluralistic society.[20] Still others make the pact between Muhammad
and the Christians of Najran an application to Christians of the principles of
the Constitution of Madinah, which had been ratified with the Jews.[21]

Ethical Issues

Another approach entirely to interreligious relations is taken by those Muslims
who choose not to treat theological questions but center their attention on ethical goals. A frequent refrain found in modern writings, one not foreign to the
text of *Nostra Aetate*, is that as believers in the one God charged with establishing His will on earth, Christians and Muslims (and Jews) have a mission to
oppose evil and godlessness in the world. The instances of this approach are too
many to cite in full,[22] but the view of Seyyed Hossein Nasr may be seen as representative. Criticizing Hans Küng's willingness to dialogue with non-believers,
he states:

The much more logical position would be to place all the religions,
including Christianity, in one world or camp before which stand the

forces of agnosticism and secularism. In fact Christianity, already scarred by several centuries of battle against humanism, secularism, and rationalism, has the choice of either returning to the universe of religion as such, to the sacred cosmos in which Islam, Hinduism, Buddhism, etc. still breathe, or attempt to bring about some kind of a wedding with the all-embracing Christian vision in the West.[23]

A number of Muslims take the struggle for liberation as a field where Christian-Muslim cooperation is to be expected and desired. Abdelmadjid Charfi sees this collaboration both in political terms of striving for the national liberation of peoples and in social terms of the structural change of oppressive social systems. Highly critical of most "dialogue encounters" between Christians and Muslims as well as of the aforementioned monotheistic battles against godless secularism, he states:

> First of all, there are those encounters which have as their goal, avowed or not, the defense of the established order. Other meetings want nothing more than crusades against dominant atheism and materialism. And we need not speak of still other congresses where one merely exchanges compliments, utters pious views, and avoids from the beginning the heart of the problem.[24]

Some Muslims are reading Christian works on the theology of liberation and have explored their relevance for the Islamic community and its mission in the world.[25] Highly critical of the rational theology represented by Afghani, Muhammad Abduh, Al-Kawakibi, and so on, Asghar Ali Engineer describes liberation theology as follows:

> The theology of liberation demands continuous struggle and striving for betterment of life and restructuring environment. Unlike the "status-quoist" theology, its primary aim is not to provide solace and justification for suffering and misery, treating them as inevitable conditions of life. Liberation theology is not theology of solace but that of struggle.[26]

Liberation is not tied to a Christian view of God and humanity, according to this author, but is also in profound accord with Islamic "stewardship" of God's creation.

> Liberation theology seeks to re-emphasize the central concern of Islam with social justice and its fundamental emphasis on liberating the weaker sections and the oppressed masses and radically restructuring society to eliminate all vested interests which could ultimately lead to the creation of classless society. It is needless to point out that the liberation theology is opposed to fundamentalist movements which seek

to emphasize traditional issues and seek to give new lease of life to traditional theology without concerning themselves with the problems of the modern world, economic exploitation, social injustices, and anti-imperialist struggles to liberate the Third World countries from the clutches of the imperialist forces.[27]

The ethical goal of common service to humanity is described by some Muslims as the purpose of dialogue. In the words of Mukti Ali, "In this search for an ethical system that will enable people to survive as civilized human beings in the coming decades, it is of the greatest importance that the various world religions continue their dialogue with each other."[28]

It is not surprising that Muslims, like others, are drawn to joining hands with people of other religions by the urgent demands of peace. Particularly, the increasing danger of nuclear war has been a catalytic factor in drawing together believers in previously unconsidered collaboration. In yet another statement critical of dominant trends in Islamic theology, Saiyadain asks:

Will Islam, will the other religions petrify into rigid dogmas and remain mainly or exclusively preoccupied with their traditional business of saving the individual soul or will they grow into dynamic movements, throwing away the flotsam and jetsam from their surface and respond to the new constructive and destructive forces in their world? Will they, for instance, be able to meet the challenge of the atom and the atomic war that hangs like a doom over mankind and teach people how to live in this atomic age?[29]

If the question is asked why Muslims believe they ought to enter into the dialogue process in any of its forms, various reasons and goals are given. One frequent response is not unfamiliar to Christians from their own experience—dialogue is a method and strategy for the propagation of Islam. The Muslim is commanded to carry out *da'wah*, proclamation of the message of Islam. In their discussion and writings in the dialogical forum, the object is to state Islamic belief to an audience who would not otherwise hear it. Basic Islamic teachings are reiterated and adapted to the concerns or prejudices of the partners in dialogue. Immediate results are not realistically expected. However, in a growing climate of understanding and goodwill, the truth of Islam, according to Muslim convictions, will be apparent to those who are open and ready for it. Ahmad von Denffer states the case succinctly:

Even though many of the Christian participants in dialogue are apparently not at all ready to accept the Muslim invitation to Islam (where it is being extended!) and hence the *da'wah* seems not to be fruitful, these Christian participants, going back to their own communities, do function as effective communicators of a new trend, which encourages

Christians generally—not only inside the arena of dialogue conferences—to at least listen to what Muslims have to say.[30]

In encounters with Christians, Muslims are not embarrassed to proclaim their beliefs in a way that seems uncompromising to others.[31] In fact, they expect the same forthrightness and conviction on the part of the Christians and sometimes complain when Christians are reticent about their personal faith convictions. As A. K. Brohi explains it:

> My experience of Christian-Muslim dialogue in some places has been one of total disappointment. The Christian theologians and philosophers treat religion sociologically, that is, view it as though they were outsiders and not as believers. So viewed, religion is denuded of all its value and relevance to life and indeed ceases to be religion. . . . I often find that modern Western philosophers and theologians, while talking to people like us who are *believers*, are conducting a dialogue which may be regarded as a dialogue between the deaf and the dumb: they are themselves deaf because their ears are not open to religious truth as it has been revealed by God, and we are dumb because what we experience as believers transcends philosophical analysis and speculation and cannot be communicated to them in the philosophical jargon which they adore, forgetting that all truth is simple.[32]

A reticence on the part of Christians stemming from an aversion to proselytizing as well as an embarrassment concerning proffering "unprovable" faith convictions in academic situations seems often to be read by Muslims as a lack of conviction and an accommodation to a scholarly distancing of oneself from one's faith.

For many Muslims, a positive goal of dialogue is the creation of an atmosphere where a frank exchange of views and even complaints can take place. A familiar relationship with Christians implies, for many, that resentments and angers that otherwise would simmer and grow can be spoken, confronted, and answered. Thus, in dialogical situations they take the occasion to complain that according to Muslims the Christian churches are still instruments of North Atlantic political/economic domination. Many feel that Muslims have a right and obligation to live in an environment where the *sharī'ah* may be fully applied and carried out, whereas Christians have never supported, and wherever possible, have campaigned against what they consider their religious duty. Others complain that Christianity has capitulated to Western civilization, sacrificing its religious and moral values. They feel that even in situations of dialogue, Christians are enthusiastic partners only when they are in a position of control and that they have not yet arrived at the willingness to risk efforts of shared initiative and responsibility. Such complaints and accusations are not disruptive of dialogue, according to many Muslim thinkers, but are of its essence.

Other approaches to the "why" of dialogue are given by various Muslim authors. According to Mahmoud Ayoub and Mushir-ul Haq, dialogue is necessary for Muslims because it is commanded in the Qur'an.[33] The views of Mohamed Talbi and Ziaul Hasan Faruqi appear to be a development of I-thou personalist philosophy that it is only through interaction that a person (and by extension a religious community) grows and becomes itself. Talbi affirms: "What dialogue can and should do in this initial stage is to help the communities to communicate with one another, to become open to each other."[34] Z. H. Faruqi stresses that by entering into another person's religious experience he comes to a more profound awareness of his own.[35] Isma'il al-Faruqi's starting point for dialogue is "What ought I to do?"

> In the circumstances in which Muslims and Christians find themselves today, primacy belongs to the ethical questions, not the theological. Dialogue should seek at first to establish a mutual understanding, if not a community of conviction, of the Muslim and Christian answers to the fundamental question, What ought I to do? If Muslims and Christians may not reach ready appreciation of each other's ideas or figurizations of divine nature, they may yet attempt to do the will of that nature, which they both hold to be one. To seek "God's way," i.e., to understand, to know, to grasp its relevance for every occasion, to anticipate its judgment of every moral deed—that is the prerequisite whose satisfaction may put the parties to the dialogue closer to mutual self-understanding.[36]

Reflecting a trend found in Christian circles in Asia, Z. H. Faruqi feels that up to now dialogue has been conducted on a Western academic agenda, but to be fruitful it must move into areas that can be called the "dialogue of life." "All agree that service to parents, kindliness to the poor, and aiding of the oppressed are things good in themselves and none holds a different view about them. Likewise, the quality of justice is acclaimed by all, even if it has to be enforced against one's own self, relatives and coreligionists."[37]

According to Abdelmadjid Méziane, what is essential is the rediscovery of the original "religious humanism" that inspired both religions. Christians and Muslims together must re-seek the monotheistic "parole commune" and the spiritual ways to which it leads. These ways find their natural expression in the sociopolitical order, where the believers in the one God are called to be forces of change and human liberation.[38]

Djohan Effendi suggests that dialogue can be a way of Christians and Muslims doing theology together. If religion is viewed as a given collection of dogmas, dialogue can mean nothing more than the juxtaposition of irreconcilable beliefs.

> However, if religion can be understood as "the path of salvation," is not religiosity a continual process of enlightenment? If this is so, then

dialogue appears to be an essential factor for stimulating our religious-ness so that it does not become static and stagnant. Such dialogue can itself be carried out in the form of a dialogue with oneself or with someone else.[39]

For Mohamed Talbi, the raison d'être of dialogue is simply the service of God on earth. It is not a tactic or a strategy toward any other goal. It is obedience to God's will and must contain no selfish agendas. "It should be radically disinterested collaboration without ulterior motive in the service of God, that is to say, of the Good and the True. In a climate without equivocation, relaxed, cleansing, and serene, dialogue in the future could be carried out to the profit of all, without exception or exclusion."[40]

This brief survey has been an attempt to bring together many of the views toward Christian-Muslim relations from the viewpoint of Muslims who have spoken or written publicly on the subject. From the great wealth of material, I have tried to select views on the basis of their representativeness of various sectors of the Islamic *ummah*, on the one hand, as well as those that, individualistic and even idiosyncratic, might serve as useful stimuli for a Christian's own reflections. Popes Paul VI and John Paul II have both often repeated that the first step at understanding those of other faiths is listening, trying to hear what others are saying as well as what they say in the silence that underlies their words. I hope that this survey has served an attempt at following that counsel.

Notes

1. Mushir-ul Haq, "The Universal Aspects of Islam," in *Towards World Community*, ed. S. J. Samartha (Geneva: W. Junk, 1975), 67.
2. Mohamed [Muhammad] Talbi, *Islam et dialogue: Réflexions sur un thème d'actualité* (Tunis: Maison Tunisienne de l'Edition, 1972), 14.
3. Fazlur Rahman, "The People of the Book and Diversity of Religions," reprinted in *Major Themes of the Qur'an* (Minneapolis: Bibliotheca Islamica, 1980), 166.
4. Haji Fadlullah Wilmot, "How Does Islam Regard Other Religions?" *The Sunday Mail* (Kuala Lumpur) July 10, 1983, 6.
5. Ibid.
6. Muhammad Hamidullah, "Islam and the Non-Muslim World," in *Relations among Religions Today: A Handbook of Policies and Principles* (Leiden: Brill, 1963), 78.
7. Isma'il R. al-Faruqi, "Islam and Christianity: Diatribe or Dialogue?" *Journal of Ecumenical Studies* 5, no. 1 (1968): 51-52.
8. Zakir Hussain, preface to *World Religions and World Peace*, ed. H. Jack (Boston: Beacon Press, 1968), vii, x.
9. Notable in this circle of thought are Frithjof Schuon (*Christianisme/Islam: Visions d'OEcumenisme ésotérique* [Milan: Arche, 1981]), Seyyed Hossein Nasr ("A Muslim's Reflections on Hans Küng," *Studies in Comparative Religion* 13 [1979]: 148-56), Abu Bakr Siraj Ed-Din (M. Lings), T. Burckhardt, and Abd al Wahid Pallavicini ("Islam and

Religious Pluralism," unpublished paper, Symposium on the Concept of Monotheism in Islam and Christianity, Rome, 1981). The Muslim contributors to *Studies in Comparative Religion* often express aspects of this point of view.

10. Pallavicini, "Islam and Religious Pluralism," 2.

11. Md. Hayath Khan, "Christian and Muslim Amity—How to Thaw the Ice," *The Bulletin of Christian Institutes of Islamic Studies* 4, no. 2 (April 1981): 78.

12. See Isma'il R. al-Faruqi, "Islam and Christianity"; *Christian Ethics* (Leiden: Brill, 1967), 211-314; *Trialogue of the Abrahamic Faiths* (Herndon, VA: International Institute of Islamic Thought, 1402/1982); "The Muslim-Christian Dialogue: A Constructionist View," *Islam and the Modern Age* 8, no. 1 (1977): 5-35; "The World's Need for Humane Humanism," in *The Challenge of Islam*, ed. Altaf Gauhar (London: Islamic Council of Europe, 1978), 82-113.

13. Faruqi, "Islam and Christianity," 54.

14. Ali Merad, *Charles de Foucauld: Au regard de l'Islam* (Lyon: Chalet, 1975), 14.

15. See Fuad Allam, "Islam e cristiani: conoscersi costruire la pace," in *Francesco: Un "pazzo" da slegare* (Assisi: Citadella Editrice, 1983), 213-22; Roger Garaudy, "Per un dialogo per un civiltà," in *Francesco*, 203-12; Muhammad Mujeeb, "St. Francis of Assisi," *Islam and the Modern Age* 13, no. 2 (May 1982): 67-75.

16. Khaled Bentounes, "Nous vivons elle et moi la même foi en Dieu," *Fraternité d'Abraham* 38 (April 1983): 9.

17. K. G. Saiyadain, "Sanctions for Peace: Islam," in *World Religions and World Peace*, ed. H. Jack (Boston: Beacon Press, 1968), 50.

18. Rahman, "People of the Book," 170.

19. Talbi, "Une communauté de communautés: Le droit à la différence et les voies de l'harmonie," *Islamocristiana* 4 (1978): 16; see Talbi, "Muhammad bani umma, dustur al-Madina," *Al-Hidaya* 3 (April 1975): 20-26.

20. See particularly Barakat Ahmad's controversial work, *Muhammad and the Jews* (New Delhi: Vikas, 1979); see also Hamidullah, "Islam and the Non-Muslim World"; Talbi, "Muhammad bani umma, dustur al-Madina"; Faruqi, "Muslim-Christian Dialogue," 5-35.

21. Abdelmadjid Méziane, "Le sens de la mubahala d'après la tradition islamique," *Islamocristiana* 2 (1976): 64.

22. See Faruqi, "Islam and Christianity"; Khurshid Ahmad, "Ten Articles for Christian-Muslim Dialogue," address at WCC/WMC Conference, Christians and Muslims Living and Working Together: Ethics and Practices of Humanitarian and Development Programmes (Colombo, 1982); M. M. Imtiazi, "How Can Muslims and Christians Work Together in the Field of 'Relief and Rehabilitation'?" WCC/WMC Conference; Sheikh al-Qattan, "Da'wat Rasul Muhammad ila al-Wahdaniyya," Symposium on the Concept of Monotheism in Islam and Christianity (see note 9); A. K. Brohi, "Some Random Reflections on the Theme of the Concept of Monotheism in Islam and Christianity," Symposium on the Concept of Monotheism in Islam and Christianity (see note 9); Sadiq Suhael, "Political Dimensions of Our Religious Concern for Man," World Conference of Religions (Cochin, 1981); Ismail Balogun, "Relation between God and His Creation: Revelation and Authority in Islam," Symposium on the Concept of Monotheism in Islam and Christianity (see note 9); Nassir El-Din El-Assad, "The Concept of Monotheism in Islam and Christianity," Symposium on the Concept of Monotheism in Islam and Christianity (see note 9); Aziz-us-Samad Ulfat, *Islam and Christianity* (Karachi: Begum Aisha Bawany Wakf, 1974).

23. Seyyed Hossein Nasr, "A Muslim's Reflections on Hans Küng," 156.

24. Abdelmajid Charfi, "Quelques réflexions sur la rencontre islamo-chrétienne de Tunis (11-17 November 1974)," *Islamocristiana* 1 (1975): 116; see Abdelmajid Charfi, "La secularización en las modernas sociedades arabo-musulmanas," *Encuentro Islamo-Cristiano* 133 (May 1983).

25. An important survey of trends in Christian liberation theology appeared in M. Habib Chrizin, "Dari Theologi Perkembangan ke Theologi Pembebasan," *Arena* (December 1979): 18-21. The title is translated "From Theology of Development to Theology of Liberation."

26. Asghar Ali Engineer, "On Developing Liberation Theology in Islam," *Islam and the Modern Age* 13, no. 2 (May 1982): 101-25.

27. Ibid., 110.

28. H. A. Mukti Ali, "Cooperation and Resource Mobilization," in *Towards World Community*, ed. S. J. Samartha (Geneva: W. Junk, 1975), 80; see Mohamed Talbi, "Signpost on a Long Road," *Towards World Community*, ed. S. J. Samartha (Geneva: W. Junk, 1975), 141-42.

29. Saiyadain, "Sanctions for Peace: Islam," 54-55.

30. Ahmad von Denffer, *Some Reflections on Dialogue between Christians and Muslims* (Leicester: Islamic Foundation, 1980), 18-19.

31. M. 'Abd al-Hadi Abou Ridah, "Al-Tawhid fi al-Islam: Shuruhuhu wa-Mazahiruhu at-Ijtima'iyya," Symposium on the Concept of Monotheism in Islam and Christianity (see note 9), 23-29; Sheikh al-Qattan, "Da'wat Rasul Muhammad ila al-Wahdaniyya," Symposium on the Concept of Monotheism in Islam and Christianity, Rome, 1981, 1-8.

32. Brohi, "Some Random Reflections," 7-8.

33. Mahmoud Ayoub, "Revelation and Salvation: Towards an Islamic View of History," paper given at Trialogue (Georgetown University, Washington, D.C., March 1983), 17; Mushir-ul Haq, "Universal Aspects of Islam," 65-73.

34. Talbi, "Signpost on a Long Road," 141-42.

35. Ziaul Hasan Faruqi, "Ways and Means of Inter-Religious Harmony and Reconciliation," *The Bulletin of Christian Institutes of Islamic Studies* 11, no. 4 (October 1976): 10.

36. I. R. Faruqi, "Islam and Christianity," 58-59.

37. Z. H. Faruqi, "Ways and Means of Inter-Religious Harmony and Reconciliation," 12.

38. Méziane, "Le sens de la mubahala," 66.

39. Djohan Effendi, "Dialog Antar Agama: Bisakah Melahirkan Teologi Kerukuman," *Prisma* (June 5, 1978): 17.

40. Talbi, *Islam et dialogue*, 35.

PART II

Christian-Muslim Dialogue

Comparative Perspectives

5

Social and Religious Factors Affecting Muslim-Christian Relations

Religious and Confessional Identification

Politics and Religious Relations

Obviously, Christian-Muslim relations do not exist in a vacuum anywhere in the world, and this is also the case in the Middle East and Asia. Political issues as well as national structures and policies impinge on relations between Muslims and Christians. It has become a cliché to say that conflicts that break down along religious lines almost always have causes and underlying motivations that are not religious. Christians and Muslims living in the same region frequently state that normal, day-to-day relations between the two communities are harmonious; the problems arise from "politics."

This reflects the common perception in both groups that, left to themselves, the two communities have historically not found it difficult to live together, nor would there be tensions and conflicts today if intrusive forces, generally denoted by the term *politics*, did not interfere. This widespread perception demands closer attention to see precisely what is meant by the intrusive factors that complicate and not infrequently damage Christian-Muslim relations.

The term *politics* indicates something broader than governments, politicians, political parties, and laws. In any analysis of conflicts and tensions, one quickly discovers that factors of demographic status as majority or minority, access to power and influence, ethnic and cultural differences, group identification, concepts of citizenship, international connections and economic stability usually lie at the heart of the problem. In this century, confessional tension and strife in the Middle East and Asia has rarely been about theology or religious belief and practice, but has almost invariably arisen from the way that groups perceive the relative status and identity of the other.

Previously published in *Islam and Christian-Muslim Relations* 8, no. 1 (1997): 53-66. Reprinted by permission.

Personal Identity and Confessional Loyalty

When the parties in a given conflict align themselves along the lines of confessional groups, in the Middle East and Asia as elsewhere, it is because religion denotes not only a system of belief and practice, but also forms the basis of identification with a recognizable group in society who shares, to a greater or lesser extent, a common history and identity. The individual's personal status and well-being are seen as tied to that of the group. If the religious group is insulted or maltreated, the individual is personally outraged. If the group is respected and honored, their personal status of the individual is recognized and enhanced.

Studies of ethnicity have shown that religious bonds form a powerful element in the make-up of ethnic identity, even for those who are not particularly "religious" in the usual sense of the term. A person who has little or no interest in God, sacred books, worship, or the moral instruction of any religion will often feel strongly that he or she is a Maronite or Copt, Sunni or Shi'i Muslim, Druze or Mandaean. When the group perceives itself to be threatened or undervalued, it is easy to see the offending group as the enemy and to vent one's anger against those members of the community who are nearest at hand, even if they be personally innocent of the offense, or to struggle, usually nonviolently, but with recourse to violence in highly polarized situations, to defend the communal cause.

The use of religious symbols and terminology to reinforce a group's self-identity and solidarity can give an observer the impression that interconfessional conflicts are mainly about religion, whereas in reality they usually have little to do with the content of the professed religions. A quick review of supposedly religious conflicts in the world today, such as Sri Lanka, Northern Ireland, Bosnia, Azerbaijan-Armenia, show this to be the case.

The Significance of Confessional Identity

If I have tended to belabor this point, it is because I believe that in parts of the world where religious profession does not usually carry implications of confessional belonging or ethnic identity, the factor of confessional attachment tends to be underrated and misunderstood. Conflicts between confessional groups are too simply dismissed as signs of primitive fanaticism.

In societies that consider religious adherence to be a personal, individual decision implying no communal participation in a distinctive societal group, changing one's religion or the profession of no religion implies no disloyalty or betrayal of one's confessional relations. Where the identification with the confessional group is strong, as in most parts of the Middle East and many regions of Asia, leaving the group through conversion and intermarriage, or failure to work for communal goals, can be considered a type of confessional treason punishable, in extreme cases, by death.

Enforcement of social ostracism is left, more often than not, to the network of extended family relations and neighbors, rather than to the state. One can document instances of a Muslim being killed by a distant cousin because he has left Islam to join a Christian church, or of a Christian father who has killed his daughter because she has entered Islam to marry a Muslim. The state's role in these affairs is usually secondary, as when it is called upon to judge the accused murderer through legal procedures.

In those societies where the link between religious adherence and confessional identification is relatively weak, as in parts of East and Southeast Asia, West Africa, much of Western Europe, and generally in North America, relations between Christians and Muslims tend to be less marked by conflict, and good relations can more easily be maintained over a long period. This is not, as is so often stated, simply the result of the secularization process, nor is it uniquely a characteristic of secularized societies. It reflects, rather, a different understanding of the link between religious profession and societal belonging.

Majority-Minority Relations

With an awareness of the importance of confessional identification, one can appreciate better other factors that influence relations between Christians and Muslims. A factor that complicates Christian-Muslim relations around the world is the fact that almost everywhere the two communities live in relationships characterized by imbalances in their status as majority or minority, access to power, and perceptions of self-sufficiency or vulnerability.

In discussions of interconfessional relations in the Middle East and Asia, the claim that "In this country, there are no minorities; we are all equal citizens," is often repeated. This is frequently correct insofar as it describes theoretical equality before the law. However, there is no denying that questions of minority, power, and influence enter into the way confessional groups regard themselves and that they color the way they regard those of the other religion. This means that in analyzing Christian-Muslim relations one cannot dismiss as irrelevant questions of numbers, power, and self-perception.

Relationships Marked by Imbalances

In the Middle East and Asia, either one or the other group is almost everywhere more numerous, powerful, wealthy, or influential, and the community in relative weakness can never forget that its well-being—political, social, or economic—is in some ways dependent on the good will of the stronger. Moreover, relationships of power and minority are often complex. One group may be more numerous, while another has greater economic or professional influence beyond its numbers, a factor that has both positive and negative repercussions on Muslim-Christian relations in many Arab countries and Iran.

In some cases, factors of ethnicity and social status come into play, where followers of one or the other religion are identified with groups considered to be at the top or bottom of the social scale. These factors influence relations between the Christian majority and Muslim minority in the Philippines and between the Muslim majority and Christian minority in Pakistan. In countries such as Lebanon, Malaysia, and Nigeria, where there is no clearly dominant majority and society is shaped by the competing claims and coalitions between various confessional groups, analysis of Muslim-Christian relations becomes even more complicated.

Sharing Minority Status

Evidence for the importance of imbalances in political, economic, and social status that overshadow and affect other aspects of the relationship can be found in those regions or nations where Muslims and Christians are *both* minorities in societies dominated by a third religious or ideological system. This is particularly evident in Asia, in countries such as Hindu India, Buddhist Burma, Thailand, and Sri Lanka, and in Confucian Singapore and officially atheist China. In the Middle East, a good example can be found in the pattern of relations among Palestinian Christians and Muslims in the Jewish state of Israel. In all these places, where both Christians and Muslims are minorities and outsiders in relation to the centers of power, communal harmony between the two is the norm, conflicts are few, and cooperation is quite easy to establish.

A similar situation applies when one treats relations between a minority group within the majority and the followers of other religions. The shared experience of being outside the centers of power helps minorities to see common interests, to sympathize with abuses of power directed against any minority, and to view the other minority not as a possible threat but as a prospective ally. One can point to many examples, such as the historical affinity between the Sunni Muslims and Orthodox Christians in Lebanon, the good relations of Christians with the Shi'a of Pakistan or Bahrain, with the Alawis of Syria or the Alevis of Turkey, the special relationship between Muslims and Roman Catholics in Presbyterian Scotland, or between Catholics and Muslims in Orthodox countries such as Greece and all the nations of the former Yugoslavia, not only Bosnia, but also Croatia, Serbia-Montenegro, and Macedonia. One might also cite the consistent leadership taken by the Protestant churches in standing in solidarity with all defending the rights of Muslims in predominantly Catholic Italy, Spain, and the Philippines.

That these generally easy relations between minorities or relative minorities are not limited to strategic alliances, but develop over time into true fellow-feeling and cooperation shows that Muslims and Christians, when issues of power and influence do not separate them, do not find it difficult to live and work together, either as individuals or as social groups.

It is essential for scholars today to focus on the difficulties and challenges faced by Muslims in mainly Christian or post-Christian societies in the West, and how they are striving, together with sympathetic Christians, to achieve their rights, dignity, and religious goals. However, the topic in this chapter concerns Muslim-Christian relations in the Middle East and Asia, the majority of whose populations are usually Muslims. Aside from those aforementioned countries where both Christians and Muslims are minorities, in all these states, except Israel, Lebanon, and the Philippines, citizens are governed by Muslim governments in nations that identify themselves either as secular states, or as states whose official religion is Islam, or as Islamic states governed according to the principles and regulations of the *sharīʿah*. Thus, our focus here must be on Christians in a minority status where Muslims are the dominant force in society and government.

Christians and the Muslim State

The State: the Third Party in the Dialogue

Any discussion of Christian-Muslim relations involves a third party to the dialogue, that is, the state. In some cases, the state consciously intervenes to regulate relations between confessional groups, to outline their respective obligations, and to define their rights and privileges. It must be remembered that those areas that were part of the Ottoman state—which include Turkey, almost the entire Mashriq, and most of the Maghrib—have inherited a four-hundred-year-old tradition of the distinctive *millet* system, which regulated the internal government of confessional groups according to their respective legal traditions. In this century, in the modern states of Turkey and Arabic-speaking countries of the Mashriq, elements of the *millet* system have been retained, particularly those that regulate matters of personal law referring to marriage, divorce, and inheritance.

The *millet* system reflects a traditionally Islamic concept of *personal law*, applicable to individuals as members of a particular confessional group, rather than a typically Western concept of a common *territorial law* meant to apply indiscriminately to all citizens within a particular area. This distinction, which is not often fully recognized by either Christians or Muslims, is relevant for determining the legal status of majority and minority communities in modern Islamic states characterized by the civil application of the *sharīʿah*. The implications of the expressly personal nature of Islamic law, the problematic of applying the *sharīʿah* as an alternative to Western-style territorial legal systems in religiously plural societies, and the possible advantages of a modern reconstructionist approach to the *millet* system are already being studied and discussed by Muslims and Christians.[1]

Christian Support for Nationalist Movements

With the emergence of modern independent nations in the region at the end of the Second World War the notion of national citizenship and systems of territorial law based on secular Western models came into force. Christian Arabs, who in the late nineteenth century and early twentieth century had been active promoters of pan-Arab nationalism, generally welcomed definitions of citizenship and legal systems based on nonreligious, secular principles on the grounds that this would remove them from the status of minority outsiders and make them equal partners in modern pluralist nations.

After independence, they supported regimes based on secular, often socialist ideologies, on the grounds that the concept of nationhood and citizenship professed by those parties and regimes transcended the principle of confessional adherence, thus offering minority groups more genuine opportunities for social and political equality.

On the contrary, they have tended to view with apprehension Muslim movements that they fear would redefine the concept of citizenship or marginalize them within the body politic. This explains Christian opposition to systems of separate electorates in nations such as the Islamic Republics of Iran and Pakistan, even though they are thereby guaranteed parliamentary representation, which they would probably not have obtained in a system of single-electorate elections. The government of Pakistan is currently considering a laudable proposal of "dual vote" for Muslim and non-Muslim minorities whereby they would vote for the general slate of candidates and also maintain reserved seats in parliament.

Christian concerns about their place in the mainstream of the national polity are expressed in Christian support for and involvement in national-based movements such as the Palestine Liberation Organization or the National Front for the Liberation of Palestine and their corresponding anxieties about Hamas. It can be seen in the support given by Christians generally to the socialist, Arab nationalist ideologies of Gamal 'Abd al-Nasser in Egypt and the Ba'ath Parties of Syria and Iraq, along with a corresponding lack of sympathy for the Front Islamique du Salut in Algeria, and in Christian backing for "secular" political parties in Turkey, Egypt, Sudan, and Jordan. In Asia, one can find Christians generally supporting religiously neutral political parties in Indonesia, Malaysia, and Bangladesh, as well as in India where both Christians and Muslims feel threatened by Hindu extremist movements and parties.

Historical developments make the relationship of Christians to each Muslim state unique. With Ataturk's establishment of the Republic of Turkey and the dissolution of the Ottoman state in the 1920s, Turkey was declared a secular nation, where no religion would take precedence or have privileges over any other. This is despite the fact that since the population exchange between Turkey and Greece in 1926, over 99 percent of the population of the Republic of Turkey is Muslim. The prerogatives of certain Christian confessional groups— the Greek Orthodox, Gregorian Armenians, and Syrian Orthodox—are further regulated by the Lausanna Treaty of 1923.

In the traditional monarchies, Christians, like others, have been subject to the policies, whether enlightened or repressive, of the ruler. Where the monar-

chy is committed to a broad application of the principles of religious tolerance
and freedom, such as in Jordan, Oman, most of the Emirates, Bahrain, and
Morocco, Christians are generally strong supporters of the monarchy.

Indigenous and Migrant Minorities

When it comes to claiming religious rights, we must distinguish between states
where Christians are part of the indigenous population, such as in Egypt, Iraq,
Lebanon, Syria, Turkey, Iran, Palestine, and Jordan, and those where the Christians are mainly foreign workers. In the latter, which includes the nations of the
Arabian peninsula and countries of the North African Maghrib (Libya, Tunisia,
Algeria, Morocco), where the Christians are not citizens and their presence is
generally temporary and voluntary, the rights of Christians have been limited to
demands for freedom of worship and the right to have religious personnel and
to offer religious instruction to their adherents.

The expectations of indigenous Christians go far beyond permission to
have churches and clergy and to perform their liturgical rites. They desire nothing less than all the rights, duties, privileges, and opportunities that accompany
full citizenship. Any intimation of second-class status is abhorrent to them, and
they judge the *sharī'ah* concept of "protected peoples" to be incompatible with
a modern understanding of citizenship and nationhood.

The reluctance of local Christians and other minorities to back political
options motivated by the Islamic revival is a recurrent source of tension in a
number of countries. Christians assume that political systems and programs
of Islamic inspiration will result in communal marginalization and suppression
of their religious prerogatives. Muslims respond that Christians are under the
influence of liberal Western prejudices, which presume that only a secular interpretation of the separation of religion and state can be the proper basis for a
modern polity.

Clichés commonly repeated by both Christians and Muslims often distort
the issue. In debates about political matters, one often hears the bromide: "In
Christianity, there is separation of Church and State. Religion is a private affair
between a person and God. In Islam, on the other hand, religion covers every
aspect of human life, including politics." Whereas modern Christian political
philosophy widely affirms the necessity of a separation of church organizational
structures and leadership from those of the state, there is a corresponding affirmation of the link between faith and politics. Committed Christians are everywhere urged to bring their religious convictions to bear upon the shaping of the
political, as well as economic and social, order.

On the other hand, Muslims do not form a monolithic block in political
matters, as the wide diversity of political systems in Islamic history and in predominantly Muslim countries today testifies. Among those who propose political options inspired by the *sharī'ah* there is wide diversity of opinion concerning
the place of religion in an Islamically guided state, and Muslim thinkers can be
quite critical of proposals put forward by other Muslims as Islamic. It is obvious

that the Islamic Republic of Iran has a very different concept of the role of Islam in public life from that of the Kingdom of Saudi Arabia, and the political programs of the Muslim Brotherhood are dissimilar from those of Jamat-i Islami. Scholars of Islamic jurisprudence hold that this diversity of political systems is not due to human stubbornness or to an inadequate understanding of Islam, but rather is presumed and promoted by the *sharī'ah* itself.

Muslim proponents of Islamist political options have often argued that the rights and status of Christians and other minorities must and will be respected in states governed according to the *sharī'ah*, but they have failed to convince most local Christian communities of this view. The experiences of Christians in *sharī'ah*-guided countries as diverse as Saudi Arabia, Iran, and Pakistan make local Christians unwilling to consider the possibility that an Islamically guided political system would in practice succeed in dialogue between Christian leaders and those of Islamist political programs, if this impasse to Muslim-Christian relations is to be resolved.

The *Ummah* and the Church: Communitarian Life

Problems of Dialogue

Turning from issues of the political order that influence Muslim-Christian relations to those that pertain more specifically to communitarian life, a factor of sweeping implications lies in the differences in the structure of the church, understood as the socially organized community of Christians, and the Islamic *ummah*, or international community of Muslims. A lack of conscious awareness of these differences can be the cause of misunderstanding, frustration, and alienation between the two communities.

Christians, especially in the highly centrally organized Roman Catholic Church and in the equally hierarchically structured Orthodox communion of sister churches, often complain that there is no corresponding structure among Muslims. No Muslim represents or speaks for another Muslim. No Muslim organization or entity, at least since the suppression of the caliphate, is indisputably recognized as representative of the whole *ummah*.

Christians consequently often express feelings of frustration in encounters with Muslims in that one can never do more than meet with a circumscribed group of Muslims who express a particular viewpoint. Any type of understandings or accords between the two communities would seem to be, from the commonly held Christian viewpoint, an impossible task. Christians ask, what is the use of trying to enter into an understanding or arrive at an agreement with a group of Muslims that will not be accepted by others?

On the other hand, Muslims often regard the Christian churches as dominated by a small group of highly committed—usually celibate clergy—who claim to speak in the name of the whole community. Muslim professors, doctors, civil servants, and business leaders who are, at the same time, deeply involved believers find it frustrating that in encounters with Christians, their counterparts are, more often than not, members of the clergy and hierarchy.

They would like to discuss the everyday problems of religious believers who are immersed in the world of earning a living, raising children to be upright, God-fearing believers, paying off housing and education loans, trying to run businesses or keep their jobs and who, at the same time, are striving to respond to the complex demands of religious conviction in today's world. It should be noted that there is more affinity between these Muslim "lay" leaders and representatives of the Protestant churches, whose structural organization and patterns of leadership are more similar to those of Muslims.

These respective frustrations must be kept in mind, as they are certain to affect the success or failure of what is called organized dialogue between Christians and Muslims. In the past thirty years, Muslims and Christians have voluntarily come together at the local, national, and international levels to study, discuss, and work together on a wide range of topics. They range from strictly theological issues, clarifying misunderstandings and delineating points of convergence and divergence between the two faiths; to academic questions of historical, philosophical and scientific interest; to broad social issues related to family, religious education, business ethics, poverty, injustice, the roles of women and men, ecology, armaments, and human development; to specific local problems of drugs, violence, corruption, and neighborhood organization.

Dialogue as a Modern Phenomenon

Dialogue encounters are characteristic of a distinctly modern understanding of Muslim-Christian relations. Certainly, Christians and Muslims down through the centuries had always lived together and had often discussed, studied, and worked together, but the need felt by both sides for conscious efforts to bring representatives of the two communities together is a recent phenomenon. Although still in its infancy, the dialogue movement has produced palpable results in creating a network of Muslim and Christian leaders around the world who know and trust one another, who can work together on issues of common concern and who, in moments of crisis or tension, can search together for mutually acceptable solutions.

Dialogue cannot solve all problems or bring all conflicts to an end, as the unhappy experience of so many Muslim and Christian Lebanese testified during the recent war. Nevertheless, dialogue efforts, of both Muslim and Christian initiative, hold out the promise that there are alternatives to conflict and violence. They operate on the hope that yet unforeseen conflicts in the future can be avoided by the two communities coming to better understanding and cooperation today.

However, if dialogue is to remain credible and not devolve into an elitist discussion club, it must reflect the real concerns of the community and strive to be truly representative of its constituencies. The need today, on the Christian side, is for lay people, business leaders, women, and youths— those groups that have been underrepresented in dialogue encounters—to take the leadership in meeting and working together with Muslim counterparts. On their side, Muslims will have to develop their "consensus theology" into stronger national and international representative structures in order to have leaders who can credibly speak in the name of more than groups of like-minded associates.

Differences in Organizational Structure

An aspect of the organizational life of the Islamic and Christian communities that has been a source of tension between Christians and Muslims lies in the divergent roles of the Christian priest and Muslim *imām*. When Muslims gather to perform their daily ritual prayer, the *ṣalāh*, any Muslim who knows the proper form can act as *imām*. Muslims often fail to appreciate the fact that for the fullest and deepest expression of Christian worship, the Eucharistic celebration, Christians, at least in the Orthodox and Catholic traditions, have need of ordained clergy. Church buildings are not necessary, and Christian worship can function without them but, at least in the Catholic and Orthodox traditions, without a priest, although Christians can read the Bible, give catechetical instruction, and pray together, there can be no Mass.

This basic difference between Islamic and Christian faiths is relevant for Christian-Muslim relations wherever Christians live in predominantly Muslim countries. It reflects well on Muslims that all Muslim governments but one permit this full expression of Christian worship. Indigenous Christian communities in the Middle East and Asia can worship freely, and most Muslim states whose Christian communities mainly comprise expatriate workers, such as Oman, the Emirates, Bahrain, Libya, and Morocco, have made generous provision for the demands of Christian worship.

The exception is the Kingdom of Saudi Arabia where, although several million Christians, mainly of Filipino and Indian origin, live and work, the presence of Christian clergy is not permitted. In speaking with Muslims in Saudi Arabia, I often receive the impression that they do not see the religious crisis for Christians involved in a prohibition of clergy. When the question of freedom of worship is raised, the response is often that Christians, like others, are free to pray in the privacy of their homes. What further need do they have of priests? This response makes sense within the context of Muslim communitarian life, in which any group of Muslims who gather to perform *ṣalāh* can choose one to be *imām* and perform the prayer.

For Christians this prohibition results in their inability to carry out a fundamental religious duty to worship God according to their faith. It is as though Muslims were told that they are free to read the Qur'an and pray forms of devotional *du'ā'* but that they may not perform *ṣalāh*. This lack of understanding of one of the principles of religious obligation, to worship God, is a factor that continues to color Christian-Muslim relations not only at the local but also at the international level. Christians feel that they are dealing with a community that does not respect one of the fundamental elements in their religion and wish that Muslims would stand in solidarity with them in urging all governments to grant true freedom of worship to all subjects.

Human Factors: The Burden of History

I have discussed factors that influence Muslim-Christian relations: confessional identification, majority-minority status, political structures, and the nature of the community. There is a final set of factors, though nebulous and difficult to define, that plays a powerful role in determining the ways in which Christians and Muslims relate. It has less to do with politics, sociology, and demography, or even with the particular characteristics of Islam and Christianity, than with universal human challenges and failings. It concerns the burden of history, distant and recent, and apprehensions about the future. It involves common human problems of how we deal with anger, resentment, frustration, and fear, how we react to suspicion and prejudice, and how we arrive at forgiveness and reconciliation. If we are to confront these human factors, it means we must speak of some unpleasant matters.

I have noted that Christian-Muslim relations do not exist in a sociological vacuum. It is equally true that they are not detached from their historical context. Any community of people can draw up a long list of the times and ways they have suffered and are still suffering at the hands of others. Indignities and injustices are not forgotten and rise up again in later generations as causes or pretexts for reprisals.

Muslim Burdens

Although they occurred almost a thousand years ago, Muslims have not forgotten the outrage of the Crusades, and the emotive power of these memories still colors their perceptions of Christians. Those opposed to the massive American troop presence in Arabia at the time of the Gulf War often referred, in speeches, articles, and radio broadcasts, to the American forces by the term *ṣalībīyūn*, Crusaders. The term, taken, as in European languages, from the word for "cross," carries in Arabic the ironic weight of those who invade and destroy under the banner of the cross, in contradiction to the express source and significance of that symbol.

Colonial Injustices and Indignities

Of more recent memory, and perhaps for that reason, more galling, is the colonial period when for more than two hundred years virtually the entire Muslim world was governed and controlled by a handful of Christian nations. The multiple indignities suffered in that period—the replacement of the indigenous and time-honored ways of behavior with new and allegedly superior codes of government, law, personal conduct, and education, the paternalistic ideologies of the "white man's burden" and "*la mission civilatrice,*" the economic exploitation, and the reduction of Islam to a "pagan" religion—are resonant memories that powerfully affect the ways that Muslims regard Christians today. Particularly hard to forget is the introduction of missionaries that accompanied colonial rule and even, through the humiliating "capitulations," affected independent nations such as the Ottoman and Qajar states.

Muslims from nations of the Middle East and Asia can provide many examples of unforgotten indignities. I will mention only two from Asian experiences of colonialism. As recorded in his autobiography, the Indonesian nationalist leader, Tjokroaminoto, was dismissed from his civil service position for a double offence: wearing shoes and remaining standing in the presence of Dutch officials. Second, in the nearby Philippines, well into this century, all Filipinos, weather Christian or Muslim, were required to kneel on the street when the Spanish bishop passed by. These were policies, not individual whims, part and parcel of colonial rule, intended to create a cultural apartheid, express a sense of European superiority, and show where the power lay. Although individual missionaries—local clergy were not encouraged— protested against many of the more degrading aspects of the colonial system, they too were often co-opted into the ruling elite.

Recalling such indignities, imposed in our own century, in the living memory of many, usually by the same nations that created and promoted the Enlightenment, Muslims cannot possibly relate to Western Christians today without the intrusion of feelings, even when well-concealed, of anger and resentment. Muslims cannot view Christianity today simply as the teaching of the holy prophet Jesus, but rather as a contributing element in a comprehensive system of oppression and cultural destruction that caused suffering and violated the dignity of their people. Muslim leaders as diverse as Muhammad Mahathir, Mu'ammar Qaddhafi, and Hasan al-Turabi, who do not hesitate to express this indignation, know that they are putting into words the deep-seated sentiments of many.

Post-Colonial Onslaughts

It is too easy for Christians to say that this is all in the past; today we live in a different era. The colonial era would be easier to forgive if it were simply part of the past, over and done with. But the perception of many Muslims today is that while the more blatant forms of colonial rule have ended, a subtle and pervasive form of neocolonialism has replaced it. Many are convinced that the West, meaning Western Europe and North America, is out to destroy Islam. This onslaught is perceived to be carried out on many fronts: political, military, economic, religious, and cultural.

The campaign is political in the formation of an international alliance against the Muslim world aimed at isolating Islamic countries much in the way that the Communist bloc had been isolated before 1989. It is military in that tactics of war—blockades, frozen assets, recourse to air attacks, and other coercive actions—are more readily directed against Muslim nations than against others. It is economic in that the old colonial regimes have been replaced by economic control, markets manipulated from the outside, political leaders bought off by international industry, and military actions threatened or taken to ensure control of resources. It is religious in the continual media presentations of Islam—in film, global television networks, news magazines, and spy novels—as a backward, fanatic, violent, xenophobic faith unable to live with others. The attack is cultural in that all things Western—education, clothing, law, manners, music, films, house furnishings, relations between sexes—are presented as superior and to be admired, imitated, and, most importantly, bought.

Reading Events in the Light of History

If this seems overstated, it reflects a widespread feeling throughout the Muslim world. The conviction that Islamic faith and Muslim culture are under attack, imperiled, threatened, explains many of the reactions among Muslims, both political and religious leaders as well as the man and woman in the street, to events that occurred during the Gulf War, after the Algerian coup d'état, and to the continuing dramas in Palestine and Bosnia.

Each of these tragedies is interpreted in the light of previous history. The Gulf War was seen as a war for control of "Muslim" oil fields, waged by a Western-assembled coalition with vastly superior technological weaponry attacking a predominantly Muslim people. The Algerian elections proved to many Muslims that a grassroots Islamic reformist political movement could succeed in being democratically elected. When these hopes were dashed by the military coup and severe repression of activist Muslims that followed, the reformers claimed that the Western powers' ready acceptance of the new government showed that their commitment to democracy in Muslim regions was mere lip-service. Israel is seen as the unilateral implantation of a Western people and ideology in the heart of the Islamic world to assuage the guilt of another group of Europeans. Bosnia is viewed as evidence that the European powers will never permit a Muslim-dominated nation, no matter how progressive, to exist in Europe.

Christian Burdens

Christian Memories in the Middle East

Just as the burdens of history bear on the way that Muslims relate to Christians, so also local Christian attitudes toward Muslims are formed and shaped by history. If Muslims retain vivid memories of the Crusades and the expulsion of Muslims from the Iberian Peninsula after the Reconquista, Christians preserve their own images of Muslims based on historical fact. Memories of the 1453 Fall of Constantinople and the destruction of some of the world's most beautiful Christian art, of Saracen raids in the Mediterranean and the *devshirme* policy when Christian boys were taken and forced to become Muslims and serve the Sultan, of atrocities committed during the Greek War of independence and elsewhere in the Balkans, of the massacres of Armenians, of the 1861 slaughter of Christians in Lebanon, are all part of Christian heritage in South and Southeast Europe and the Eastern Mediterranean.

The Christian historical memory in the Middle East is as complex as it is unhappy. If Christians remember the events in which they were victims of Muslim governments and armies, they remember also the 1099 Sack of Jerusalem by the Crusaders when Eastern Christians as well as Muslims were butchered in the Holy City, and the first, perhaps more destructive, Sack of Constantinople by armies of European coreligionists in 1204. Feeling that, through sharing the same religion, they have often been regarded unjustly by Muslims as allies of European invaders, as collaborators with the colonial powers, and as local promoters of modern liberalism, Middle East Christians are also conscious of the many ways they have been dismissed, disregarded, and patronized by their fellow Christian believers of the West.

Cultural Alienation in Asia

Except for South India, whose Christian tradition is very ancient, Christians in Asia make up younger churches exposed to the weight of a different history. These churches are rooted in the missionary efforts of the colonial period. They are descendants of those who accepted Christian faith by conviction, often at great hardship, but also of "rice Christians" whose Christian commitment was compromised by material benefits such as promises of food, land, better education, health care, and social status.

Becoming Christians did not save them from multiple indignities. They were denied posts of leadership in the church and regularly refused admission to religious orders. It was not until the 1930s that prominent religious orders in the Philippines accepted Filipino members, although the country had already been predominately Catholic for centuries. In mission schools they were frequently forbidden to speak local languages and wear national dress; following local customs and celebrating popular festivals were condemned as participation in pagan rites. Christians in Asia are conscious that Muslims, like Hindus and Buddhists, tend to regard them as a continuing unwanted reminder of the colonial project. They are seen as communities who have abandoned the ancient culture, traditions, and religion of the place and adopted, along with the "European" religion, a European way of life, values, and expectations.

No matter what their origins may have been, the Christian churches of Asia today profess a faith that is as deep as in the regions from which it was brought, and often more vibrant and active. For these Christians, the challenge is to find ways to integrate their Christian faith into national cultures and traditions to create something that is both culturally valid and authentically Christian. For this reason, the churches of Asia have been in the vanguard of dialogue with Muslim and followers of other religions. It can be safely said that in no part of the world have Christians devoted so much time, expense, training, and expertise to the study of other religions and encounters with their followers in Asia.

Christian Concerns

When we listen to the concerns of Christians in the Middle East and Asia it is clear that it is with some apprehension that they regard the Muslims with whom they live and by whom, in many cases, they are governed. Their concerns, more often than not, revolve around the basic necessities of everyday life. Is preference given to Muslims in jobs, university seats, housing, positions in the civil service and military? Can Muslim preachers get away with public diatribes against Christianity, while Christians have to be cautious about any criticism of Islam or Muslims? Can blasphemy laws be used, as many Christians believe to have been the case in the widely publicized case in Pakistan this year, to settle scores and appropriate property? Are Christians forced to study from textbooks that present Islam as the final, complete religion and Christianity as a superseded, corrupt form of prophetic religion? Is it possible for Christians, as a community, rather than as isolated individuals, to play a fully active and constructive role in the shaping of society, or are they merely to be "tolerated" and "protected"? These are issues that local Christians discuss among themselves and that color their attitudes toward Muslims.

Christians in the Middle East and Asia feel vulnerable, dependent on the good will of Muslim majorities and governments. In times of international crisis, when Muslim public opinion is indignant at the actions of one or another Western power, their anger is frequently directed, not at those distant Christian nations of the West who are safely beyond their reach, but toward local Christians. Examples within the past decade could be given of churches in Pakistan and Egypt that were burned by angry mobs in protest against American policies directed against Iran and Iraq. Local Christians, who may or may not agree with such policies and who, in any case, have no power to influence them, are angry that they are used as scapegoats for events of which they are innocent and over which they have no control.

Anger at being treated as second-class citizens and feelings of insecurity within their own societies are often directed by Middle East Christians at their fellow believers in the West. In discussions with representatives of the Vatican and the World Council of Churches, questions like the following are repeatedly raised: Why do Christians in Europe and America grant Muslims full religious rights and assistance to Muslims in the West when Christians in predominantly Muslim areas meet with continual discrimination? How can the Vatican permit the construction of a huge mosque and Islamic center in Rome when Christians are not allowed even the smallest church building in Saudi Arabia? How can you enter into dialogue and cooperation with one or another country when Christians of that country are deprived of the right to express themselves freely?

Reconciliation: A Universal Human Challenge

In my opinion, it is these "human factors," which, being the most deeply rooted, are the most difficult to overcome, and thus will be the strongest obstacles to establishing good Muslim-Christian relations in the twenty-first century. It is no more or less difficult for Christians and Muslims to move beyond the injustices of the past and concerns of the present to arrive at a stage of mutual trust, forgiveness, and reconciliation than for people of other religions or of no religion. One needs only think of the weight of the history of wrongs that

Jews must face if they are to forgive and live in peace with European Christians. The anger of Koreans and Chinese toward the Japanese, of Irish toward the English, of black Africans toward both Arabs and Europeans, of Russians and Poles toward Germans shows that collective resentment is a universal human phenomenon, but it is for this reason no less important as a factor complicating and hindering Christian-Muslim relations. Put simply, the problem is how can victims and victimizers both move beyond the past?

Christians and Muslims are called to mercy and forgiveness by their faiths. Both the Qur'an and the Bible are filled with exhortations to compassion, pardon, and acceptance of others. We all know that a deeply felt injury can become like a cancer of the spirit, eating away at an individual or a community until it can seem greater than our powers to withstand or overcome. Christianity and Islam, however, both teach that we are not prisoners of the past, nor hostages of our present situation, and thus, it is possible to live together better in the twenty-first century than we often have in the past and than we have in this century. But there are no easy answers. It is possible to find ways to live together, first, if we do not minimize the problem and, second, if both communities are willing to look self-critically at our pasts. What Muslims and Christians can accomplish together by living together in harmony and cooperating for the good of all is too important to be thwarted by old grievances and suspicions.

By way of conclusion, I may add, as a Catholic Christian, that this is the task solemnly given to Christians and Muslims by the Second Vatican Council, which states:

> Although in the course of centuries many quarrels and hostilities have arisen between Christians and Muslims, this most sacred Synod urges all to forget the past and to strive sincerely for mutual understanding. On behalf of all humankind, let them make common cause of safeguarding and fostering social justice, moral values, peace, and freedom. (*Nostra Aetate* §3)

Notes

1. See Tayyib Z. Al-Abdin, "The Implications of *Shari'ah*, *Fiqh*, and *Qānūn* in an Islamic State," and Bert F. Breiner, "*Shari'ah* and Religious Pluralism," in *Religion, Law and Society: A Christian-Muslim Discussion*, ed. Tarek Mitri (Geneva: World Council of Churches Publications, 1995), 20-26 and 51-62.

6

Toward a Dialogue of Liberation with Muslims

At their first continental meeting in Manila in 1970, the Catholic bishops of Asia noted three elements of Asian realities that form the societal context in which Christian faith must be lived. They are the undeniable facts that (1) Christians in Asia live amid millions of committed followers of other religions, (2) that they belong to ancient and rich Asian cultures of which they are heirs and stewards, and (3) that they live in societies in which crushing, oppressive poverty is still the daily lot of the majority of people. The mission of the churches in Asia, they proposed, must be the task of dialogue of the Gospel—and thus the people of the Gospel—with these three realities, that is, the triple task of interreligious dialogue, intercultural dialogue, and dialogue with the poor and marginalized.

Setting the Practical Goals of Dialogue

In the decades that have passed since this declaration, the triple dialogue has been reiterated and elaborated in many forms by the Catholic churches in Asia and by our sister churches of the Christian Conference of Asia. This awareness has engendered Asian theological movements such as *dalit* theology and *minjung* theology, and specifically Asian forms of feminist theology and indigenous theology. In recent decades, new elements of the Asian context have come to the forefront of our consciousness, most notably the fact that Asian societies are part of a globalizing market economy, made possible by the technological and informational revolution, rooted in liberal philosophical values of modernity, and promoting a secularizing process that touches the life of every religious group and culture and every suffering individual. Globalization is a dynamic process that appears to be even stronger than individual nation-states and national cultures, and adds a fourth element to the "triple dialogue." This

This is a slightly different version of the essay by the same title previously published in *Visioning New Life Together among Asian Religions* (Hong Kong: Christian Conference of Asia, 2000), 26-42. Reprinted by permission.

reality challenges Christians to involve themselves in dialogue with the "movers and shakers" of modern Asia if more just, humane, and harmonious societies are to be built.

My personal involvement in this task of the churches in Asia, a region where I was not born but which I consider my home for the past thirty years, is in the area of dialogue with Muslims. It was in Asia, specifically in this city of Yogyakarta, that I first came to know Muslims in 1969, and it is in Asia where I have sought to discover the meaning and purpose of Christian-Muslim dialogue in subsequent years. Although the results have not always been encouraging, my experience has strongly convinced me that this task must be continued.

One thing that I have learned in the course of time is that interreligious dialogue or, more specifically, Muslim-Christian dialogue, must never be separated from dialogue with cultures and, even more importantly, from the centrality of ongoing dialogue with the poor. Interreligious dialogue can too easily become an elitist exercise in which scholars and religious leaders create among themselves a clubby brotherhood—and I use the gender-specific term intentionally—across religious lines to perpetuate and, in the worst cases, justify the economic and social status quo. Too often in interreligious gatherings, the daily concerns of the poor are simply ignored, as if they were nonexistent, or mentioned and passed over as though the indignities and injustices they experience daily were irrelevant or even an embarrassment in the context of the lofty religious concepts and ideals expressed. The excluded voices of the poor, of women, of indigenous peoples, of children and—dare I say it?—of the unborn, undermine the whole effort of dialogue and prevent it from becoming an effective means of social transformation.

I am convinced that what is needed in Asia today is an interreligious dialogue that begins from the needs and concerns of the poor and is oriented toward true human liberation. In a world where decisions that affect the lives of millions are made on the bases of market policy, spreadsheets, realpolitik, and demographic projections, religious groups are challenged to provide an alternative reading of social situations by drawing on the liberative elements of our specific traditions. It is either in this area where the religious traditions in Asia can make a unique and much needed contribution to the transformation of society, or nowhere. If we "fumble the ball" in failing to voice the genuine longing of the masses of the Asian poor for dignity and justice, we simply contribute to the malaise of values that secular modernity inexorably propagates.

Turning specifically to dialogue with Muslims, Christians must not hesitate to draw upon the strong prophetic tradition of our Scriptures, exemplified by Amos, Jeremiah, Isaiah, John the Baptist, and the Epistle of James, upon the sapiential insights of Job and Qoheleth (the Preacher), and most of all, upon the lessons of our Master's Sermon on the Mount, his parables of unjust stewards, foolish empire-builders, the rich man in hell and his impervious brothers, as well as Jesus' observations on poor widows and repentant women, and his example of sharing food with lawbreakers and unwashed masses.

I have rarely heard—and must confess, to my shame, that I have too rarely expressed—such central elements of the Christian tradition in situations of Christian-Muslim dialogue. One wonders why we are more inclined to formulate Jesus' relationship to the Father or God's Trinitarian life than to deal with basic Gospel teaching concerning the majority of our neighbors who daily "hunger and thirst for justice," whose demands, our Master teaches, *will* be satisfied. Part of the reason, obviously, is that most of those who engage in formal dialogue are well-fed, well-housed, well-educated, and well-placed in society.

Liberative Elements in Christianity and Islam

Different elements of the Gospel have personal impact on different people, depending on their particular situation of life. Let me give an example from my early experience in Yogyakarta. When I first arrived in Yogya in 1969, I was approached to celebrate the Eucharist with the political prisoners who were detained here in the city. Some were in the prison of the *benteng*, but there were still in those first years of the New Order so many prisoners that makeshift prisons, three for men and one for women, were set up in police stations and army barracks in various places.[1] The Catholics were few, but they wanted Mass, so taking turns with others on the team, I went twice-weekly to preside at the worship.

There were no restrictions on who attended, but in fact almost all the prisoners—nominal or committed Communists, sympathizers, or members of left-leaning trade unions—took part. I believe that the vast majority of the prisoners, nominally Muslims, did not carry out the practice of any organized religion. They had probably never encountered any Scripture reading or passage of the Qur'an. The religiosity of most centered about meditative exercises of Javanese mysticism. Why did the non-Christians take part? I think that the reasons were varied: a mixture of curiosity, boredom (there was nothing else to do), and a need for spiritual nourishment at a moment in their lives when they had lost everything: homes, families, livelihood, and hope for the future.

As I said, for most, it was the first time they had ever heard any passage of the Gospel. Over and over, I had an amazing experience while reading the Gospel of the day. It was as if I had dropped out of the scene, and God was directly communicating with these prisoners through Christ's words at a moment of extreme crisis in their lives. One day, for example, the reading was a passage from the Sermon on the Mount: "Do not be afraid; you are worth more than many sparrows" (Matt. 10:31, outside the Sermon on the Mount, or Matt. 6:26, which is in the Sermon of the Mount), and "Set your heart first on God's kingdom and justice and all these things will be given to you" (Matt. 6:33). On hearing these words, a prisoner spontaneously burst out in heaves of emotion, followed by another and another. I had heard those verses many times since my childhood and found them comforting, but they never triggered in me the deep emotional response that they did in these men.

Through Christ, God was telling them that, despite the apparently hopeless situation they were in, they were precious in God's sight and that God would one day bring also to them a time of liberation. The situation reminded me of Ezekiel's preaching to the Jewish exiles in Babylon, whose situation was not very different from these prisoners. In Ezekiel's message, the sharp sword of the prophetic message became the comforting and hope-filled words of a tender mother.

These are the kinds of things that I should and do talk about with Muslims. These are the aspects of our faith that we need to be in communication about. Muslims need to know about the liberating aspects of Christian faith, and it is just as important that we Christians learn about the elements of liberation and transformation that the Muslim poor, who are far more numerous in Asia than Christians, find grounds in their Islamic faith for strength and hope and consolation. We need to discover the strong prophetic tradition carried on in the Qur'an and the elements of liberation found in the pillars of Islam and in the *shari'ah*, the Islamic way of life.

It is a sign of our ignorance that many Christians respond, "I didn't know that there were liberating elements in Islam. I thought Islam was oppressive of the poor, of women, of sinners. I have the impression that Islam is impassive and fatalistic in the face of injustice and wrongdoing." Yet thirty minutes in any Muslim bookshop will reveal titles such as *Transformative Islam*, *Islam: The Religion of Justice*, and *Islam and the Liberation of Women*. It is sobering, but small consolation, to remember that Muslims are usually no better informed about our faith than we are about theirs, and are normally surprised to find that Christianity has any concern for human liberation. They often regard Christian faith mainly as a justification for power and wealth.

Christians also need to learn how to listen to Muslims, especially to poor Muslims. They often frame and phrase their hopes and struggles in terms different from ours. All over Asia, Muslim scholars and activists are rediscovering the liberative elements in the Qur'anic teaching and in the *hadith* reports that stem from Muhammad. In the past, Muslim efforts to elucidate the social message of Islam were often hampered by a literalism that made it difficult to apply Qur'anic passages to the very different social and economic structures of today. However, what we find in writings of Muslim scholars like Asghar Ali Engineer of India, Chandra Muzaffar of Malaysia, Abdurrahman Wahid (d. 2009) of Indonesia, or the feminist activist Mucha Shim Quiling of the Philippines, and what might be called the cooperative projects of groups like the Asian Muslim Action Network (AMAN), may be properly described as attempts to draw out the societal and economic implications of the Islamic sources and to implement them in modern Asian societies.

An obstacle that prevents Christians from appreciating and entering into dialogue with Muslims on elements of liberation is the sad fact that in several parts of Asia, Christians and Muslims are locked in confessional conflicts in which religious affiliation, while not the cause of the conflict, plays an important role in pitting one against the other. This unhappy situation too often leads us to see "the Muslim" as a threat to our well-being or even the enemy to be defeated, just as it leads Muslims to regard Christians as inimical to Islam and Muslims. An understandable concern with political Islam, Islamic state, and application of the *sharī'ah* can blind us to the reality that, for the vast majority of ordinary Muslims, Islam is first and foremost a response to God, a way to encounter the Creator and to do God's will on earth. These Muslims are not interested in politics or revolution or communal conflict, precisely because they are far too busy trying to provide for their families, raise their children to be God-fearing people, and eke out a measure of God's abundant gifts, blessings for humankind, but very unequally distributed within the human family. It is with such Muslims that we must enter into dialogue concerning the One God who is able to liberate people from sin and from the oppressive structures that we have fashioned.

Justice, Equality, and Personal Responsibility in the Qur'an

Without pretending to do justice to the transformative exegesis done by Muslims today, I would like to point out some of the Qur'anic passages that are inspiring some Muslims to propose and carry out a liberative agenda in the context of the social realities of modern Asia.

The Qur'anic ideal that has influenced millions of Muslims down through the centuries is that of a simple, family-oriented lifestyle that rejects both consumer-oriented displays of wealth and the piling up of material possessions. This, even critics of Islam are ready to admit. The Qur'an teaches that what God has given is good and can be enjoyed, but within strict limits of moderation. "Eat and drink," states the Qur'an, "but *do not be extravagant*. [God] does not love those who go to excess" (7:31; also 6:141). Wealth and property are considered blessings from God, but must be used properly. Those obsessed with seeking, multiplying, and displaying wealth are even accused of being in the same family as demons who are not grateful to God for God's gifts. The Qur'an teaches, "Do not squander [your money] extravagantly. *Spendthrifts are the devils' brethren* and Satan has always been ungrateful to His Lord" (17:26-27). The call to a modest way of life underlies, for example, the prohibition against men's wearing gold ornaments such as rings, bracelets, chains, and the like.

The Qur'an was first preached to a people who were no less imbued with a dog-eat-dog mentality than our own modern societies. It teaches that aggressive economic activities and amassing personal wealth serve to distract people from what is truly important in life: to do God's will in all things and to stand before God in patience and humility. "*Competition has distracted you*, until you visit graveyards. Nevertheless, you soon will know" (102:1-3). The message is clear: the day is coming when people will discover, too late, that their desperate passion for wealth has led them astray and they will have nothing to show for their life's work. Whole civilizations have gone under because of their lack of restraint in regard to material possessions, and all that remains of them are deserted monuments and ruins. As the Qur'an states, "How many civilizations have we wiped out who were reckless in their way of living. Their dwellings have been inhabited only occasionally since then" (28:58).

The Qur'anic ideal of a virtuous life contrasts sharply with that of the "modern advertising ideal" of constantly pursuing fortune, power, beauty, prestige, and eternal youth, and restlessly searching for new and exciting pleasures. A famous Qur'an passage sums up what Islamic life is about; it is about faith, generosity, and effective concern for the poor, patience in times of distress, and fidelity:

> Virtue does not mean that you turn your faces towards the East or West, but [true] virtue means to believe in God, the Last Day, the angels, the Book and the prophets; and to give one's wealth away out of love for Him to relatives, orphans, the needy, the migrant and beggars, and towards freeing captives; and to keep up prayer and pay the tax for the poor; and those who keep their word whenever they promised anything, and are patient under suffering and hardship and in time of violence. Those are the ones who are loyal, and those are the ones who are heedful [of God's message]. (2:177)

Islam constantly teaches that those who have been blessed with sufficiency or, a fortiori, abundance, have a serious obligation to those who are lacking the basic essentials. It is not merely a matter of good will or feelings of sympathy for the poor, but an obligation that corresponds to a divinely acknowledged right of the poor. In more than one place, the Qur'an states unequivocally: "*The beggar and the destitute have acknowledged right to a portion of people's wealth*" (70:24-25; see also 51:19).

The concept does not remain simply a good idea, but structures have been created in the religion itself to carry out this injunction. The *zakāh*, the fourth obligatory pillar of Islam, is intended to provide for the poor of the community. Sometimes mistranslated as *almsgiving*, the *zakāh* is more accurately understood as a *poor tax*. It is a tax of a specific percentage of a Muslim's income (2.5%) or harvest (10%) and is levied expressly for those classes of society who cannot provide for themselves. In the list of recipients of *zakāh*, the Qur'an always puts in the first place near relatives, particularly one's aged parents, and goes on to list other categories of those whose circumstances put them at the mercy of others: the biblical orphans and widows, beggars, and migrants. Addressing what has in recent times become a significant class of Asia's suffering poor, the Qur'an commands that assistance is also to be given to "*refugees who have been expelled from their homes and property*" (59:8).

While *zakāh* is intended to provide for all members of the Muslim community, charity or alms to anyone in need, Muslim or non-Muslim, is highly encouraged in the Qur'an. Such free will offerings, called *sadaqah*, are to be used "for the poor, the needy, those working at [collecting and distributing it], those whose hearts are being reconciled, for [freeing] captives and debtors, for those [struggling] in God's way, and for the migrant, as a duty imposed by God" (9:60). The Qur'an knows that charity can too easily bear its own reward in that the giver is seen and praised as a person of means who is nevertheless bountiful to the poor. The true charity proposed by the Qur'an should be performed as faithful obedience to what God commands, and as such, it need be seen by no one but God. Thus, in a passage reminiscent of Jesus' teaching in the Sermon on the Mount on giving alms, the Qur'an teaches: "If you give *sadaqah* (alms) openly, that is good, but *if you conceal it and give it [directly] to the poor, that is better* for you" (2:271).

Zakāh is commanded of every Muslim, and in addition Muslims are urged to perform *sadaqah*. An example of how *sadaqah* can be used to supplement *zakāh* can be found in the action taken by the Organization of Islamic Conference (OIC) during the severe drought in the Sahel region of Africa in the 1980s.[2] The OIC used funds collected from *zakāh* payments by Muslims to aid the predominantly Muslim nations affected, and then contributed $1,000,000 in *sadaqah* or alms to Cabo Verde, a mainly Christian nation. More recently, a friend who is an aid worker in El Salvador said that, after the 2001 earthquake in that virtually 100 percent Christian country, the most effective organizations in supplying fast and much-needed assistance were the Christian organization Caritas and the Islamic Relief Worldwide. Both were on the job within a week of the earthquake and offered their services to all in need with no proselytism or other strings attached.

Islamic Relief Worldwide (IRW) operates in over twenty-five countries and offers not only disaster relief but development projects on water and sanitation, literacy, business loans, reintegration programs for returning refugees, projects for women's economic empowerment, mother and child care, computer centers, mobile clinics, orphanages, homes for the aged, etc.[3] It is significant that the projects in which IRW is engaged read very much like a list of projects by various Christian welfare agencies—and, one might add, international Jewish relief agencies. Should it be any cause for wonder that the same prophetic tradition, when its teachings are actually put into practice, would result in very similar approaches to the person in need?

Zakāh is not intended only as temporary emergency relief for those brought low by personal, familial, or natural tragedies, but as a type of ongoing income redistribution. The Qur'an explicitly speaks of wealth being extended "to relatives, orphans, the needy and the migrant, *so that it will not circulate merely among the wealthy among you*" (59:7).

This goal of a periodic redistribution of wealth underlies the intricate Islamic laws of inheritance. The Qur'an states: "Men shall have a portion of whatever parents and near relatives leave, and women shall have a portion of what parents and near relatives leave. No matter how small or how large it be, a portion is stipulated for them. When near relatives, orphans and paupers are present at the division [of inheritance], *provide for them from it and treat them politely*" (4:7-8). Repeating the same injunction in the same words underlines the inadmissibility of ignoring female heirs or cheating them out of their share.

Still more surprising is the Qur'anic inclusion of "relatives, orphans and paupers," who also have a right to a portion of the inheritance. These latter are not to be treated as interlopers or unwanted guests, for they have a certain right to be present at the redistribution of funds. No doubt referring to the abuse to which such outsiders are commonly subjected, the Qur'an adds pointedly, "and treat them politely."

Not only are the pillar of *zakāh* and the laws of inheritance oriented to reminding Muslims of their duty to the poor, but celebration of the central Islamic feasts would not be complete without providing for the poor. At 'Eid al-Fitr, the great feast that celebrates the end of the fasting month of Ramadan, Muslims are commanded to pay the *zakāt al-fiṭrah* so that the poor of the community can also celebrate the feast properly. At 'Eid al-Adha, the Feast of the Sacrifice, commemorating Abraham's willingness to sacrifice his son, Muslims are commanded to give one-third of the meat of the sacrificed animals to the poor.

The underlying view of wealth presumed by such Qur'anic teaching is that a person's wealth is not simply a private fortune to dispose of in any way one wants. God has a say in the matter and wants to ensure that the person's spouse, children, relatives, as well as helpless and dependent sectors of society receive their proper share. Thus, along with the wealth that one has received from God goes a responsibility to provide for others, beginning with one's closest family ties and extending all the way to those whose claim is based solely on common humanity.

Wealth and inequalities in economic status are seen in the Qur'an as a test of one's fidelity to God. The Qur'an states: "He is the One who has placed you as overlords on earth and raised some of you higher than others in rank *so that He may test you* by means of what He has given you" (6:165). And again, "God has favored some of you more than others in providing [for them]. Yet those who have been allowed to excel are not willing to hand over their provision to those under their control so that they become equal partners in it. Do they not thus abuse God's favor?" (16:71; see also 64:15; 8:28). In the God-centered universe envisioned by the Qur'an, the fact that some are wealthy while many are poor is not simply an accident of history, nor the inevitable result of economic determinism or class struggle, but a means by which believers are tested in their fidelity to God's word, in their generosity, sense of responsibility for the neighbor, and humility in recognizing that all that they possess comes from God's bounty.

The Qur'an saves some of its harshest warnings for those who are selfish and egotistic in using what they have been granted. "Announce *painful torment for those who hoard gold and silver* and do not spend them for God's sake" (9:34). And "How terrible it will be for everyone who backbites and slanders, and for *him who amasses wealth and keeps on counting it.* He reckons that his wealth will make him immortal, but he will be flung into [hell]" (104:1-4).

The Qur'anic warnings do not stop with personal selfishness, but extend as well to those who fail in their responsibilities to teach generosity and social concern. "God does not love someone who is conceited and boastful, nor those who are tight-fisted and encourage others to be stingy" (4:36-37). One of the strongest condemnations in the whole Qur'an is directed at the person who refuses to believe God's message and fails to teach the necessity of taking care of the poor. "Take him off and handcuff him. Padlock him to a long chain. Then let him roast in Hell. *He neither believed in God Almighty nor encouraged others to feed the needy*" (69:30-37).

The message is clear and uncompromising: God is deadly serious about the importance of "feeding the needy," with all that is implied in that obligation, and about the importance of encouraging others to do likewise, and God will not treat lightly those who neglect this duty. We must not allow the hyperbolic language (reminiscent of some of the prophet Amos's more stringent warnings or of Jesus' injunction to pluck out your eye or cut off your hand, if they cause you to sin) to distract us from the passage's unequivocal message. Failure to integrate what we today call "social concern" into personal and communal religiosity is placed right alongside the refusal to believe in God. Those who promote an unbridled consumerism as well as theologians and other teachers of religion might do well to hear this warning and tremble!

Given the force of the Qur'anic strictures against an unrestricted use of wealth and the obligation to "give away a part of it" (2:177), it should come as no surprise that a disproportionate number of Muhammad's early followers were women, slaves, and people without means, while his main opponents were the prosperous merchants of Mecca whose financial comfort was connected with the city's role as a flourishing pilgrimage site of the pagan religion.

The Qur'an, however, sees Muhammad's rejection by the wealthy classes of Mecca as indicative of a more general unwillingness to accept the prophetic message on the part of those overly attached to material possessions, those whose security is based on what they "have" rather than what they "are" before God. The Qur'an states: "Whenever we sent a warner to civilizations, the wealthy elite said: 'We do not believe in what you have been sent with.' They say, 'We have more wealth and children [than you]; we will not be tormented'" (34:34-35).

The Christian scholar from Sri Lanka, Aloysius Pieris, has called Jesus "God's defense pact with the poor." In Christ, he sees God displaying, to use the modern phrase, "a preferential option for the poor" and a promise to defend them from the arrogant and unjust use of power on the part of the rich. I agree with this view but feel that it could be extended to cover the major thrust of the whole prophetic tradition since the time of Abraham and Sarah.

The Qur'anic attitude to an economic system in which "the big fish eat the little fish" is twofold. On the one hand, there are strict warnings against "devouring the wealth of others" through exploitation and manipulation. On the other hand, there are strong expressions of God's commitment to defend the defenseless against those who would take advantage of their vulnerability. One passage displays a knowing awareness that economic aggressiveness and official corruption often go hand in hand and reveal the same Godless mentality. "*Do not devour one another's wealth* to no good purpose," states the Qur'an, "*nor try to bribe authorities with it* so that you can aggressively consume a share of other people's wealth, even while you realize [what you are doing]" (2:188).

Economic competition where the only rule is that of profits and annual returns is strongly condemned. What is foreseen, instead, in an Islamic way of life, is economic activity in which both partners freely consent and which is mutually beneficial. "You who believe, do not use up one another's wealth to no good purpose, unless it is for some business based on mutual consent among you" (4:29). The idea that, in business affairs, one takes whatever one can get is not the way that those who obey God's word must deal with one another.

Profiting from the needs and weaknesses of others underlies the Qur'an's prohibition of interest-taking. Debts that cannot be repaid should be postponed or, better yet, written off rather than imposing unbearable burdens on debtors. The Qur'an states: "Listen to God and *write off anything that remains outstanding from lending at interest* if you are [true] believers. If you do not do so, then be prepared to face war declared by God and His Messenger. If you repent, you may retain your principal. Do no wrong and you will not be wronged. *If any debtor suffers hardship, then postpone [repaying] it*, until conditions become easier [for the debtor]. And *if you treat it as an act of charity, it will be better for you*" (2:278-280; cf. also 2:275). In today's world where crushing international debts are causing untold suffering for millions in poor countries, I need not elaborate the relevance of this teaching.

The second side of the Qur'an's teaching is the promise of God's punishment of those who exploit the weak and defenseless. Here again, the Qur'an is repeating the consistent prophetic tradition. From the early prophets like Nathan confronting David and Elijah condemning Ahab and Jezebel, through the writings of the Hebrew prophets, and into the teaching of John the Baptist and Jesus, the prophetic word has consistently taken "widows, orphans, and strangers" as paradigmatic of all those groups in society who are at the mercy of others. The widows and orphans must rely on the strength of God's word to protect them from injustice, exploitation, and oppression. The widows and orphans in Asia today include indentured laborers, factory workers, street children, sex industry workers, child laborers, tenant farmers, and fishing folk.

The Qur'an reiterates the prophetic word by calling for a change of heart in people, urging them to join the defenders, rather than the oppressors, of the weak. The Qur'an focuses particular attention on the plight of orphans. Many commentators have pointed out that this concern might well reflect some of the misery and indignities to which Muhammad had been subject as an orphan (cf. 93:4-5). If revelation is granted in the context of a prophet's own life experience, this could well be the case. What is clear is the strong Qur'anic condemnation of those who would exploit the orphan and the needy. "Those who live off orphans' property unjustly will only suck up fire into their bellies, and they will roast in the Blaze" (4:10).

There are too many passages in the Qur'an on this theme to cite them all, and any reader of the Qur'an will find justice to the orphan to be a motif that runs throughout the Sacred Book. For example, "*The orphan must not be exploited*; and *the beggar should not be brushed aside*" (93:9; cf. also 6:152; 4:36; 59:7; 4:5-6, 8; 2:215; 90:13-14). One might go so far as to say that, according to the Qur'an, a key indication of whether one is accepting or refusing the divine message is the way one treats the orphan and the pauper. The Qur'an states: "Have you seen *someone who rejects religion? That is the person who pushes the orphan aside and does not encourage feeding the needy*" (103:1-3).

Similar to the orphan is the unfortunate child whose parents are more interested in material comfort than in the divine gift and responsibility that are children. In passages that are often cited to oppose the practice of abortion, the Qur'an states: "Do not kill your children out of fear of poverty. We will provide for them and for you. Killing them is a serious sin" (17:31; see also 6:151, 140). A poignant passage notes that, on the Last Day, the baby girl who has been destroyed because she would be an economic burden "will be asked for what offence she had been killed" (81:8-9). The shameful practice of selling one's children, particularly young girls, into prostitution, which is so prevalent in certain regions of modern Asia, was apparently also quite common at the time of Muhammad. The Qur'an categorically condemns this practice: "*Do not force girls, if they want to preserve their chastity, into prostitution*, so that you may seek worldly benefits" (24:23).

Other social concerns that the Qur'anic teaching raises for Muslims include: *dishonesty* in business practice ("It will go badly for cheats who insist on full measure when they have people measure something out of them; yet whenever they measure or weigh things for others, they give less than what is due" [83:1-3]); *manipulation of markets* and the use of power to obtain *unjust advantages* ("You use your oaths in order to snatch at advantages over one another, just because one nation may be more prosperous than another" [16:92]); *partiality and favoritism* in judicial systems ("Whenever you judge between people, you should judge on [the principles of] justice" [4:58]); *racism and ethnic chauvinism* ("You who believe, do not let one group of people sneer at another set; perhaps those others are better than they are. Women should not ridicule other women; perhaps those others are even better than they are themselves. Nor should you debase yourselves by insulting one another and calling names. It is bad to use evil names [about others] after [entering] the faith" [49:11-12]).

I conclude this introductory study with a few words on the duty of those who believe in God to work for *peace and reconciliation*. The Qur'an allows the Old Testament principle of "an eye for an eye, a tooth for a tooth" as a limit of strict justice, that is, one cannot requite compensation greater than the crime (i.e., never demand two eyes for an eye or two teeth for one), but at the same time, the Qur'an encourages believers to go beyond strict justice and operate instead on principles of mercy and forgiveness . . . to move beyond a legalistic mentality of demanding strict justice to a God-centered spirituality in which people are invited and urged to treat others as God treats us. Here I call your attention to several passages of the Qur'an that point in this direction:

The payment for an injury should be a proportionate injury. But *anyone who pardons offences and makes reconciliation shall be rewarded by God*. Those who defend themselves after being wronged will not be blamed for that. Only those who mistreat others and act arrogantly on earth, and have no right to do so, will be held blameworthy. (42:40-42)

A good deed and an evil deed are not alike: *repay [evil] with something better (iḥsān)* and see how someone who is separated from you because of enmity will become a bosom friend! (41:34)

Repay *evil with something that is fine*. (23:96)

Let those among you who have wealth and resources give something to relatives, paupers and those who are refugees for God's sake. They should *forgive and be indulgent*. Do you not want God to pardon you? God is forgiving and merciful. (24:22)

Cooperate with one another for virtue and heedfulness, but do not cooperate with one another for the purpose of vice and aggression. (5:2)

In conclusion, I hope that for Christians learning about these elements of the Qur'anic message, many of the phrases and attitudes expressed will ring bells with Gospel passages that we are struggling to live out in our churches in Asia. Some of you might be thinking, "These are lofty ideals, but we do not see them put into practice by Muslims in our countries. Our Muslim political leaders seem to be as rapacious and unconcerned about the plight of the poor as non-Muslims. Our Muslim scholars seem less interested in teaching these elements of the Qur'anic message than in preaching domination and intolerance. Muslims with economic power act with the same ruthlessness and greed as those of other religions or of no religion."

The reactions are similar when I teach about Christianity to Muslims. My Muslim students repeatedly say that they have no quarrel with the teachings of Jesus or with the way he lived what he preached. He is, after all, considered "the Seal of Holiness" by Muslims. But they regret that this is not what they see when they look at the behavior of Christians around the world. Gandhi's famous phrase: "Christianity is a beautiful thing; it's just never been tried," is a challenging half-truth.

The sad reality is that both Christians and Muslims are constantly struggling to live in obedience to the prophetic message we have received. We are constantly failing, constantly being called back to repentance (Bible: *metanoia*, Qur'an: *tawbah*) and God's forgiveness, constantly standing in need of God's grace which alone can transform our personal and communitarian lives. Moreover, we must not overdraw the picture. I could point to countless examples of Muslims and Christians who concretely seek to care for the poor, to support their just causes, to oppose dehumanizing and unjust systems of economy and government, and to work for true human liberation. There are millions of Muslims and millions of Christians throughout Asia who are striving, often together, to put into practice the message contained in the prophetic word.

But is this not exactly what Christians and Muslims ought to be talking about together—our magnificent ideals and our all-too-often sad realities, our sincere efforts as well as our shameful failures, our wonderful experiences of God's love and our selfish refusal to share that love with others? I suggest that this is what dialogue is all about. I conclude with a verse from the Qur'an: "If God had wanted, He could have made you one community. So *compete with one another in doing good deeds*, so that He may test you by what he has given you" (5:48).

Notes

1. *Benteng* is the name of a prison, and the "New Order" refers to Suharto's regime (1966-1998) and the dictatorial powers he assumed as opposed to the democratic potential that existed in the previous regime of Sukarno, the first president of Indonesia after independence from the Dutch.

2. For more on the work of this organization, visit http://www.oic-oci.org (accessed August 15, 2009).—Ed.

3. For an updated account of their activities, visit http://www.islamic-relief.com (accessed August 15, 2009).—Ed.

7

Hagar

Biblical and Islamic Perspectives

Abraham as a Bond of Unity

In recent years, Jews, Christians, and Muslims have explored the person and role of Abraham as "father in faith" for the followers of these three religions. For example, John Paul II, the leader of my own Christian tradition, that of the Catholic Church, has often had recourse to the figure of Abraham as a bond of unity between the three religions. His first visit outside Rome after becoming pope was to Ankara, Turkey, in 1979. Speaking to the Christians at the Mass, the pope stressed both the spiritual unity of the three communities descended from Abraham and the importance of striving for an active faith like that of their spiritual ancestor. He said:

> Faith in God, which the spiritual descendants of Abraham, Christians, Muslims, and Jews profess, when it is lived sincerely so that it penetrates life, is an assured foundation of human dignity, brotherhood, and freedom and a principle of rectitude for moral conduct in life and society. As a consequence of this faith in God the transcendent Creator, human beings find themselves at the summit of creation.[1]

On February 9, 1998, when the Muslim leader Fethullah Gülen visited Pope John Paul II in the Vatican, he proposed that the ancient site of Harran, near the modern city of Urfa, traditionally regarded as the birthplace of Abraham, become a center for Jewish-Christian-Muslim understanding, a proposal that still merits serious consideration. At the symposium held in Harran and Urfa on April 13-16, 2000, the Intercultural Dialogue Platform brought together an international group of scholars of the three religions who affirmed the faith of Abraham as a bond of unity. In preparing for that symposium, I discovered that "Abrahamic associa-

Previously published as "Hagar: Mother of Faith in the Compassionate God," in *Islam and Christian-Muslim Relations* 16, no. 2 (2005): 99-105. Reprinted by permission.

tions" made up of Jews, Christians, and Muslims already exist in over ten countries, including Bosnia, Canada, France, Germany, Indonesia, Ireland, Israel and Palestine, Sweden, the United Kingdom, and the United States.

It has become accepted in circles of those who want to build understanding, respect, and peace among the followers of the three religions that they possess a common spiritual patrimony, faith, and obedience to the One God who called Abraham and his family from Ur, through whom "all nations in the world" would be blessed. Today I would like to call attention to one member of that family to indicate some ways in which she might be regarded as our common "Mother in faith." I am referring to Hagar,[2] the mother of Abraham's oldest child, Ishmael.

Hagar in the Bible and in Islamic Sources

As wife of a prophet, mother of a prophet, and distant ancestress of Muhammad, the Prophet of Islam, Hagar has always been highly regarded by Muslims. She is referred to by Muslims with reverence as "Sitti Hajar" (my Lady Hagar), and her travail in the desert is relived by those who make the pilgrimage to Mecca. However, Hagar has been somewhat eclipsed in the attentions of Jews and Christians by Sarah, the first wife of Abraham, mother of Isaac, and ancestress of the Jewish people, including the Jew whom Christians regard as Savior, Jesus Christ.

I believe that despite the importance of her role as wife and mother, Hagar's deeper relevance for our understanding of God, particularly in today's world, is founded on her own experience of the Divine. By meditating together on the figure of Hagar, all of us—Jews, Christians, and Muslims—can gain insights into God's nature and God's will for us. I will concentrate on what we might learn about God from the story of Hagar as found in the Bible and as elaborated on in Islamic traditions.

The Jewish, Christian, and Muslim traditions agree on the main lines of the story of Hagar, but each tradition presents unique elements for our understanding of her significance in the history of God's revelation to humankind. All focus on the compassionate care shown by God to Hagar and her child when she was alone and helpless in the desert.

In the Christian New Testament, the only reference to Hagar is in Paul's letter to the Galatians (4:21-25), where Hagar and Sarah are said to represent the First Covenant that God made with the Jews on Sinai and the New Covenant established in the person of Jesus Christ. In this passage, Paul does not treat Sarah and Hagar in their historical setting but uses the biblical characters allegorically or "figuratively" to affirm the spiritual freedom of those who accept God's new covenant in Christ.

The story of Hagar is not recounted in the Qur'an but is told in hadith from Muhammad related by Ibn 'Abbas and found in Bukhari's authoritative collection of sound hadith.[3] The Qur'an does refer indirectly to the story of Hagar in speaking of Abraham and Ishmael laying the foundations of the Ka'bah (2:127) near the site in Mecca where God had saved Hagar and her child by producing the spring of Zamzam. There is also a Qur'anic reference (14:39) to God's answering the prayers of Abraham by blessing him with the birth of Ishmael and Isaac in his old age.

The Textual Question of the Biblical Accounts

The most important biblical accounts of Hagar are two and present a textual difficulty. Both accounts are found in the Book of Genesis (Gen. 16:1-15; 21:8-21). A straightforward reading of the Genesis narrative would seem to indicate that Hagar was cast out *twice* into the desert, both times at the instigation of Abraham's wife, Sarah. The first time was when Hagar was still pregnant with her unborn child, the second time after the birth and weaning of Isaac, almost sixteen years later.

Although it is possible to reconcile the two accounts into one ongoing narrative, modern biblical scholarship, by use of historical-critical methods, offers an alternative suggestion. It is now accepted by most biblical scholars that the accounts in Genesis are the result of editing by later redactors of narratives that originally developed independently of one another.

This hypothesis, which can be neither proved nor disproved, is illustrative of the way in which much of the biblical text came into its present form. Since this historical development might be unfamiliar to Muslims, whose Qur'anic scripture came about through a very different process of revelation, I will trace the outlines very briefly. Most scholars today accept the view that the Jewish people orally preserved and handed on the stories of Adam, Noah, Abraham, Moses, David, and the other great figures of their past. As the stories were told and retold from generation to generation, they came to take on the form of longer consistent narratives, which, in the divided reign after the time of David and Solomon, developed separately in the northern kingdom of Israel and the southern kingdom of Judah.

Sometime around the tenth century B.C., the southern narrative was written down by an unknown author, as was that of the north in the following century. One of the distinguishing characteristics of the two narratives is the use of the sacred name "JHWH" in the earlier narrative, and the generic name for God "Elohim" in the northern account. Thus, scholars commonly refer to the first as the J tradition and the second as the E tradition.

Several centuries later (in the eighth to sixth centuries B.C.), these two accounts were woven into one, with new material ("D") added, by the proponents of a reform movement called the Deuteronomic reform. Still later, after the return of the Jews from Babylon, the earlier accounts were put into their final form by a group of Priestly authors, whose contributions are referred to as the P source. Jews and Christians believe that this complex process by which the actual biblical text was produced from four originally independent sources (J, E,

D, P) was guided by God and that it is the final redaction that we have today that deserves to be called God's revealed message.

All this is what lies behind my statement that the two stories of Hagar in the Book of Genesis may in fact be parallel accounts referring to the same event.

Hagar Meets "the God Who Sees" in the Desert

According to the account in Genesis 16, Hagar was an Egyptian servant working in the house of Sarai and Abram (their names would be changed after the birth of Isaac). Since both were advanced in years and it appeared that the couple would have no children of their own, Sarai allowed Abram to sleep with Hagar in the hope that, as she stated: "perhaps I can build a family through her" (Gen. 16:2). Abram agreed and Hagar became pregnant with Ishmael. However, Sarai became jealous of Hagar, as the mother of Abram's only child and heir, and mistreated Hagar (16:6) to the point that Hagar finally fled into the desert.

In the desert, (the angel of) God found Hagar near a spring of water and appeared to her. In these early accounts in Genesis, "the angel of God" is an indirect, respectful way of referring to God's own self. God said, "Hagar, servant of Sarai, where have you come from, and where are you going?" "I am running away from my mistress Sarai," she answered. God tells Hagar to return and submit to Sarai, for God intends that Hagar will also be the mother of "descendants too numerous to count."

God also tells Hagar that he understands her misery and encourages her by predicting the birth of Ishmael. At the climax of the story, Hagar, who has found comfort and courage in God's concern for her plight, speaks boldly to God and gives God a new name. "She gave this name to the LORD who spoke to her: 'You are EL ROY: the God who sees me.'" She said, "I have now seen the One who sees me" (Gen. 16:13).

The parallel account in Genesis 21 differs in detail but bears the same message. The story takes place after the birth of Isaac. Abraham gave a great feast on the occasion of Isaac's weaning, when Isaac would have been about three years old and Ishmael already in his teens. On seeing Ishmael playing with Isaac, Sarah once again became jealous and said to Abraham: "Get rid of that slave woman and her son, for that slave woman's son will never share in the inheritance with my son Isaac" (Gen. 21:9). The Bible says that Abraham was upset because of his love for Ishmael, but God told Abraham to send Hagar away, promising him that both Isaac and Ishmael would be the fathers of great nations (Gen. 21:12-13). God's promise must have reassured Abraham as it guaranteed the survival of Ishmael.

So Abraham gave Hagar and Ishmael some food and water and sent them off to the south into the desert. The biblical narrative continues:

> When the water in the skin was gone, she placed the boy under a bush. Then she went off and sat down nearby, about a bowshot away, and

thought, "I cannot watch the boy die." And as she sat there, she began to sob. God heard the boy crying, and [the angel of] God called to Hagar from heaven and said to her, "What is the matter, Hagar? Do not be afraid. God has heard the boy crying as he lies there. Lift the boy up and take him by the hand, for I will make him into a great nation." Then God opened her eyes and she saw a well of water. So she went and filled the skin with water and gave the boy a drink, and God was with the boy as he grew up. (Gen. 21:15-20)

Hagar in the Islamic Traditions

Against the background of the two biblical accounts, we can see points of similarity with the story as told in Islamic traditions. The story is told in many versions, but Bukhari's collection of sound hadith forms the basis of the accounts. As narrated by Ibn 'Abbas, when Abraham had differences with his wife because of her jealousy of Hagar, he led the two of them away through the desert until they reached the region of Mecca. He gave them a full waterskin and left them under a tree and returned home. Hagar called out: "Abraham, to whom are you leaving us?" He replied, "[I leave you] in the care of God." Hagar answered, "I am satisfied to be with God" (*Sahih al-Bukhari* 4.584).

In another account, also related by Ibn 'Abbas, the story is even more poignant:

In those days there was nobody in Mecca, nor was there any water. So he made them sit down and placed near them a leather bag with some dates, and a small waterskin containing water, and set out homeward. Ishmael's mother followed him saying, "Abraham! Where are you going, leaving us in this valley where there is no one whose company we may enjoy, and there is nothing [to eat or drink]?" She repeated that to him many times, but he did not look back at her. Then she asked him, "Has God ordered you to do this?" He said, "Yes." She said, "Then God will not neglect us." (*Sahih al-Bukhari* 4.583)

After Abraham's departure, when their water was gone, Hagar went to look for help, climbing the hill of Safa, then that of Marwa, going back and forth between the two hills, each time stopping in the valley to check on Ishmael. He was close to death from thirst and Hagar could not bear to watch him die, so even though she herself was dying of thirst she climbed Safa once again to look for help. At that point, she heard a voice, although she saw no one. She cried out, "Help us if you can!" It was Gabriel she had heard. Gabriel struck the earth and water gushed out and the mother and child were saved. Later, some passing Arabs found them and gave them a home with them. Ishmael, when he reached the age of marriage, married one of the women from the tribe.

Still later, Abraham told his wife that he wanted to visit Hagar and his son in Mecca and found Ishmael mending arrows near the well of Zamzam. He told Ishmael that God had ordered him to build a house for God and that Ishmael should help him. Ishmael agreed and the two built the Ka'bah, praying in the words of the Qur'an: "O Lord! Accept [this service] from us. Truly, You are the All-Hearing, the All-Knowing" (2:127).

Other hadith traditions add more details to the Islamic account, but the main lines are similar to those above. The Islamic traditions give the name Zamzam to the well mentioned in Genesis 21:19 and relate the construction of the Ka'bah by Abraham and Ishmael. Muslims on the pilgrimage still perform the *sa'y*, running between Safa and Marwa to reenact Hagar's distress; they take water from the well of Zamzam to recall how God saved her and her son from death.

Significance of Hagar as "Mother in Faith"

I believe that Hagar is a key religious figure and that meditation on her story can enrich the understanding of Jews, Christians, and Muslims concerning the nature of the God whom we worship and what it means to do God's will in contemporary societies. The image of Hagar and her child in the desert is part of today's reality. The low-born, hard-working domestic laborer, used and misused and cast out by her employers, the single mother abandoned by the father of her child, the foreigner and refugee far from her native land, desperately trying to survive, frantic in her maternal concern for the safety of her child—this Hagar I have met many times.

I see Hagar in the Filipino domestic workers that often make up the bulk of our Catholic parishes in Amman, Dubai, Rome, Chicago, and Hong Kong. Women far from home, working long hours at thankless tasks for poor pay in other people's houses, rearing and showing love to other people's children, often defenseless against personal assaults, without the means to defend their legal and human rights, supporting distant families by their labors. The Hagars of our day are not only Christian Filipinos—they might be Pakistani or Indonesian Muslims, they might be Buddhists from Sri Lanka or Hindus from India.

It goes without saying that not all those for whom Hagar is a model of faith are women. The poor man who trusts in God, who strives against odds to support his family, whose desperation never turns to despair or hatred or violence, he is also a child with the faith of Hagar. But because of their vulnerability, because their social and economic resources are more limited than those of men, it is preeminently the poor woman in whom we can see the modern figure of Hagar.

All these have one thing in common. Abandoned and desperate in the desert of our modern metropolises and rural areas, they are emblematic of the poor people of this world for whom God has special care, whose dignity is recognized by God, to whom God shows compassion in their distress. It is significant that in the Bible, Hagar is the first one to whom God is revealed as "the God who sees." It is Hagar who gives God this name. What does God see? God sees Hagar's distress, comes to her aid, shows compassion, treats her with kindness and saves her. In God's encounter with Hagar in the desert, we see for the first time that God is a God who has special care for those who suffer.

What God began to teach us through Hagar has become a central theme of the prophetic tradition of which we Jews, Christians, and Muslims are heirs in faith. A central element of the teaching of the Hebrew prophets like Nathan, Amos, Isaiah, and Elisha is that God is the champion of the poor, the mistreated, the defenseless— the "orphan, widow, and wayfarer." For example, it is the poor widow's oil jar that the prophet Elijah is sent by God to replenish.

Jesus carried on the message of the Hebrew prophets by declaring that it is to such people, the poor of every age, that God's reign belongs (Luke 6:20). They are "blessed" because in their misery they rely on God and God never fails to respond to their trust. It is to such that Jesus brought God's healing and consolation and whose demons he cast out. It is their faith that he recognized and defended in parables such as that of the widow whose insignificant temple offering, he says, was worth more in God's sight than the superfluous wealth of the rich.

The Qur'an forthrightly notes that concern for the widows and orphans in our midst is an indispensable part of faith in God. The poor are not simply objects of charity but have a right to a portion of the wealth of others. *Zakāh* is an obligation in Islam. In the distribution of wealth that occurs in the division of inheritance, the poor have a prescribed portion. In a strong condemnation, the Qur'an consigns to Hell the person who "neither believed in God almighty nor encouraged others to feed the needy" (69:30-37). Because of her faith, Islam uplifts the status of Hagar from being a servant girl to being honored as "the Lady Hagar," and, by performing the *sa'y* between Safa and Marwa, Muslims bear witness to God's saving response to her faith.

The image of Hagar invites us all to look at God through the eyes of the Egyptian domestic who could say in the words of the hadith: "I am satisfied to be with God." Hagar challenges modern believers to ask ourselves if we respond to the plight of the poor with the respect their dignity deserves, with the compassion shown by God, with the concrete assistance provided by God and symbolized in the water of Zamzam. We must examine ourselves honestly to inquire whether we who worship El Roy, "the God Who Sees" the plight of the poor, fail to see the contemporary daughters and sons in faith of Hagar in our societies.

Notes

1. Pope John Paul II, Homily at Mass, Ankara, Turkey, November 26, 1979.
2. Abraham (Ibrahim), Hagar (Hajar), Ishmael (Ismaʿil), Isaac (Ishaq) are English derivations of the cognate names taken respectively from Hebrew and Arabic. Jews and

Christians tend to use the Hebrew form, Muslims that of Arabic. To be consistent and avoid clumsiness, I will refer to all these by their biblical names taken from Hebrew.

3. Al-Bukhari's collection of hadith (recorded sayings of Muhammad) is regarded as second only to the Qur'an in aiding scholars and believers alike in contextualizing the meaning of the text of the Qur'an. For an online access to the text of *Sahih Bukhari*, please visit http://www.usc.edu/schools/college/crcc/engagement/resources/texts/muslim/hadith (accessed August 15, 2009).—Ed.

8

Christian and Muslim Fundamentalism

In speaking about Christian and Muslim fundamentalism it should be noted at the beginning that I am referring to a derogatory term, one that today no religious group claims for itself. In the first half of the twentieth century, there were Christians who proudly referred to themselves as "fundamentalists," but as the term came to carry connotations of narrow-mindedness, an intolerance of all those outside their group, and a rejection of science, rational thought, and modern life, erstwhile fundamentalists came to refer to themselves as "evangelicals."

Muslims reject the term even more strongly, which they see as part of a media and political campaign to denigrate and isolate Muslims in the modern world. There are Islamic terms, as we shall see, by which Muslims themselves refer to phenomena and attitudes within the Islamic community that are often dubbed "fundamentalist" by the news media. Thus, we should be aware at the outset that we are using a term that, although it has become so current as to be inescapable, is not respectful of the beliefs and perspectives of those to whom it is applied.

In order to bring this very broad topic into sharper focus, I will attempt to answer the following questions: What are the characteristics that distinguish Christian and Muslim "fundamentalists" from other Muslims and Christians? On what points might we as Catholics find ourselves in agreement with such groups? Where do we differ? What makes fundamentalist religious attitudes attractive in the modern world and results in fundamentalism as a growing phenomenon in the world today? Finally, what pastoral responses might be proposed to this reality?

Christian Fundamentalism

The origins of the term are well known. At the American Biblical Congress held in Niagara, New York, in 1895, a group of conservative Protestant churchmen

Previously published in *Christian Response to the Phenomenon of Violence in South Asia* (Kathmandu: n.p., 1997); reprinted in FABC Papers, no. 82, Hong Kong, 1998. Reprinted by permission.

who were disturbed by trends in biblical scholarship and liberal theology drew up a list of "fundamentals" that they affirmed: verbal inerrancy of Scripture, the divinity of Christ, his virgin birth, the doctrine of vicarious expiation, and the bodily resurrection at the Second Coming of Christ. (The resurrection of the body and the Second Coming of Christ are sometimes counted as two distinct fundamentals, giving a total of six.) These theses were developed in a series of tracts, which popularized and systematized their views in American Protestant circles. Their strong missionary thrust (it is estimated that between 70 and 80 percent of missionaries are evangelicals) brought their particular understanding of Christianity to many parts of the world, so that today evangelical Christianity is a worldwide phenomenon, growing quickly throughout Asia, Africa, and Latin America.

Christian fundamentalism is not a united movement, but rather an outlook on modern life formed by a distinctive reading of Scripture and the role of Christians in world history. Some reject all denominations and have no ties to any ecclesial organization. Others form fellowships of independent local congregations that recognize no higher authority. Still others are members of recognized "historical" churches. The characteristic features of Christian fundamentalism can be viewed under four headings: (1) their understanding of Scripture, its inspiration, interpretation, and authority; (2) a unique history of salvation; (3) eschatology; and (4) critique of modernity.

Scripture: Its Inspiration, Interpretation, and Authority

The 1993 document of the Pontifical Biblical Commission, *The Interpretation of the Bible in the Church*, with a preface by Cardinal Ratzinger, surveys various aspects of the historical-critical approach to the Bible. It treats textual criticism, literary genre, tradition and redaction criticism, rhetorical, narrative, and semiotic analyses, canonical criticism, Jewish methods of interpretation, and aspects of sociological, anthropological, psychological, and psychoanalytic approaches to Scripture. The document examines both the strengths and limitations of liberationist and feminist uses of Scripture. Of all the varied approaches to the Word of God, only the fundamentalist use is described as "dangerous."

Fundamentalists might state their position as follows: Scripture is inerrant because it is inspired by God (2 Tim. 3:16), who is Truth. Thus, Scripture cannot contradict itself. The inerrancy of Scripture flows from the truthfulness of God—to challenge one is to challenge both. Because Scripture is inerrant, its authority cannot be contested. There is only one correct interpretation of Scripture, that which comes from a literal reading of the text.

The fundamentalist understanding of inspiration not only presumes divine authorship but denies any role to human reflection and creativity. The Bible, they hold, is not a product of the human community. It originates, rather, from God and was transmitted to the community by chosen agents such as prophets and apostles. Some subscribe to the "dictation theory," by which God takes possession of the imagination and faculties of the individual authors, dictating words and ideas and preserving them from errors that could arise from ignorance or deception. The inspired authors are regarded as passive, receptive secretaries of God's Word.

God moved the biblical authors to write and inspired every detail of the original text. Many hold that God also preserved from error those who prepared "official" translations (such as the King James Version in English) from Hebrew and Greek. There are no tales or myths to distort the revelation, no need for later reinterpretation or further theological development. In contrast to the Catholic and Orthodox position that the Bible is to be interpreted by ecclesiastical officials in the light of church tradition, and the liberal Protestant view that biblical teaching must be evaluated in the light of Christian reason, fundamentalists hold that the Bible is self-contained and self-interpreting. The biblical word is complete and comprehensive, providing all that needs to be known for salvation, and containing within itself the principles of its own interpretation.

This appeal to the self-authenticating nature of the Scripture also distinguishes Scripturalist evangelicals from Pentecostals, who claim that the individual Christian believer will be guided by the direct action of the Holy Spirit to interpret the Scripture. Throughout most of this century there have been mutual suspicions and antagonisms between evangelicals and Pentecostals, with the Scripturalists holding that the fullness of salvific knowledge contained in the Bible renders superfluous all private revelations that arise from Spirit possession. Pentecostals, on the other hand, hold that the charismatic gifts of the Spirit, including that of interpretation, were meant to be ongoing blessings in the Christian community. By repudiating them, the Scripturalists lack the fullness of the apostolic experience. However, in the last twenty-five years, there has been a cross-fertilization between evangelicals and Pentecostals, and the formerly sharp distinctions between the two interpretations are blurred.

Because the Bible is inspired, it is not subject to any historical limitations. Thus, fundamentalists oppose all critical biblical interpretation and reject the conclusions that arise from critical-historical methods. This view, which the document of the Pontifical Biblical Commission describes as "naïve literalism," is opposed to the Catholic position, which holds that "the historical-critical method is the indispensable method for the scientific study of the meaning of the ancient texts."

The difference between the two views would seem to lie in understanding the meaning of the term "literal." Fundamentalists contend that "the Bible says what it means and means what it says," thus making no distinction between what the words say and what they mean. Since the revealed Word is not limited by historical expression, they do not take into account the change of meaning in words that occurs in the course of time. They presume that words and ideas today have exactly the same significance they had for the original authors.

Historical-critical scholars also seek to affirm the literal meaning of Scripture, by which they mean the way these words were understood by the biblical authors, editors, and communities. They do not presume that this meaning has remained unchanged over the centuries. Thus, critical scholars do not question the God-given and authoritative character of the Bible, but they insist that Scripture is not comprehensive, self-contained, or self-interpreting.

Finally, it must be recognized that Catholics and evangelicals share many of the same biblical concerns and interests. Both regard the biblical teachings as normative and seek to live their lives in accord with them. Both hold that the Holy Spirit has been with the church since the beginning and guides its understanding of revealed truth. Both agree that church tradition is important and offers invaluable assistance and insight in explaining biblical teaching. It is on the international implications of the role of the human author in the production of Scripture that they differ.

History of Salvation: Dispensationalism

One of the most distinctive features of the fundamentalist reading of the Bible is the doctrine of the seven dispensations. This scheme, which dates from the nineteenth century, was set forth in the notes to the Scofield Reference Bible (1909)[1] which, through its many reprintings, translation into many languages, and study in Bible colleges, has been one of the main vehicles for the spread of dispensationalist doctrine. Dispensationalist theory divides the world into seven epochs, each of which is characterized by a specific way in which God brings about human salvation. The seven epochs are:

1. innocence (the Garden of Eden). Adam and Eve were sinless while in the Garden.
2. conscience (the Fall to Noah). People were saved by following their conscience.
3. human government (Noah to Abraham). Obedience to human rulers.
4. promise (Abraham to Moses). Salvation through the promise.
5. law (Moses to Christ). Salvation by perfect adherence to the Law.
6. grace (the death of Christ to the present; "the Church Age").
7. millennium (begins with Christ's Second Coming; "the Kingdom Age").

Of particular interest is the relationship between the last three dispensations. The "70 weeks of years" (Dan. 9:20-27) are divided into four periods. The 69th "week" ended with the death of Christ and the destruction of the Temple in the year 70. With the death of Jesus there came into being two peoples: the "worldly" people of God, the Jews, and the "heavenly" people of God, the Church. The Church Age, in which we now live, is a hiatus during which the Gospel is preached to the Gentiles. When this has been accomplished, the world will enter the 70th week, at which time the fulfillment of all the prophecies will occur.

A peculiar feature of dispensationalism is the belief that the Gospel preaching of Jesus took place under the dispensation of the law, while the epistles are addressed to the Church and are fully applicable to the dispensation of grace. The Scofield Reference Bible states that "the doctrines of grace are to be sought in the epistles, not in the gospels." Jesus' earthly preaching, including the Sermon on the Mount, the Lord's Prayer, and so on, is seen as calling people to enter the dispensation of grace. It does not contain the full teaching of the Church Age. For example, in the Lord's Prayer, forgiveness is dependent on forgiving others, but under grace, God's forgiveness is unconditional—Jesus, under the dispensation of the law, teaches: "Not everyone who says 'Lord, Lord' will enter the Kingdom of heaven, but the one who does the will of my Father in heaven" (Matt. 7:21); but Paul, in the time of grace, teaches: "Everyone who calls upon the name of the Lord will be saved" (Rom. 10:13).

There is no contradiction between Jesus and Paul, since Jesus taught under the law, while Paul wrote in the dispensation of grace. What is important in dispensationalist thought is not the earthly teaching of Jesus but rather his death, which expiated for all sins committed by humankind and ushered in the new dispensation, the age of grace. This, they claim, is faithful to the approach of Paul himself, who admittedly refers, but rarely, to Gospel teachings and parables, and is more concerned with the effects of Christ's death and resurrection as the inauguration of the "new and eternal covenant" and God's unconditional free gift of salvation.

Eschatology: The Final Days

The doctrine of divine dispensations sets the stage for one of the best-known elements of fundamentalist thought, the imminent Second Coming of Christ. Until the 1920s, most fundamentalist Protestants accepted the historical optimism of the time, that Christians would be successful in transforming the world through evangelical values, overcoming ignorance, poverty, and injustice through scientific advances. Christian missionaries from technologically advanced countries saw themselves as bringing the benefits of Christian civilization to all peoples. Their efforts were to be ultimately crowned with the Christian millennium, a thousand-year reign of peace and prosperity on earth. At the end of this period, Christ would return and set the divine seal of approval on the Christian transformation of the world. The technical term for this view in which Christ returns after the millennium is called *postmillennialism*. In the early part of this century, most fundamentalists were postmillennialists.

The experience of World War I, with Christian armies using modern scientific weapons to annihilate one another, brought a profound disillusionment with modernity and technology. More and more, they began to turn to a *premillennialist* schema, which presumes that the world is headed inexorably to disaster. The signs are all around, "for those who have eyes to see." At the point when things cannot get any worse, Christ will return and inaugurate the millennium. Thus, in the premillennial schema, Christ returns before the millennium.

Relying on obscure passages in the prophecies of Daniel, Jeremiah, Ezekiel, and the Book of Revelation (the Apocalypse), fundamentalist thinkers attempt to predict the coming eschatological crisis. The Antichrist, an ecclesiastical and political tyrant supported by the apostate Christian churches, will appear and lead many astray. World history will degenerate to a seven-year period called the Great Tribulation (Matt. 24:21-29). However, before the beginning of the Tribulation, Christ will return to take those who have been "born again" and call upon the name of Jesus out of this world so they will escape the coming sorrows. This is called the Rapture (see 1 Thess. 4:16-17), and it is expected quite literally. The Tribulation will culminate in the Battle of Armageddon, after which Christ will come to establish the millennium.

The broad outlines of this worldly eschatology were already sketched in the Scofield Reference Bible in 1909, but were given wide diffusion and concrete application with the publication in 1970 of Hal Lindsey's *The Late Great Planet Earth*,[2] which has sold over twenty million copies in more than forty languages. This work attempts to apply the fundamentalist eschatology to current events. The first sign of the imminent approach of the Last Days is the establishment of the state of Israel (Dan. 9:20-27). The Antichrist's appearance is seen in the appearance of the Beast, which Lindsey identifies with the European Union. A Russian-led Arab coalition is expected to attack Israel, which will be defended by the European Union led by the Antichrist. The Antichrist will enter the Temple in Jerusalem and demand to be worshiped. This is the beginning of the Great Persecution, followed by "the greatest battle of all time," Armageddon. At this point the Rapture will occur, and those who have remained faithful and accept Jesus as their personal Savior will not have to suffer the terrible events to follow.

China will invade Israel, and the whole world will be caught up in a nuclear war. After much suffering, sickness, and famine, Christ will return with an army of angels and saints, defeat the Antichrist and all Gentile powers, and usher in his thousand-year millennial reign. At the end of this final dispensation, God will free Satan from his bonds, and he will make a final effort to overthrow the Reign of Christ. Christ will totally defeat Satan, who will be hurled into the lake of fire, and the New Jerusalem will descend from heaven.

There are, of course, religious and political implications to this fanciful scenario, which might be amusing were it not for the fact that so many Christians take it as a literal prediction of coming events. Much of the zeal of evangelical missionaries in all corners of the globe is motivated by the belief that the Final Cataclysm cannot take place until the Gospel has been preached to all the Gentiles. With the fall of the Soviet Union, evangelicals lost no time in sending specially trained missionaries into Russia and the neighboring republics. At the political level, rather than fearing a nuclear holocaust, dispensationalists look forward to it. They themselves will not suffer the consequences, since they will have been raptured into heaven. Thus, they tend to support excessive military budgets and oppose nuclear-arms limitation treaties. There are no stronger supporters of the state of Israel than fundamentalist Christians, because they see its existence as a necessary prerequisite for the Final World Crisis. Every year at the Jewish feast of Succoth, thousands of evangelicals visit Jerusalem and pledge their support for the state of Israel.

Anti-Modernist Social Critique

Perhaps the key element that unites Christian fundamentalists of various churches and ecclesial communities is their opposition to "modernism." By modernism is not meant modernity. Fundamentalists are not opposed to advances in technology, health, and education. They are often skillful and innovative in the use of media, including its most advanced applications, such as satellites, e-mail, and the Internet, to promote and disseminate their message. What they object to, strongly and angrily, is the modernist philosophy of life, which, in their view, offers an antireligious understanding of the human person, the universe, and society, and proposes a system of values meant to replace a religious "theocentric" outlook with an anthropocentric humanism.

The element of anger in the fundamentalist rejection of modernist values stems from what they consider to be a "liberal hegemony" that controls decisions and public opinion on a global scale. They hold that all centers of power, from government ministries and international organizations such as the United Nations, the European Union, and the World Bank, to university faculties, NGOs, research centers, family planning and development programs, the arts, popular entertainment, and communications media are controlled by "liberals" and "secular humanists," who have substituted human values for those revealed by God. Fundamentalists feel that their own views are ignored by this international liberal establishment, that their concerns are dismissed as devoid of serious consideration, and that their religious outlook caricatured as "fanatic" and "obscurantist."

Modernist Values in Fundamentalist Perspective

Fundamentalists often preach and write against secular humanism, a line of thought they trace from the European philosophers of the Enlightenment. It introduces a religious relativism founded on the invalidity of metaphysics and theology (Kant). Religion is reduced to an ethic (for example, in Asia, many countries have replaced religious instruction with "moral education"). Religiosity is seen as a characteristic of primitive man; in mature, modern societies it should be superseded (Comte). For mature people in mature societies, reason, not revelation, is the sound basis for arriving at truth. Secularism is presumed as the basis of social life. Religion is a private affair and has no place in the public life of politics, economy, and social affairs.

A scientific, rational attitude is one of objectivity and affective disinterest, an indifference to the consequences of truth. Scientific research does not treat ultimate questions but is oriented, rather, toward solving problems. Primacy is given to the individual over and against society. This leads to self-fulfillment being regarded as the highest of human goals and to a burning concern for human rights. The social values of the French revolution—liberty, fraternity, equality—are societal ideals to be striven for with "religious" fervor.

Finally, modernism proposes a historical optimism, an evolutionary vision of history, with a firm conviction of the inevitable victory of the forces of reason, progress, and liberty over those of superstition, obscurantism, and slavery. The downside of this optimism in social, political, and economic life is a Darwinian "survival of the fittest" that divides the world into "winners" and "losers." It provides a philosophical underpinning for the "New World Order" in which success validates ideology—gold cards are the sign of ultimate achievement, and the losers get what they deserve. While the winners are rewarded with wealth, power, and prestige, the losers are left to enjoy the destructive and self-destructive pleasures of alcohol, drugs, and sex.

The Fundamentalist Vision of Society

The vision of the fundamentalists is quite different. There is one God, one moral universe, one Scripture. Truth is not founded on human reason, but has been revealed in the Scripture, which offers a clear, comprehensive, incontrovertible guide by which societies and individuals can order their lives according to God's will. Success in life is based not on a university education, a high salary, and traveling first class, but on accepting Christ as one's personal savior and being preserved from the tribulation to come.

Fundamentalists hold that modern progress has been achieved at the cost of religious and moral values, and results in dehumanization, the breakdown of families, and promiscuity. The modernist plan of society they compare to a plant fed with supernutrients that are growing too fast, wildly, directionless, out of control, into a monstrous being, devouring everything within its grasp. As a result, modern society values quantity more than quality, pragmatism more than truth, efficiency more than beauty.

Pastoral Challenges

Catholics must admit that the fundamentalist critique is not entirely without basis. Serious Christians, of whatever tendency, cannot accept uncritically the modernist value system proposed by such diverse sources as *Time*, *Asiaweek*, CNN, popular films, family-planning agencies, business schools, and the advertising industry. Fundamentalists challenge Catholics to be aware that secular principles of society and humanist causes are not value-free.

Fundamentalists often accuse the main-line churches, including the Catholic Church, of having sold out to modernist ideals and allowing themselves to become the servants of society's "winners." It cannot be denied that one of the reasons for the fundamentalists' rapid growth in the world today is their appeal to society's "losers." The fundamentalist outlook meets the felt needs of people on the bottom end of the social and economic scale. It helps them overcome immediate suffering due to human failure, frustration, and sin, by enabling people to deal with alcoholism, family discord, and mental anguish. The close-knit, mutually supportive communities of evangelicals provide havens of faith and encouragement in environments that are felt to be impersonal and hostile. The values of honesty, frugality, and discipline instilled through sermons and popular religious literature enable people to survive amid a rapidly disintegrating social order. Finally, their religious experience is fervent and emotionally satisfying and allows for an enthusiastic release of tension in ecstatic prayer gatherings.

In addition to the ways in which fundamentalists challenge Catholics today, we must also be conscious of the weak points in their system. Fundamentalists tend to idealize or romanticize the past and do not face up to the contradictions and cruelties of every period of human history. Some evangelicals want to have it both ways and preach "the Prosperity Gospel," with born-again Christians bearing witness how once they had given their lives to Jesus they were rewarded with jobs, windfalls, good health, and peace of mind. Fundamentalists employ a selective and often fanciful reading of Scripture. Not all Scripture is equally cited and meditated upon. The most difficult element of fundamentalist belief to accept is the bloodthirsty image of God presented in their eschatological scenario, one who is willing to allow millions to suffer and die in a nuclear catastrophe, and then suffer eternal damnation because they did not accept Christ as their savior. This is an appalling departure from the message of Christ.

Muslim Fundamentalism

The similarities of outlook between Muslim revivalists and Christian fundamentalists are most apparent in their understanding of scriptural inspiration and authority, and in their social critique. The correspondence is most acute in their common rejection of secular humanism although the Muslim critique has its own history, emphases, and concerns.

The concept of Islamic fundamentalism is more problematic than its Christian counterpart. As we have seen, fundamentalism is a part of Christian history in the last century. It was the invention of certain Christians who saw the term as properly descriptive of their views. By contrast, when one speaks of fundamentalism among Muslims, one is using a term that has no proper origin or history within the Islamic tradition, but is applied pejoratively to Muslims by others. Moreover, it is not careful scholars who refer to Muslims as fundamentalists, but rather journalists, politicians, and casual observers. Thus, the term "Islamic fundamentalism" does not have the same precision as when it is applied to Christians, but is rather a catch-all for many diverse and often contradictory movements and interpretations of Islam.

Muslims and other observers often use the term "fundamentalism" to indicate movements based on the principle of *salafīyah* (following the interpretations of the earliest generations of Muslims), or *'usūliyah* (purifying religion according to its original roots). These terms indicate a different emphasis from that of Christian fundamentalists. The emphasis of Muslim revivalists is on "beginnings," "return," and "purifying" religion. The basic supposition is that Islam has moved away from its origins, and in doing so has lost its pristine purity, which can be regained by returning to the original interpretation of the "Fathers" (*salaf*).

This explains one type of fundamentalist movement, for example, that of the Wahhabis in Saudi Arabia or the Jama'at-i Islami in the Indian subcontinent, but other so-called fundamentalist movements, such as the revolutionary ideology of Iran, are diametrically opposed to those movements. If we were to single out elements that characterize the many diverse and often incompatible movements of Islamic fundamentalism, three would stand out: (1) desecularization (antisecularism); (2) the priority of divine law over human law; (3) sectarian protest (alternative Islam.)

Origins of Islamic Fundamentalism

Whereas the origins of Christian fundamentalism may be traced to a nineteenth-century reaction in conservative Protestant circles in America, Islamic fundamentalism finds its roots in a religious response to the loss of sovereignty. When Muslims looked around the world at the beginning of the nineteenth century, they were forced to ask, "What went wrong?" From having possessed, in previous centuries, the world's most powerful, advanced, and prosperous states, in the Ottoman, Safavid, and Mughal empires, Muslims had by 1800 succumbed almost everywhere to the rule of others.

In South and Southeast Asia it was Christian European powers—first the Portuguese, then Dutch, British, Spaniards, Russians, and Americans—who came to dominate Muslim regions. In the same period, Chinese, Thai, and Burmese Buddhists incorporated Muslim regions into their domains. In Asia, only Afghanistan was able to remain independent, due to its topological isolation and a skillful playing off of Russian designs against those of England. In the Middle East and North Africa, the British and French were locked in a power struggle over regions inhabited by Muslims, with the other European powers holding on to whatever enclaves they could. Iran and Turkey, while remaining nominally independent, had to accept humiliating capitulations that gave European powers rights to intervene, interfere, and impose their will.

How did the Muslim world fall so far so fast? A radical response was provided by Muhammad ibn 'Abd al-Wahhab (d. 1792) in Arabia, who held that Muslim peoples were reduced to their low state because they had deviated from the true Islamic path. When Muslims abandoned Islam in its original purity, God left them to the consequences. Ibn 'Abd al-Wahhab felt that nothing less than a return to the pure, original Islam would permit Muslims to achieve their past glory. In his analysis, Ibn 'Abd al-Wahhab was not devising a new theory, but drawing on a minority strain of thought (Khariji, Ibn Hanbal, Ibn Taymiyah) that had been present in the Islamic community from the beginning as a protest against secularizing tendencies.

Those who took up his views were called Wahhabis.[3] They wanted not only to purify Islam of accretions and novelties that had wrongly been accepted as Islamic in the course of time; but they held that the Sufi preoccupation with

Islam as a personal, spiritual path to God was in itself a distortion of the original intent of the religion. They claimed that Islam was meant to be a program for building a humane society whose every aspect was to be lived in accord with the will of God. Many hajjis making the pilgrimage to Mecca encountered Wahhabi ideas in Arabia and brought these views back with them to their homelands in Asia.

The Wahhabi analysis had political implications. If God intended the Islamization of society in all its social, economic, and political aspects, this could only be accomplished if Muslims themselves were in control of the political systems. Their political theory held that the state existed to permit Muslims to foster the Islamization process, to forbid deviations, and to punish wrongdoing. They felt that the Sufis, in their efforts to draw up interior spiritual paths aimed at mystical union with God, ignored political realities and held Muslims back from the task of forming society according to God's will. In this way, the Muslim revival linked religious and political concerns. In order to pursue their societal ends, they sought to create a state that would favor and implement these goals. The first objective, therefore, was to achieve liberation from non-Muslim rule. Wahhabi-inspired movements, such as that of Sayyid Ahmad Barelavi (d. 1831) in north India, worked for the overthrow of colonial regimes in order to create an Islamic state that would implement the aims of Islamization of society.

Geopolitical Factors Influencing Islamic Revival

After 1945, two organizations emerged to articulate the concept of the Islamic state in modern societies. In Egypt and other Arab countries, the Muslim Brotherhood, insisting that rule by Muslims did not ensure the creation of an Islamic state, worked to counter nationalist feelings that they felt divided rather than united the Islamic *ummah*. The harsh repression of the Brotherhood in Egypt and Syria convinced many that the new regimes were as opposed to the creation of an Islamic state as the colonial powers had been. In South Asia, the Jama'at-i Islami held that Islam offered the world an Islamic solution to every modern problem. There was already an Islamic science, economics, politics, legal system, and educational program. Muslims had only to search in their own early tradition to find the ingredients necessary to develop Islamic alternatives to these secular fields.

As one Muslim nation after another achieved independence in the years after World War II, the revivalists hoped that Islamic states would be set up. What actually happened was quite different. Muslim rule replaced the colonial regimes, but the ideals of the Islamic state were far from being implemented. The new ruling class throughout the Muslim world generally created nation-states on a European nationalist model. Legal codes were based on those of Western nations and were often merely revisions of colonial law. On the grounds that it was more egalitarian and would prevent the abuses of uncontrolled capitalism, socialist policies of a one-party state, state ownership of industries, and centrally planned economics were adopted. Cultural mores, as well as development concepts, were borrowed from the West.

In the first years after World War II, many Muslims were enthusiastic about the creation of Pakistan, which they considered a model for the modern Islamic democracy. When it gradually became clear that Pakistan's Islamic identity did not enable the country to overcome ethnic clashes, economic mismanagement and corruption, military takeovers, and equitable distribution of wealth, many Muslims claimed that the Pakistan model was a failed experiment. A truly Islamic state would have to undergo a more revolutionary societal restructuring.

The emergence of the state of Israel in 1948 had great influence on the thinking of militant Muslims. Seen as a stage for non-Muslim Europeans created in the Arab heartland by Western powers to assuage their guilt for Europe's treatment of its Jews, Israel, in expelling and oppressing the Palestinians, provided the imagery of oppressed Muslims achieving liberation through armed rebellion. The Palestinian cause engendered a conviction that the West, despite its professions of concern for the development of Muslim countries, was in fact opposed to Islam, and that Arabs and Muslims generally were victims of injustice perpetrated by inimical Western powers.

The disastrous 1967 war was a watershed in modern Muslim thought. Egypt, the cultural capital of the Arab world, led by the charismatic Gamal 'Abd al-Nasser, sustained by alliances and financial backing from other Arab countries, went down to quick and ignominious defeat by tiny Israel. Not only were Nasser and the ideology of pan-Arab nationalism discredited, but also the military. Corrupt and ineffective in its role of defending the nation, the military was seen as a costly expenditure that existed mainly to preserve the internal status quo and to enable the ruling elite to govern by force, in many cases, against the will of the people.

The lingering hopes that the Western powers would provide the assistance needed in Muslim regions were dashed when those states supported Israel both financially and in international diplomatic fora, such as the United Nations. In response to these reversals, many began to question the efficacy of nationalist thought and turned to religion to furnish more effective means to govern Muslim peoples.

The 1979 Iranian revolution gave concrete shape to these grievances. The world was amazed when religious solidarity enabled Iranian Muslims to overthrow with apparent ease a wealthy and unpopular Muslim regime, one which had been presumed to be of unassailable stability. The facts that the Shah's regime was a strong proponent of secularization and closely allied to the West were not lost on Muslims. The Islamic Republic of Iran replaced, in the thoughts of many, the failed Pakistan as the model of an Islamic state. All observers, whether sympathetic or not, agreed that the government of Ayatollah Khomeini was truly revolutionary in rethinking and reorganizing every aspect of social life according to the principles of Islam.

Later events in the Muslim world encouraged the growth and spread of revivalist ideals. The 1991 Gulf War and the continuing blockade against Iraq, along with economic and diplomatic measures taken against other outspoken Muslim nations, confirmed for many that the West, particularly the United States, intended to isolate Muslim countries much as Communist states had previously been isolated. For others, the electoral victory of the Front Islamique du Salut in Algeria in 1992 showed that a grassroots Islamic political movement could succeed through democratic processes. The uncritical welcome given to the military coup and dictatorship in Algeria confirmed for many Muslims the hollowness of European rhetoric about democracy and its implacable enmity toward Islam.

Critique of Traditional Islam in Asia

Muslim fundamentalists reserve some of their harshest criticism for the way that Islam has developed and been expressed in traditional Islamic societies. While this is a universal phenomenon, I will focus my remarks on Islam in Asian societies. Islam was brought to Asia not by religious scholars, but rather by traders and Sufi holy men. The main exceptions to this pattern are Central Asia and the northern part of the Indian subcontinent, where Muslim armies, led by a Turkish-Mongol warrior caste, were decisive in spreading Islamic rule. Even there, the eventual conversions of local peoples to Islam were mainly due to Sufi itinerant preachers. Although Muslims had been present in Asian coastal cities as foreign trading colonies almost since the first century of Islam, the great age of the spread of Islam in Asia was in the fourteenth through sixteenth centuries, which saw widespread conversions of local peoples across northern India, Bangladesh, western China, and the mainland and islands of Southeast Asia. The Sufi orders and their mystical interpretation of Islam represented the most dynamic force in Islam at the time; and it was the collaboration between Sufi and merchants—in the Indian Ocean and on the Silk Road between Iran and China—that was responsible for the dramatic spread of Islam.

The point relevant for understanding traditional Islam in Asia is that neither the Arab and Persian businessmen, nor the Turkish military conquerors, nor the Sufi saints were deeply knowledgeable about Islam, nor extensively read in orthodox Islamic thought. They were often devout and zealous Muslims, but their understanding of Islam did not often have a strong doctrinal basis. The Sufis, who occasionally were well versed in Islamic literature, reemphasized religious experience as the basis of an interior union of love with God, and viewed the practices of the *shari'ah* and the study of Islamic law as either peripheral or preliminary to the real project of Islam, which was the path to union of love and will with God.

All of this made Muslims flexible in tolerating pre-Islamic Asian religiosity, expressed in visits to local shrines and holy sites such as the tombs of holy persons, banyan trees, caves, mountains, and cemeteries, accompanied by an offering of flowers, incense, rice, and fruit to the local spirit who dwelt in the place. Once Islam was established in a region and began to have its own holy men and women—in many cases the missionary who brought Islam to the region—the tomb of the holy person either replaced or was joined to the already existing pilgrimage site. Islamic practice distinguished Muslims from the non-Muslims with whom they lived in basic ways: one God, the prohibition of pork and alcohol, the Ramadan fast. But in other matters—dress, marriage customs, village organization, even religious architecture—Muslims followed local norms.

Given their desire to arrive at a personal, loving union with God, the Sufis tended to focus on individualized interior religious practice, and they correspondingly deemphasized the social and political aspect of religion. Islam was seen as a way of life that could be lived in any form of government, in any culture or nation. Even when Muslim regions came to be governed in the colonial period by non-Muslim rulers, traditional Islam was politically quietist and found a workable, if uncomfortable, *modus vivendi* with the new realities. In the creation of Pakistan and in independence movements in Indonesia, Malaysia, and the Philippines, it was not the traditional Muslim scholars who were in the forefront, but rather the reformist lay leaders, usually trained not in the religious sciences but in secular disciplines.

The easy accommodation of traditional Islam with Asian cultures was challenged by some Muslims. They understood the purpose of Islam to be the construction of a society in accord with God's will, rather than one based on human likes and dislikes. The Islamic community was to be distinguished from others not simply by a certain number of specific injunctions (e.g., the five prayers, fasting during Ramadan) or prohibitions (e.g., from alcohol or pork) but by a way of life that embraces every aspect of personal behavior and social relations.

To the reformers, it was not simply a matter of correcting the accommodations that traditional Muslims had made with pre-Islamic Asian cultures. What was needed was nothing less than a reorientation of understanding the nature of Islam. For the reformers, Islam was a social program aimed at building a certain kind of society, not, as many Sufis had seen it, a spiritual path to union with God. The guidelines for what society should be like, the reformers held, are found in a careful study of the *sharī'ah*. The Islamic way of life is not limited to spiritual personal perfection, but extends to societal relations, economic affairs, and political systems.

The earliest reform movements in Asia were undertaken by the Sufi orders themselves, particularly the Naqshbandi. These Sufis envisioned the Islamization of society as a lengthy but irreversible historical process. Islamization was not achieved at the moment that most of the people in a given region became Muslims. It was rather an evolutionary process that began with the first preaching of Islam and would go on for centuries.

The role of the state was to "enforce good, prohibit evil." This meant, negatively, that the state must not put any obstacles in the way of the project of Islamization. It must not command that which is forbidden, nor prevent Muslims from carrying out the social and ritual prescriptions of Islam. Many reformers added that the role of governments included positive promotion of Islam.

In the colonial period, this understanding of the role of the state brought Muslims regularly into conflict with colonial administrators, and reformist Muslims played a prominent role in the struggle for independence. They believed that, until Muslims were themselves in control of the political apparatus and government of their own nations, the state could not play its proper role in Islamizing society. After independence, reformist movements discovered that the new rulers, liberal fellow-Muslims, were not interested in promoting Islam.

Muslim Reformist Critique of Modernity

Many factors underlie the emergence of militant Muslim movements. There is a criticism of the Sufi roots of Islam in Asia, and a desire to reorient the inner-directed thrust of Sufism toward an activist program of social reform. The political philosophy of Muslim militants holds that the state should be an instrument in the promotion of an Islamic way of life. In many countries, a revivalist approach to Islam is an attractive alternative that promises to resolve the crises in existing institutions: the lack of effective and representative government, the wasteful yet ambiguous role of the military, the failure of socialist central planning and management of the economy, and the institutionalization of the traditional *'ulamā'*, which made them servants of the governments rather than spokesmen for the people.

This is accompanied by a harsh critique of modernity. Militant Muslim objections to modernity are similar to those of Christian fundamentalists but have their own slant. Among Muslims, the focus of protest is secularism, and their social program could be called "desecularization" or "the sacralization (or Islamization) of society." Like their Christian counterparts, Muslims are ready to accept and use modern technology of communications, transportation, and consumer goods to promote their cause. In Western secular humanism, they perceive a postreligious ideology that seeks to overturn a God-centered, community-based understanding of human life. They see modernity as an egoistic, individualist approach to life that relativizes religion, exalts the individual, and divides the world into masters and subjects, advanced and underdeveloped. Ethics is reduced to market expediency, while family values and moral choices are left to the private decision of the individual. The natural world is simply raw material to be economically exploited. Muslim reformers claim that modern societies have abandoned God and regard a religious outlook as an outmoded relic from former times. In this secular age, the need for God has been superseded, and religion is seen as typical of "primitive, immature, backward, superstitious" societies. This is symptomatic, the reformers hold, of human arrogance, of the view that man is capable of all things, sufficient unto himself, the measure of good and bad, right and wrong. Domination, power, wealth, sex appeal, and conspicuous consumption are signs of success, evidence that someone is an "achiever."

In the highly individualistic modernist outlook, it is not society or the social group, not even the family, that counts. It is the individual person who makes his or her own morality, autonomous in moral code and decisions. Human rights are equated with "the rights of the individual." Muslim revivalists stress the prior "rights of God" to determine proper societal relations. God's revealed Word gives precedence to "the rights of society," to the overriding prerogatives of the collectivity over the desires of the individual.

Another characteristic, which the Muslim reformers share with Christian fundamentalists, is the harsh anger of the outsider, of those who are excluded from the elite "in-group" who both promote and profit from modernity. The Muslim reformers perceive this liberal elite to be occupying the seats of power—the great international bureaucracies at the UN, WHO, and IMF, government ministries, even in Muslim countries, the universities, schools, and departments of education, think tanks and consultancy boards, and the owners, promoters, and personalities of the mass media. In short, they hold that the "liberal consensus" has created an environment in which the only viewpoint to be taken seriously is their own, while other points of view are simply dismissed as unenlightened, backward, or fanatic. In the view of the reformers, the liberal elite not only express public opinion, they create it and dictate it.

According to Muslim reformers, what is at stake is a fundamental conflict of values. On the one hand, in a secular value system, the individual person is conceived as the center of the universe. Fulfilling to the utmost one's potential, capabilities, and legitimate desires is considered the highest human goal, and individuals must be free to achieve these aspirations. The only limitation on human freedom is that in pursuing one's personal objectives, no one must violate the rights of others to pursue and achieve their own goals.

While secular liberalism does not deny the existence of God or reject religion as such, it is skeptical of the ability of any religious system to attain truth; and it is opposed to the role of religion in public life. Religion can be admitted as the personal choice of some individuals who feel they need some moral direction in their private and familial lives, but it has no place in public affairs. The marketplace, social interaction, and, above all, government are autonomous spheres that must exist and operate outside the influence of religious thought.

Against secular values, Muslim revivalists propose their own theocentric value system. For them, God has revealed a proper way for humans to live, and has laid down the principles on which society is to be built. They take the moral will of God very seriously and view as enemies those who would propose incompatible ethical values. They are called on to struggle (the root meaning of jihad) against secular, meaning anti-God, antireligion, antimorality forces propagated first and foremost by American and European societies.

The Direction of History

In their reading of recent historical events, Muslim revivalists find points of agreement with Christian fundamentalists, but also their own distinctive vision. They hold that the modernist ideology, with its anti-religious component, scored its first successes in intellectual circles in Europe, and was then taken up and spread throughout the world by America. Having gotten its start in predominantly Christian regions, the first victim to modernist philosophy was Christianity, which Muslim reformers are convinced is dead in its medieval homeland.

Muslim activists are convinced that the goals of secular advocates are ambitious and inimical to Islam. They believe that the West is out to destroy Islam as the last bastion of the religious worldview, and perceive the onslaught to be carried out on many fronts. The campaign is political, in the sense that the Western alliance intends to isolate Islamic countries much in the way that the Communist bloc was isolated before 1989. It is military, in that tactics of war—blockades, frozen assets, recourse to air attacks, and other coercive actions—are more often directed against Muslim nations than against others. It is economic, in that the former colonial domination has been replaced by economic globalization, markets manipulated from the outside, political leaders bought off by international industry, and military action threatened or taken to ensure control of resources. The attack is religious, in the constant presentation of Islam in film, global television networks, newsmagazines, and spy novels—as a fanatic, violent, xenophobic faith that is difficult for all others to live with. The attack is cultural, in that all things Western—education, clothing, law, manners, music, film, house furnishing, and relations between sexes—are presented as superior and to be admired and imitated. They see the alleged cultural superiority of the West, which presents itself as the unique font of truth, liberty, and progress, as an implicit attack on their faith, culture, and traditions.

If all this seems overstated, and even somewhat paranoid, it reflects a widespread perception in the Muslim world. The conviction that Islamic faith and Muslim culture are imperiled explains many of the reactions among Muslims, of political, intellectual, and religious leaders, as well as of the man and woman in the street, to recent events such as the Gulf War, the Algerian coup d'état, and to the continuing dramas in Palestine and Bosnia. Each of these tragedies is interpreted in the light of the preceding critique of modernity. The Gulf War was seen as a war for control of "Muslim" oil fields, waged by a Western-assembled and controlled coalition attacking a predominantly Muslim people with vastly superior technological weaponry. Israel is seen as the unilateral implantation of a Western people and ideology in the heart of the Islamic world. Bosnia is taken as evidence that the European powers will never permit a Muslim-dominated nation, no matter how progressive, to exist in Europe.

Like Christian evangelicals, Muslim revivalists regard the direction that history has taken in this century as the temporary triumph of the forces of evil. When Ayatollah Khomeini referred to the United States as the "Great Satan," he was not simply engaging in invective, but making a theological statement. The course of current history, they feel, is a threat to morality and a God-centered life. Unlike dispensationalists, Muslims foresee no scenario of imminent eschatological crisis. They are optimistic that they will be successful in withstanding and eventually overcoming anti-God forces, although it will require struggle, sacrifice, and suffering on their part. Many claim that the God-given task of Islam today is to save the world from the onslaught of Western liberal hegemony.

Bases for Dialogue

The Muslim critique of modern secularism is a challenge to Christians. For Muslims, it is God who is the center of the universe, at the heart of human life and every human activity. Any way of life that reduces faith to private morality and ritual is unacceptable, an affront to God's majesty and holiness. They regard modern Christians' easy acceptance of secular society and humanist ethics as a compromise with the essence of religious faith. Muslims repeatedly affirm that they have no argument with "true" Christians, to whom they look as natural allies in the struggle against modern secularity, but they feel that Christians have too often "sold their birthright" in order to present themselves as modern and progressive. It is tempting for Christians to feel complacently that we have been successful in reconciling our religious faith with the demands of modern life. We can even be tempted to boast that we are "modern," while Muslims are "backward." Yet we may not be conscious of the extent to which we have compromised our faith with incompatible elements of modern or Western culture. We may be unaware of the ways in which the Christian churches have been wounded in the course of their encounter with liberal values.

Yet it is precisely on these grounds that Christians must engage in dialogue with Muslims on the question of modernity. We accept the challenges posed by modern values, such as the liberal critique of religion as often being a factor of oppression, inequality, and patriarchy in human societies. We uphold a commitment to the legitimate human and civil rights of all, a commitment that does not entail a blind acceptance of everything that is claimed to be a human right. In dialogue, we must challenge Muslims to engage, with us, in a constructive and critical encounter with modern liberal philosophy, in order to disentangle its positive humane values which are confirmed by religious faith from the destructive, divisive, and egoistic elements, which are by-products of secular and modernist thinking and policy.

Notes

1. Published by Oxford University Press; first rev. ed. appeared in 1917.
2. Grand Rapids, Mich.: Zondervan, 1970.
3. Wahhabism as a movement today refers not to a single unified group but to certain puritanical reformist tendencies that became widespread in the twentieth century.—Ed.

9

The Ethics of Pardon and Peace

A Dialogue of Ideas between the Thought of Pope John Paul II and the *Risale-i Nur*

At international congresses around the world, there are always many papers and speeches about peace. We hear the speakers of each religious group profess that their religion wants peace, teaches peace, builds peace. The leaders of various nations say how they are committed to peace among nations, peace in their regions, civil peace within their societies. There is a human paradox here that we must face. It seems like everyone is in favor of peace, no one ever admits to being against peace, and yet there is very little peace in the world. The problem, I believe, lies in the fact that we are all in favor of peace *in the abstract*, but without saying in what peace consists, and without examining what is involved in building peace.

Of those religious thinkers of modern times who have attempted to study the concept of peace to explore what is involved in establishing and maintaining peace, I want to compare the thought of two persons who have made a remarkable contribution to the topic. One is a Christian, Pope John Paul II, leader of the Catholic Church, and the other a Muslim, Bediuzzaman Said Nursi, the author of the *Risale-i Nur*. In this paper I hope to bring together the thinking of these two scholars and religious teachers into a kind of dialogue on the theme: "the ethics of peace." I will do this by summarizing the position of John Paul II as the basis or point of view from which I will then read and explain the views of Said Nursi as found in the *Risale-i Nur*.

Previously published in *Globalization, Ethics, and Islam: The Case of Bediuzzaman Said Nursi*, ed. Ian Markham and Ibrahim Ozdemir (Burlington, VT: Ashgate, 2005), 37-47. Reprinted by permission.

John Paul II: Peace Rests on Two Pillars: Justice and Forgiveness

As he did every year since becoming pope, on January 1, 2002, Pope John Paul II sent a message for the World Day of Peace at the beginning of the New Year. In this message, the pope proposed that true peace must rest on two pillars: *justice* and *forgiveness*. Without these, you cannot have real peace. Both justice and pardon are necessary. One element without the other is not enough.

The pope's reasoning was like this. Any real peace, if it is to be more than simply a cease-fire or temporary cessation of hostilities, has to get to the heart of the conflict and try to heal the breach in human relations that was ruptured. When peoples are at war, when individuals are estranged and alienated from one another, they are angry, suspicious, and resentful of one another. They see the other as an enemy to be overcome, defeated, the object of retaliation, rather than a fellow-human with whom one ought to be reconciled. Thus, no talk about peace can proceed effectively without addressing the issue of broken relationships and without taking positive steps to repair those relations.

If one group or individual is being oppressed or treated unjustly by another, one cannot hope for peace between the two until there is justice. The pope sees justice in two ways: first, as a "moral virtue," that is, as a human quality that a person can acquire and develop with God's powerful assistance (which Christians call *grace*), and second as a "legal guarantee," that is, part of the functioning of the national and international rule of law.[1] The aim of justice, both as a personal quality and as an element of the international system of relations among peoples, is to ensure "full respect for rights and responsibilities" and to carry out a "just distribution of benefits and burdens."

Justice is thus a first, indispensable condition for peace. Unless one person treats another justly, that is, with respect for the other's rights and duties and by giving them their proper share of what is due to them, there will be no peace between them. The same holds true between social groups, ethnic groups, peoples, and nations. Where there is aggression, oppression, occupation, transgression, there can be no peace. First, justice has to be established, then peace can be built.

All of this the pope had said before. However, in his Day of Prayer for Peace message, he added another element that he saw as intrinsic to the peace-making process. This is *forgiveness*, which goes beyond strict justice to strive to heal the historical burdens brought about by one individual's or one group's injustice and wrongdoing toward another.

Every nation, every religious or ethnic group, can draw up a long list of grievances that we have against one another, of wrongs that our group has suffered at the hands of the others. This is the human burden of past misdeeds and experiences that we bring into our relations with others, that complicate the way we relate to individual members of the other group, that can poison all efforts at cooperation and reconciliation, and that can flare up into violence at the slightest provocation. Justice alone is not sufficient to heal these wounds; we need to exercise forgiveness. Forgiveness is, as the pope states, "a personal choice, a decision to go against the natural instinct to pay back evil with evil." In doing so, it always involves an *apparent* short-term loss, but brings about the possibility of achieving a *real* long-term gain. "Violence," the pope notes, works exactly the opposite: "opting for an apparent short-term gain, but involving a real and permanent loss."[2] "Forgiveness," the pope notes, "may seem like weakness, but it demands great spiritual strength and moral courage."

It should not be surprising to discover that both Christianity and Islam lay great importance on the notions of justice and forgiveness, if these are to be the indispensable preconditions of peace. In the Gospel, Jesus taught his disciples: "You have heard it said, 'Love your neighbor and hate your enemy,' but I say to you 'Love your enemies and pray for those who persecute you'" (Matt. 5:43-44). In a similar vein, the Qur'an permits vengeance up to the limits of strict justice but no farther, and then always adds: "But it is better to forgive" (42:40).

Social Ethics in the *Risale-i Nur*

When we turn to the *Risale-i Nur*, we find that for Said Nursi, as for Pope John Paul II, ethics, as the study of what is good and bad, is primarily oriented toward the social sphere. In the thought of both men, a religiously based ethical system above all must treat questions of right and wrong in society, and only secondarily regard the goodness or evil of acts of private morality. Moreover, both root this primacy of social ethics in the scriptural teaching of their respective faiths. For Said Nursi, ethical systems drawn up by philosophers and put into practice by public and private welfare associations fail to reach the levels of social commitment demanded by the teaching of the Qur'an. He states: "Together with all its associations for good works, all its establishments for the teaching of ethics, all its severe discipline and regulations, [society] has not been able to reconcile these two classes of mankind [the rich and the poor], nor heal the two fearsome wounds in human life."[3] The evils of which he is speaking here are *social complacency* on the part of the wealthy who feel no responsibility to share what they have with the poor and needy, and *class struggle* on the part of the poor who seek to take by force from the rich what they will not give freely. "The Qur'an, however," Said Nursi continues, "eradicates the first [social irresponsibility] with its injunction to pay *zakāh*, and heals it, and uproots the second [class struggle] by prohibiting usury and interest, and cures that. Indeed, the Qur'an stands at the door of the world and declares usury and interest to be forbidden. It reads out its decree to mankind, saying: 'In order to close the door of strife, close the door of usury and interest!' and forbids its students to enter it."[4]

Instead of the ethics of the jungle where the rich and powerful take what they can and defend what they have by use of force, and those of class struggle in which the poor and oppressed seek to obtain their rights by force, Said Nursi sees the Divinely guided ethic proposed by Islam as one in which truth, justice, and harmony are paramount.

The civilization the *sharī'ah* of Muhammad (PBUH) comprises and commands is this: its point of support is truth instead of force, the marks of which are justice and harmony. Its goal is virtue in place of [selfish] benefit, and its characteristic marks are love and attraction. Its means of unity are the ties of religion, country, and class, in place of racialism and nationalism, and the mark of these are sincere brotherhood, peace, and only defense against external aggression. Its life is the principle of mutual assistance instead of that of conflict, and its mark is accord and solidarity.[5]

Said Nursi holds that philosophically based ethical systems fail to reach the heights of moral teaching proclaimed by the Qur'an because they fail to take into account an essential element of the human reality, that is, human weakness. If an ethical system presumes that people know what they want and will always work to achieve their desired goal, it will miss the point, for in fact people often act against their best interests out of anger, timidity, and so forth, and for reasons of selfishness, laziness, ignorance, and the like fail to achieve what they desire.

However, a religious outlook, exemplified in Qur'anic teaching, takes into consideration and allows for the reality of human failure by urging believers to return to God in repentance, seeking forgiveness, and starting over. Thus, he calls on believers to be shaped by a "God-given ethics," which he holds to be an essential element in the message of all the prophets. "Be distinguished by *God-given morals* and turn towards God Almighty with humility, recognizing your impotence, poverty, and defectiveness, and so be a slave in His presence."[6] Philosophically based ethical systems, he holds, tend to ignore this element of human nature and selfishly aim at perfection through human efforts alone. This Nursi sees as basically self-deception. "The essence of humanity," he states, "has been kneaded with infinite impotence, weakness, poverty, and need, while the essence of the Necessarily Existent One is infinitely omnipotent, powerful, self-sufficient, and without need."[7] He concludes:

> The aim of humanity and duty of human beings is to be molded by God-given ethics and good character, and, by knowing their [own] impotence to seek refuge with Divine power, by seeing their weakness to rely on Divine strength, by realizing their poverty to trust in Divine mercy, by perceiving their need to seek help from Divine riches, by seeing their faults to ask for pardon through Divine forgiveness, and by realizing their deficiency to be glorifiers of Divine perfection.[8]

Thus, if they are to act in an ethical way people need to be informed and guided by God's revelation and to be supported by God's strength or grace. These two elements (Divine guidance and Divine strength) are often ignored in philosophically based ethical systems that do not take into account elements of God's revealed word.

Inner Peace

1. *How does the concept of peace fit into Said Nursi's ethical thought?* In the *Risale-i Nur*, he treats various aspects and elements of peace, not from a theoretical perspective, but as a practical guide for those who seek to pursue peace. In the first place, he treats of peace as the ultimate goal of human life, almost synonymous with salvation. Specifically, it is the final destination of the collective personality of those who study the *Risale-i Nur*. He sees the *Risale-i Nur* students, through their efforts carried out in solidarity and sincerity, as contributing in their diverse activities to the building of an eternal realm of peace and happiness:

> O *Risale-i Nur* students and servants of the Qur'an! You and I are members of a collective personality . . . like the components of a factory's machinery which produces eternal happiness within eternal life. We are hands working on a dominical boat which will disembark the community of Muhammad (PBUH) at the Realm of Peace, the shore of salvation. So we are surely in need of solidarity and true union, obtained through gaining sincerity.[9]

This concept not only gives meaning and direction to individual acts, but in this way the believer also achieves a kind of conquest over death.

> Through the mystery of true brotherhood on the way of Divine pleasure . . . there are spirits to the number of brothers. If one of them dies, he meets death happily, saying: "other spirits remain alive, for they in effect make life continue for me by constantly gaining reward for me, so I am not dying. By means of their spirits, I live in respect of merit; I am only dying in respect of sin." And he lays down in peace.[10]

2. *A second way in which the* Risale-i Nur *looks at peace might be called the psychological sense, as tranquility and peace of mind, an inner confidence born of faith that enables the religious believer to face adversity without anxiety or despair.* Particularly when one is facing the approach of death, the believer can attain a peace of mind that will enable the person to overcome spiritual turmoil and fear.[11] Reflecting on the long periods of his incarceration, he notes that his close companions, students of the *Risale-i Nur*, who were imprisoned with him did not waste their time or give in to selfish expressions of worry, complaint, or pride, or try to change what cannot be altered, but they achieved a peace of mind and steadfastness that bore witness to the spiritual values and dignity that they had achieved.[12]

This interior peace, not only of individuals but of whole societies, he sees as one of the marks of Islamic civilization. Along with justice, harmony, brotherhood, solidarity, human progress, and spiritual advancement, peace should characterize the Islamic community.[13] It is peace as the basis of societal relations that should be the force that attracts others to Islam.

3. *A third aspect of peace studied by Said Nursi is universal peace.* Particularly in his rewriting of the Damascus Sermon in the years immediately following the Second World War, he reflects the widespread conviction of the time that humankind can sink no lower in criminality toward its own kind and expresses the longing for a time of peace and prosperity for all. This Said Nursi sees as the specific mission of Islam, that "God willing, through the strength of Islam in the future, the virtues of civilization will prevail, the face of the earth cleaned of filth, and universal peace be secured." He is optimistic that this hope for peace through Islam is no vain desire, but that people may confidently "expect from Divine mercy to see true civilization with universal peace brought about through the sun of the truth of Islam."[14]

It is in his analysis of peace, based on truth, as the only viable alternative to the use of brute force that the thought of Said Nursi prefigures that of Pope John Paul II. Said Nursi notes that wars and violence can never resolve ethical conflicts concerning who is in the right. All that wars and violent actions can accomplish is to show which party has access to reserves of force that it can use to coerce others to obey and to punish the recalcitrant.[15] Truth, on the other hand, is characterized by justice and harmony and seeks goodness and virtue instead of selfish gain.[16] He sees a tendency in modern governments and rulers that is relevant for the discussion of globalization. He criticizes modern governments for fomenting a kind of false nationalism, which in reality amounts to a type of racism, by picturing those of another nationality or religion as the enemy against whom war must be waged. Meanwhile, the governments concentrate on providing amusements to gratify the senses and favor consumerist policies to "create needs." The result, he states, is "a sort of superficial happiness for about 20 percent of mankind and casts 80 percent into distress and poverty."[17] By contrast, the Qur'an, he states, takes truth rather than force as its starting point. Hence the Qur'an proposes an alternative to the use of force in resolving conflicts, that of negotiation, compromise, and uprightness, rather than the employment of brute force with the very limited aim of "winning."

Said Nursi's opposition to war as an inhumane and ultimately useless endeavor was highly controversial in his time, for in any nation all citizens are expected to support whatever wars are decided and carried out by their governments, and anyone opposing war is accused of being disloyal. In fact, ruling parties and cliques have been known to *foment* conflict and war in an attempt to increase their popularity and rally support for unpopular or incompetent government. In *The Flashes Collection*, Said Nursi notes that he was often challenged because of his commitment to peace. Critics claimed that war against British and Italian incursions provided an opportunity to revive Islamic zeal and to assert the moral strength of the nation. They charged Said Nursi, who proposed prayers for peace and negotiated settlement, as indirectly supporting the invaders' aims.[18]

In response, Said Nursi held that he wanted release from the attacks of aggressors, but not by using the same methods the attackers were employing. In other words, he rejected the practice of opposing force by force. Religion teaches people to seek truth and uprightness, not to try to achieve their aims by use of force. In consequence, he felt that the students of the *Risale-i Nur* could better use their time studying the Qur'an than by engaging in military service. Later in his life he was asked whether freely relinquishing one's rights for the sake of peace could not be considered a form of compromise with wrongdoing. Again reflecting on his prison experiences, he responded that "A person who is in the right, is fair. He will sacrifice his one *dirhem*'s worth of right for the general peace, which is worth a hundred."[19]

In the long run, he concludes, the preoccupation with current events and international crises is of secondary importance to seeking the personal, interior transformation of peace that comes through the study of Scripture. Said Nursi carried this principal to an extreme degree, as he recounts:

> For a full two years in Kastamonu and seven years in other places I knew nothing of the conflicts and wars in the world, and whether or not peace had been declared, or who else was involved in the fighting. I was not curious about it and did not ask, and for nearly three years did not listen to the radio that was playing close by me. But with the *Risale-i Nur* I triumphantly confronted absolute unbelief, which destroys eternal life, and transforms the life of this world even into compounded pain and suffering.[20]

This attitude, which places a higher value on interior peace, which is based on the study of God's Word, than on current events, presents a challenge to modern people for whom the daily newspapers and evening news on television are fixed appointments in their daily schedules. However, when one reflects on the degree to which the news media is slanted by the prejudices, policies, and propaganda, not only of individual journalists but also of those who own and direct the communications industry, one can see in Said Nursi's practice the freedom of the honest individual who renounces an obsession with transitory events, which will be forgotten in a few years, in favor of the search for eternal, unchangeable truth presented in the Word of God.

The irony here is that Said Nursi was often accused of being a trouble-maker guilty of disturbing the peace and inciting his followers to revolt. He was accused of "working secretly in Emirdag. He poisoned the minds of some people giving them the idea of disturbing the peace."[21] In defending himself against false accusations of fomenting public disorder, he also defends the students of the *Risale-i Nur* against similar charges. "In twenty years, six courts of law and the police of ten provinces . . . have not recorded any incident involving the disturbance of public order and breaching of security in connection with the 20,000 or perhaps 100,000 people who enthusiastically read copies of the *Risale-i Nur*."

He asserts that this reputation of being a troublemaker and rabble-rouser is based on fear that nonreligious people have of those who take religious faith seriously.

> "The worldly" are exceptionally and excessively suspicious of me. Quite simply, they are frightened of me, imagining non-existent things in me, which even if they existed would not constitute a political crime and could not be the basis of accusation, like being a shaykh, or of significant rank or family, or being a tribal leader, and influential, and having numerous followers, or meeting with people from my native region, or being connected with the affairs of the world, or even entering politics, or even the opposition. Imagining these things in me, they have been carried away by groundless fears.[22]

He makes it clear that his silence must not be interpreted as agreement with all decisions made by public officials, but should be understood rather in terms of passive resistance. He states:

> I support neither intellectually nor on scholarly grounds the arbitrary commands, called laws, of a commander, which have made Aya Sophia into a house of idols and the Shaykh al-Islam's Office into a girls' high school. And for myself I do not act in accordance with them. But although for twenty years I have been severely oppressed during my tortuous captivity, I have not become involved in politics, nor provoked the authorities, nor disturbed public order. And although I have hundreds of thousands of *Risale-i Nur* friends, not a single incident has been recorded involving the disturbance of the peace.[23]

Along with Gandhi and Martin Luther King, Said Nursi must be seen as one of the twentieth century's great exponents of nonviolent resistance.

Peace and Forgiveness

When we turn to the question of the relationship between peace and forgiveness, the similarity of thought between Said Nursi and the later views of Pope John Paul becomes even more striking. He analyzes the nature of wrongdoing. In the case of a crime such as murder, the killer might derive a momentary satisfaction by having taken revenge on his enemy, but he pays for it over and over by suffering the consequences, not only of imprisonment, but of fear of retaliation by the relatives of the murdered person. The result is fear, anger, anxiety. "There is only one solution for this," states Said Nursi, "and that is reconciliation, which the Qur'an commands, and which truth, reality, benefit, humanity, and Islam require and encourage."[24] He notes that Islam commands that "one believer should not be vexed with another believer for more than three days," and that so long as there is no reconciliation, "both sides perpetually suffer the torments of fear and revenge." His conclusion is that "it is essential to make peace quickly."[25]

Often a person's unwillingness to forgive arises, according to Said Nursi, from a lack of self-knowledge, a resistance to finding in oneself many of the same qualities that one condemns in the other. If someone is unwilling to confront the defects in one's own attitudes and actions, it is much easier to demonize the other and regard them as an enemy. Said Nursi's advice is to "Look at the defect in your own soul that you do not see or do not wish to see. Deduct a share for that too. As for the small share which then remains, if you respond with forgiveness, pardon, and magnanimity, in such a way as to conquer your enemy swiftly and safely, then you will have escaped all sin and harm."[26] Thus, self-awareness should lead to repentance, repentance to forgiveness, forgiveness to reconciliation, and the seeds for a lasting peace are laid.

So long as no reconciliation takes place, the wounds to the human relations fester and grow and turn into resentment. Discord produces more discord, violence engenders even greater violence, and the state of conflict is perpetuated. The only way out of a spiraling succession of violent reactions and counter-reactions is for one party to take the initiative to reconcile. Reconciliation heals what force can never heal, the suspicion and resentment caused by wrongdoing one against another. As Said Nursi puts it, "A minor disaster becomes a large one," and continues, "But if they make peace, and the murderer repents and prays continuously for the man he killed, then both sides will gain much and become like brothers. In place of one departed brother, he will gain several religious brothers."

Said Nursi's analysis of peace and reconciliation is very similar to the words of the pope with which I began this talk:

> Forgiveness is a personal choice, a decision to go against the natural instinct to pay back evil with evil. In doing so, it always involves an *apparent* short-term loss, but brings about the possibility of achieving a *real* long-term gain. Violence works exactly the opposite: opting for an apparent short-term gain, but involving a real and permanent loss. Forgiveness may seem like weakness, but it demands great spiritual strength and moral courage.

Here we find a strong convergence between these two great religious teachers.

So important is the element of forgiveness in human relations that Said Nursi commands the students of the *Risale-i Nur* to pardon one another's faults speedily. In fact, mutual forgiveness should be a characteristic mark that identifies students of the *Risale-i Nur*. "It is absolutely essential," he states,

> that you completely forgive each other. You are brothers closer to each other than the most devoted blood brother, and a brother conceals his brother's faults, and forgives and forgets. I do not attribute your uncustomary differences and egotism here to your evil-commanding souls, and I cannot reconcile it with the *Risale-i Nur* students. I rather con-

sider it to be a sort of temporary egotism found even in saints who have given up their souls. So on your part, do not spoil my good opinion through obstinacy, and make peace with each other.[27]

Since the study of the *Risale-i Nur* creates a relationship even closer than that of blood brothers, there is no offense so serious that it should go unforgiven among its students. Said Nursi goes so far as to state, "I swear that if one of you were to insult me most terribly and entirely trample my honor but not give up serving the Qur'an, belief, and the *Risale-i Nur*, I would forgive him and make peace with him and try not to be offended."[28]

Said Nursi sees a relationship between God's abundant forgiveness of the faults of humans and the need for believers to forgive one another. Just as God is generous in forgiving anyone who repents, so Said Nursi encourages the students of the *Risale-i Nur* to imitate these Divine qualities by acting with love and forgiveness toward those who wronged them.

> Your sincerity, loyalty, and steadfastness are sufficient reason to disregard one another's faults. . . . For the powerful brotherhood within the *Risale-i Nur* is such a good thing it causes one to forgive a thousand evils. Since at the Last Judgment when good deeds will preponderate over evils, Divine justice will forgive, you too, seeing that good deeds preponderate, should act with love and forgiveness.[29]

One must even forgive one's enemies and those who have done one wrong. Said Nursi repeatedly expressed his forgiveness for the prison wardens, judges, government officials, law officers, and civil authorities, who had treated him unjustly during his period of courtroom trials and subsequent imprisonments.[30] His point in forgiving others is that the relationship of enmity created by the wrong done by one person to another can only be overcome and superseded by forgiveness. Otherwise, one becomes a prisoner of circumstances, events, and the deeds of others, and history becomes a string of injustices and retaliations. This chain of evil and violence can only be broken by one who is willing to take the initiative to forgive.

In conclusion, I might mention that according to Said Nursi forgiveness and peacemaking should not be limited only to students of the *Risale-i Nur* or, more generally, to fellow Muslims. He argues that members of the People of the Book, Jews and Christians, if they want to make peace, should be allowed to do so. "A Christian may," he states, "accept some sacred matters and may believe in some of the prophets, and may assent to Almighty God in some respects."[31]

A Convergence of Ideas

When I examine the thought of Pope John Paul and that of Said Nursi, I am struck by the many similarities. Both understand peace to be not only a universal human longing but also a cornerstone of the Message that God has revealed to humans. It is not only that human beings long for peace, but that God desires and intends that people live in peace. Both are convinced that the use of violence and force can never be the true path to peace. Both hold that societies can succeed only if they are founded on the principles of justice and harmony. Both agree that the cycle of injury and revenge, wrongdoing and retaliation, violence and counter-violence can be broken when people take recourse to forgiveness and pardon. This act, which seems to be a sign of weakness and to result in a short-term loss, is in fact a courageous effort to move beyond past conflicts and establish reconciliation. Both agree that true forgiveness is beyond humankind's unaided resources and is possible only by the guidance and strength that come from God.

The human race would certainly be facing a better future if people would heed the advice of these two great moral teachers.

Notes

1. John Paul II, "No Peace without Justice, No Justice without Forgiveness," *Message of His Holiness Pope John Paul II for the World Day of Peace, 1 January 2002* (Vatican City: Libreria Editrice Vaticana, 2002), 5.

2. Ibid., 12.

3. Bediuzzaman Said Nursi, *The Words: On the Nature and Purpose of Man, Life, and All Things*, trans. Sükran Vahide (Istanbul: Sözler Publications, 1998), Twenty-Fifth Word, First Light, Third Ray, 422.

4. Ibid.

5. Bediuzzaman Said Nursi, *The Damascus Sermon*, trans. Sükran Vahide (Istanbul: Sözler Publications, 1996), 106.

6. Nursi, *Words*, Thirtieth Word, First Aim, 564.

7. Ibid.

8. Ibid., Thirtieth Word, First Aim, 563.

9. Bediuzzaman Said Nursi, *The Flashes Collection*, trans. Sükran Vahide (Istanbul: Sözler Publications, 1995), Twenty-First Flash, On Sincerity, 214.

10. Ibid., 215.

11. Bediuzzaman Said Nursi, *The Rays Collection*, trans. Sükran Vahide (Istanbul: Sözler Publications, 1998), Ninth Ray, 203.

12. Ibid., Thirteenth Ray, 343.

13. Bediuzzaman Said Nursi, *Letters 1928-1932*, trans. Sükran Vahide (Istanbul: Sözler Publications, 1997), Seeds of Reality, 548; Nursi, *Damascus Sermon*, 106.

14. Nursi, *Damascus Sermon*, 29, 38, 39, 43.

15. Nursi, *Words*, Twenty-Fifth Word, First Light, Third Ray, 422.

16. Nursi, *Letters*, Seeds of Reality, 548.

17. Nursi, *Words*, Twenty-Fifth Word, First Light, Third Ray, 422.

18. Nursi, *Flashes*, Sixteenth Flash, 144.

19. Nursi, *Rays*, Thirteenth Ray, 345; Nursi, *Flashes*, Twenty-Eighth Flash, 362.

20. Nursi, *Rays*, Fourteenth Ray, 373.

21. Ibid., Fourteenth Ray, 447.

22. Nursi, *Letters*, Addendum to the Sixteenth Letter, 96.

23. Nursi, *Rays*, Fourteenth Ray, 417.

24. Ibid., 484.

25. Ibid.

26. Nursi, *Letters*, Twenty-Second Letter, First Topic, 316.

27. Nursi, *Rays*, Thirteenth Ray, 369.

28. Ibid., Fourteenth Ray, 510.

29. Ibid., Thirteenth Ray, 355.

30. Ibid., Fourteenth Ray, 395, 416, 460, 487.

31. Nursi, *Letters*, Twenty-Ninth Letter, Seventh Section, 512; Nursi, *Flashes*, Seventeenth Flash, Seventh Note, 168.

PART III

A Christian View of Islam

10

Jesuit Writings on Islam in the Seventeenth Century

Neglected Polemical Works

Several articles in the journal *Islamocristiana* have presented a wealth of material that together forms a historical bibliography of Christian works on Islam and Muslim works on Christianity, including the controversialist writings of both Christians and Muslims. Taken as a whole, this material confirms what has been clear since Christian-Muslim polemical literature was first treated as a specific genre of religious literature,[1] that is, that it is the two "ends" of the chronological spectrum—the earliest centuries and the most recent—that have received the greatest attention from scholars.

Of those works still extant from Ummayad and Abbasid times, most, both Muslim and Christian, have received the benefit of scholarly study. In later periods, the Arabic treatises that date from the fifth/eleventh to the eighth/fourteenth centuries (Hijri/Gregorian) have begun to receive the attention that they deserve. Much work has also been done on Byzantine polemics up to the fall of Constantinople as well as on the Christian works about Islam of Medieval Europe.[2]

However, with the rise of the "New Islamic Empires" of the Ottomans, the Safavids, and the Moguls on the one hand, and the Renaissance and Baroque periods in European civilization on the other, the scholarly world has only scratched the surface in studying the many writings produced by Christians and Muslims concerning each other's religion. And yet, when one moves from the Enlightenment into the colonial period of the nineteenth and early twentieth centuries, studies in modern scholarship again enrich our view of how Muslims and Christians have regarded each other's faith.

Part of the reason for the sixteenth-seventeenth century hiatus may be explained by the tradition of scholarship as it has developed in the Western world. Pride of place has been given to the study of manuscripts, whose restoration through critical editions and textual analysis is easily recognized as a

---

Previously published in *Islamochristiana* (Rome) 15 (1989): 57-85.

123

worthwhile academic project. By contrast, those writings composed after the advent of printing seem already "available" and, because of their very accessibility, modern; yet, at the same time, those works appear to be too distant from our times and culture to have contemporary relevance.

When we look at the Christian writings on Islam from the late Renaissance and Baroque periods, further reasons for this scholarly neglect present themselves. As Levi della Vida has perceptively noted concerning the *Refutatio Alcorani* of Ludovico Marracci, the best known and most ambitious of seventeenth-century Christian studies of Islam, the work was virtually ignored in the eighteenth and nineteenth centuries. When the work was referred to by the encyclopedists and the Romantic scholars, it was with scorn for his "deficient notion of the historical development of the theological doctrines of Islam, for his indiscriminate use of sources of diverse provenance and diverse value and . . . his bitterly polemical character towards Islam and its founder."[3]

The Baroque writings on Islam represent the final stage of the development of European Christian polemic before the "epistemological shift" that took place in Western society during the Enlightenment. For example, the strong reliance on argumentation from miracles in the seventeenth-century polemics as a proof of the divine claims of Jesus and the church he founded remains as unconvincing to the modern reader—whether Christian, Muslim, or other—as it must have been to the Muslim "adversarius" of that day. In fact, it may well appear more specious to the Christian of today than it did to the Muslim of that time.

The care that the apologists took to translate the subtleties of patristic and scholastic trinitarian formulations into apologetic arguments in everyday speech and simple metaphors is lost on the modern reader for whom scholastic argumentation, with its passion for careful definition and distinctions and its method of proceeding with relentless logic from first principles or biblical texts to appropriate foreordained conclusions, seems both presumptuous and dishonest.

The use of Scripture in the sixteenth- and seventeenth-century Christian polemical writings is subject to criticism. The Scriptures are utilized primarily as the source of "proof texts," and the polemicists are not beyond adapting or even distorting the original meaning of the biblical texts to fit their polemical intents. Thus, the primary role of Scripture in forming the faith of the Christian community and serving as the timeless norm of the integrity of that faith is reduced in these controversialist works to providing bases, more or less suitable, for dogmas whose historical development can only be traced to later ages.

Another reason for the unattractiveness of the sixteenth- and seventeenth-century polemics is their effort to intellectualize religious faith and make it demonstrable by rational arguments. Antecedent to the Kantian critique concerning what of God's nature and activities can be known by human reason, these works presume that the adversary can be led step by step through the proper use of logic, from the starting point of whatever intellectual principles are affirmed or whatever religious convictions are held, to an absolute, irrefutable knowledge of the truth of the Christian faith as historically professed by the Catholic Church.

Presented with this unbroken chain of logical argument, an opponent's refusal to accept the truth of Christianity and subsequently to enter the community of truth through baptism can only be due to worldly factors of stubborn pride, considerations of family or social position, or sentimental attachment to traditional beliefs. Three of the works to be studied in this article, those by Thyrso Gonzales, Sanz, and Nau, proceed in this fashion.

Earlier Works by Jesuits on Islam

The Society of Jesus, commonly known as the Jesuits, established as a recognized religious order within the Catholic Church by papal bull in 1542, took an interest in Islam almost from its inception. As active promoters of the counter-reformation renewal within the Catholic Church, Jesuits devoted their energies to combating Protestant reform in Western Europe and working for reunion of the Orthodox churches with Rome and for the conversion of persons of other faiths to Christianity. This was done by the development of new centers directed toward these ends, the establishment of colleges in key regions, and the production of great amounts of controversialist literature.

The Jesuits took an interest in Islam from the beginning. One year after their formal approval by the pope, Ignatius of Loyola, the founder and first general superior of the Society, opened the "Casa dei Catechumeni" in Rome, which was designed to provide instruction for Jews and Muslims who desired to embrace Christianity.[4] In 1554, Ignatius directed that the houses of the society purchase Islamic books and that Jesuits study the Qur'an in order to be prepared to enter into religious discussions with Muslims. To this end, Ig. Lomelini (1561-1645) made a translation of the Qur'an into Italian.[5] An Arabic-speaking Jesuit house was set up in Messina, Sicily, and an Arabic studies program introduced into the college there. Another Arabic college was begun at Monreale, also in Sicily, as well as an Arabic studies program for the Jesuit college on Malta. Ignatius laid plans for founding colleges in Beirut and on Cyprus. At the invitation of the Sheikh of Djerba (in modern Tunisia), plans were made to open the first Jesuit college in a Muslim land.

Of the early efforts begun by Ignatius, none stood the test of time. In the years after his death, however, Jesuit houses were opened in many predominantly Muslim regions. The first Jesuit community was founded in Istanbul in 1582, and from this political capital of the Ottoman Empire, Jesuit activities in Ottoman realms were directed.[6] By 1650, with the permission of the Sultan and under the protection of the French ambassador, Jesuits were living and working in many parts of the Ottoman realm: in Izmir, Aleppo, Damascus, Sidon, and Lebanese Tripoli, and on the Aegean islands of Chios, Naxos, and Santorini. Although already in the time of Ignatius, J. B. Eliano (d. 1589) had spent time in Cairo, the first Jesuit house was not erected there until 1697.

In India, Jesuit contacts with Muslims developed earlier. In 1578, the Mughal emperor Akbar sent a delegation to the Jesuits in Goa inviting them to his court at Fatehpur Sikri. The emperor had erected a house of worship for religious debates, and there Jesuits and representatives of other religions held religious discussions with Muslim leaders. The Jesuits in Fatehpur Sikri (later in Lahore) recommended that a school for learning Persian and Urdu be founded for Jesuits who would work in North India.

One of the first questions that presented itself to Jesuits as guests in Islamic lands was the religious attitude that they were to take toward their hosts. Early generals such as Laynez, Borgia, and Acquaviva instructed Jesuits to refrain from proselytizing or entering into polemics with Muslims, but rather to direct their attention exclusively toward offering spiritual service to Christians living in those regions. The idea was not to provoke disputes with Muslims, which might compromise their service to the Christian population.

Nevertheless, from the time of the first generations, some Jesuits became proficient in Arabic, Turkish, and Persian, and produced both descriptive and controversialist writings about Islam. The first writings by Jesuits on Islam grew out of personal involvement and experience. J. B. Eliano, a convert to Christianity from a prominent Jewish family of Alexandria, wrote the earliest Jesuit polemical treatise on Islam, in which he introduced the novel technique of a discussion between two Muslim scholars in order to disprove the revealed nature of the Qur'an and demonstrate the unique truth of Christian faith.[7] Ignatius de las Casas (d. 1608), himself of a morisco family, wrote a fair-minded and sympathetic treatise entitled "Información acerca de los moriscos de España" in order to inform Pope Clement VIII of the beliefs, religious practices, and cultural traditions of the Muslims and Muslim converts to Christianity in Spain.[8] A. Possevino (d. 1611) included a long treatise on Islam in his Ratio Studiorum, which had great influence on the educational program offered in Jesuit colleges.[9]

One of the earliest controversialist works by a Jesuit on Islam was "The Fountain of Life" composed in 1596 by Jerome Xavier at Akbar's Court in Lahore. Xavier wrote the work in Portuguese and translated it himself into Persian.[10] The work sparked a polemical exchange between Muslims and Christians that continued throughout the seventeenth century. An Iranian Muslim scholar, Ahmad b. Zayn al-'Abidin (d. ca. 1651), wrote a refutation of a Persian summary of Xavier's work that was circulating in Iran. When a copy of Zayn al-'Abidin's work reached Rome, the Propaganda Fide commissioned two Catholic scholars to prepare responses. These were a Latin treatise by B. Malvasia (1628) and a work in Arabic by F. Guadagnolo (1631). Subsequently, in 1656, A. Chézaud, a Jesuit missionary living in Isfahan, Iran, who knew personally Ahmad b. Zayn al-'Abidin, wrote a two-volume rebuttal in Persian to the Muslim's work, which the author debated publicly with Muslim scholars. The manuscript of Chézaud's work was still being recopied in Iran during the eighteenth century.[11]

The seventeenth century saw a number of theological polemics by Jesuits intended to strengthen Christians in their religious debates with Muslims. Many of these works are lost. At the time of the general suppression of the Society of Jesus in 1774 and in the local suppressions that preceded that event, Jesuit libraries and archives were confiscated, records destroyed, and books dispersed and lost. Often the loss was haphazard, with the new owners interested in only a part of the acquired library, selling or discarding those volumes that did not interest them or for which they had no space. Among these lost writings on Islam were a three-volume work by S. Arator[12] (d. 1612), a treatise in French written in Syria by J. Amieu[13] (d. 1653), a work in Cebuano by A. Lopez[14] (d. 1655), Spanish treatises by F. de Aléman[15] (d. 1644) and J. de Almarza[16] (d. 1669), a work in German by B. Christel[17] (d. 1701), and works in Polish by T. Rutka[18] (d. 1700).

The final decades of the seventeenth century witnessed a number of Jesuit writings on Islam. These were all more or less directly occasioned by the religio-political relationships of the time between the European states and the Ottoman Empire. The Christian states of Western Europe perceived the Ottoman siege of Vienna in 1683 as a threat to Christendom itself. Pope Innocent XI ordered special prayers of petition to be offered in all Catholic churches, and a military alliance of German, Polish, Venetian, Papal, Russian, and Austro-Hungarian troops was formed to oppose the Ottomans. The siege was lifted when the Ottoman armies withdrew in September 1683; this event, followed by a rapid series of victories over the Ottoman army, was interpreted as a divinely granted confirmation of the supreme truth of Christianity, specifically in its Roman Catholic tradition. Many Catholics believed that the tide had turned; now Christianity was ascendant and Islam on the defensive. Some writers went so far as to predict the imminent demise of Islam as a heretical faith and a cultural unit inimical to European Christianity.

In the euphoria that followed upon the raising of the Turkish siege of Vienna, Jesuits produced a number of polemical treatises on Islam. The four works studied in this article date from this period. They are:

1. *Manuductio ad conversionem mahumetanorum* by Thyrso Gonzales (1689);

2. *Breve trattato nel quale con ragioni dimostratiue si conuincono manifestamente i Turchi* by Emmanuele Sanz (1691);

3. *Le moderne prosperità della Chiesa Cattolica contro il Maccomettismo* by Nicolò Pallavicino (1688); and

4. *Religio christiana contra Alcoranum per Alcoranum pacifice defensa ac probata* by Michel Nau (1680).

The *Manuductio* of Gonzales

Thyrso Gonzales de Santalla, *Manuductio ad conversionem mahumetanorum. In duas partes divisa. In prima, veritas religionis christianae catholicae romanae manifestis argumentis demonstratur. In secunda, falsitas mahumetanae sectae convincitur* (Dilingæ: Joannis Caspari Bencard, 1688).[19]

The most ambitious of the four works treated here is the *Manuductio* of T. Gonzales, written when he was a theology professor in Salamanca, but published shortly after he was elected superior general of the Jesuits.[20] His work is valuable historically for the many contemporary sources cited and the information provided on early contacts between Jesuits and Muslims. Theologically, there is little advance on the polemical tradition that had preceded. However, Marracci praised the work highly in the preface to his *Prodromus*.[21]

The work is explicitly written as a handbook for Christian preachers to lead Muslims to accept the Christian faith and baptism. The author has compiled it from his many years of experience in preaching missions to Muslims,[22] reinforced by his years of training as a theologian and professor of theology. Part I is a presentation of the claims of Roman Catholic Christianity to be the unique revelation from God, which can lead a person to eternal salvation. Part II is directed specifically toward giving his readers background information on the life and teaching of Muhammad, the religious tenets and practices of Islam, and a refutation of Muslim objections to Christianity.

General Argument

At 866 pages, this is by far the most extensive of the early Jesuit polemics. Gonzales begins his first part *in medias res*. The opening words are taken from John 8:24, "If you do not believe that I am he, you will die in your sins." The author believes that the most effective way to lead Muslims, Jews, and pagans to faith in Christ is by confronting his hearers immediately with the alternative to acceptance of Christian faith, which, in the theological understanding of the time, was eternal damnation.

This first topic treated is a demonstration of the divinity of Christ, mainly through an elaboration of the miracles worked by Christ and by his followers, both in apostolic times and down through the centuries, in his name. The miracles confirm the claims that Jesus makes concerning himself in the Gospel. Against those who would deny the possibility of miracles, he strives to show the rational credibility of the Christian faith and to prove God's power to supersede the natural order.

Although the preoccupation in these works could be understood as a reaction of religious faith against the nascent rationalism of the time, Gonzales's concern seems to be more with Reformation theology. The Reformers generally agreed that miracles ceased soon after the Apostolic period; the Apostles were granted power to perform miracles so that the church could be established. Medieval and modern apparently miraculous occurrences were either frauds or delusions, a mark of the church of the Antichrist.

The Reformers were objecting to what had become an excessive cult of thaumaturgic saints and to exaggerated miraculous claims made at sites of pilgrimage. D. P. Walker, in discussing this question, notes the weak Scriptural basis for the Reformers' views. "There is nothing whatever in the New Testament to indicate that the miraculous power conferred by Christ on the Apostles, and those whom they could convert, were limited in time. The only Patristic support consists of remarks by latish Fathers, such as Chrysostom and Augustine, on the diminishing frequency of miracles as the faith becomes established."[23]

Gonzales moves to a discussion of the nature of faith, in which he shows the necessity of revelation for humankind and that the only religion in fact revealed by God has been that of Christians. Among the forms of Christian religion, there is only one that can claim to be true and founded by Christ, the Roman Catholic. This concluding section is centered on a refutation of the claims of Eastern Orthodoxy and the Reform theology of Luther and Calvin.

It is Part II of this work, entitled "Guide to the Conversion of Muhammedans, in which the falsity of the Muhammedan sect is convincingly shown," which is most pertinent to the subject of this present study. This part is divided into six books with a total of eighty chapters (514 pages).

Sources

The author begins by listing his sources. Most of those cited by Gonzales are known to historians: the works of Ricoldo de Monte Croce,[24] Peter de Cavalleria,[25] John Torquemada,[26] the letter of Pope Pius II,[27] Peter the Venerable, Dionysius (Denis) the Carthusian,[28] William Postel,[29] Bartholomaeus Hungarus, P. Possevin,[30] the *Panoplia* of the Orthodox monk Euthemius, St. Peter Paschal, the *Cribratio* of Nicholas of Cusa, Bishop Gienensis, and, especially, the works of Juan Andrea and Lupus de Obregon Abulensi (a priest of Avila). This last work I have not been able to identify, nor those by Bishop Gienensis and Bartholomaeus Hungarus.

For historical materials, he relies on Cardinal Baronius's *Annales*, Roderick of Toledo's *General History*, and Thomas Erpenius's translation of George Almacinus's version of Kamāl al-Dīn Armunaeo's edition of Muhammad Abū Jafar's *History*, published in Lyon in 1625. He is aware of Bukhari's collection of hadith and the *tafsīr* of Jalalayn, probably not directly, but through citations in his Christian sources.

In his presentation of the daily life and religious practices of Muslims, he cites pilgrim guides, travel books, and descriptive literature to supplement his personal experience among Muslims. Works of the Franciscan Anthony of Castille, Thomas Bozium, Joannes Antonius Menavinus of Genoa, Theodorus Spanduginus Cantacuzenus, and Joannes Leo Africanus provide such descriptive material.

Origins and Principles of Islam

The first topic treated is the life and preaching of Muhammad. Gonzales takes pains to provide precise historical information, comparing the accounts in his various sources and offering his own opinion on the relative merits of each. For example, he cites no fewer than thirteen Christian authors in attempting to determine the dates of Muhammad's birth and death, which he complements by presenting the views of "the Muslims of Spain" (Part II, 6). The result is a "Life of Muhammad" that is surprisingly accurate in its historical outlines. Following earlier writers like Nicholas of Cusa and Juan Andres, he holds that Muhammad, reared in the pagan environment of Mecca, rejected the local cult and turned to the worship of the one God; however, at that point, he came under the influence of the Arian (or Nestorian) pseudo-monk Sergius[31] who was responsible for teaching him a corrupted version of Christianity.

Some of his information comes from personal contact with Muslims in Spain and North Africa. It was a Muslim in Oran who corrected his European-ized pronunciation of "Mahomam," to the more accurate "Muhammad" and informed him that the correct name of the religion was not "Mahumetanism" but rather Islam and that its followers were not Mohammedans but "Muslims," which means, he adds, "those handed over to (or saved by) God." Since that time, he states, he has always used the correct terms in his discussions with Mus-lims "so as to gain their good will" (although in the *Manuductio* he continues to employ the more common corruptions). His treatment on the origins of Islam is concluded with an objective, even sympathetic, summary of Islamic faith and practices.

> Turks[32] believe in one God, but in only one person, Creator of the heav-ens and earth, the rewarder of good deeds and the punisher of evil who established Paradise for rewarding good things and Hell for the final and extreme punishment of sins. They firmly believe Muhammad to be the greatest prophet of God, delegated by God on earth so that he might teach men the way of salvation.[33]

He gives the *shahādah* in Arabic and its Latin translation, explains the times for *ṣalāh*, the manner of ablution, the rules for the Ramadan fast, the celebra-tion of 'Eid al-Fitr, *ḥajj*, the pillars of *īmān*, Sufi *zāwiyahs*, and the differences between Islamic beliefs and those of Christians. He makes the curious observa-tion, "Except for circumcision, they have no sacraments."

Theological Arguments

In Book II, Gonzales begins his arguments against Islam. If Muslims say that one must be saved by following the Islamic law, what about all those who lived between the time of Christ and the preaching of Muhammad? There were in those days three religions: paganism, which Muslims and Christians agree to be an abomination; that of the Jews who were waiting for a Messiah whom Mus-lims and Christians agree to have come in the person of Christ; and the Chris-tian religion. God, who does not leave the world without a means of salvation, must have made salvation possible through the Christian law.

His second argument is directed against the Qur'anic passages that imply that each is saved by following his own religion, Jews Judaism, Christians Christianity, and Muslims Islam. In his response, he follows Bellarmine in arguing that all the other laws are error and thus unable to conduct one to truth and salvation. He adds a second argument of his own. Although the Qur'anic teaching is ambiguous and may admit the salvation of non-Muslims, the Christian teaching is clear and decisive that "*extra Christi Ecclesiam homines salvari non posse*" ("Outside the Church of Christ, humans cannot be saved"). Certitude has a pragmatic advantage over uncertainty, not necessarily at the level of truth, but in the sense that if Islam allows the possibility of others' being saved, but Christianity does not, one is more certain to attain the goal of salvation by following "the narrower path."[34]

His next argument seems to reflect the social pressures on Muslims in Spain after the Reconquista to convert to Christianity. He argues that while Muslims sometimes become Christians, it is unheard of that a Christian become a Muslim. Gonzales is not unaware that captured slaves, on both sides, were "forced" to accept the religion of their masters; but, he says, Christians make an outward profession of Islam while remaining interiorly Christians, whereas Muslims actually, upon conversion, become good Christians. He then gives a number of instances, some from his personal experience, of apparently sincere conversions of Muslims to Christianity, the most celebrated case being that of Balthasar of Loyola, "the king of Fez" who became a Christian and eventually a Jesuit. Gonzales sees fit to cite verbatim Balthasar's own account of his spiritual journey (Part 11, 54-58).[35] He concludes this section with an explication of his opinion that conscientious persons would be naturally attracted to the asceticism of Christianity after having experienced the "voluptuous sensuality" of Islam.

The next section (Book III) is strictly theological, with Gonzales attempting to prove the divinity of Christ from the statements about Jesus in the Qur'an. His method is to take the passages of the Gospels that speak of Christ's divinity and argue that the Qur'anic teachings logically lead to the same conclusion. This is followed by a parallel effort to show that the teaching of the Qur'an rationally concludes in the Christian position on the trinitarian nature of God.

At this point he deals with the Islamic objection that God, who has no wife, could not have a son. In his defense of the Incarnation, Gonzales begins from the Johannine verse, "And the Word became flesh," to give account of the Christology of the early councils. He accuses Muslims of having been historically influenced by the Arian heresy (which he claims to be recurrent in Christian history, under various names and movements); this has blinded Muslims to the genuine teaching of the early councils.

His next argument is based on the honor and reverence that both Muslims and Christians give to Mary. A Muslim with true respect for Mary should be led to Christian faith by seeing the many miracles that God has worked through Mary in Christian history. Such miracles are evidence of God's confirming the truth of Christian faith. Gonzales returns to the question of the Trinity and argues against the Muslim charge that Christians worship three gods. He responds with a summary of the Trinitarian theology of Augustine and Thomas to show that the three persons of the Trinity do not compromise the essential unity of God. He supports this classical argumentation with a long account of a dialogue between himself and a Muslim named Hamid Sulayman that took place in Malaga in 1669, twenty years previously.[36]

> "Do not think," I told him, "that we Christians hold in one God three persons so distinct and separate as one man is distinguished from another. Among us, where there are three distinct persons, it is necessary that there be three men. Each person has his own human nature distinct from that of the other, as well as a distinct body and distinct soul. Three human persons are three men, because they have three bodies, souls, and human natures. . . . But the three divine persons have the same divine nature, the same perfections: intellect, will, power, and other perfections. Whence, although the persons are three, there are not three gods, but one God, who does not have three essences, but only one most simple (essence)."[37]

This brief example must suffice to indicate Gonzales's efforts to "translate" the subtle and precise formulations of the theologians into living discussion between believers. However, it is in the frequent recounting of his personal discussions with Muslims that his work comes alive and is distinguished from the more theoretical polemics to which he frequently refers. It must be remembered that this work is a "handbook for preachers," intended to be used by Christians with the express purpose of leading Muslims to the Christian faith.

It is interesting to note Gonzales's frank admission that his interlocutor was ultimately not convinced by the Christian's reasoning and decided to remain a Muslim. As Hamid Sulayman was about to take his leave, Gonzales said to him:

> Friend Hamid, before God you will not be able to plead ignorance; I have manifested the truth to you. If you still doubt the truth of what I have said, ask God to show you the truth, so that He may illuminate the darkness of your mind and lead you to salvation. After having heard all these arguments, if you remain doubtful that the religion of Christ is necessary for your eternal salvation, ask God to enlighten you. So that you be worthy of His light, avoid vices, practice piety, love God above all things and your neighbor as yourself, and diligently keep the Ten Commandments, for to these things all men are obliged. And then, after many signs of love and a friendly embrace, the Moor went away. Although I have not explored the matter further, I still carry the greatest hope that he will die a Christian.[38]

Book IV is short and attempts to prove, against Muslim objections, that Christ was truly crucified and died on the cross and raised to new life. This is the least original section of the book, relying mainly on Nicholas of Cusa and Peter de Cavalleria. In what seems to have been Gonzales's own predilection, he adds of his own, as an argument parallel to the miracles worked through Mary, an account of the miracles worked in Christian history through the cross as divine confirmation of the reality of the crucifixion. Book IV closes with a refutation of Muslim objections that the Bible of Christians has been corrupted.

In Book V, Gonzales abandons the apologetic stance of defending Christian teaching from the objections of Muslims; taking the offensive, he tries to show, from contradictions, errors, moral lapses, and injustices that he finds in the Qur'an, that Muhammad could not have been a true prophet, but in the ministry of Satan.

Following a common preoccupation in his Christian sources, he tries to show that Qur'anic permission of polygamy, being against the natural law, has led many Muslims into sinfully licentious practices that will result in eternal damnation, and that the prohibition of virginity prevents its adherents from following the highest spiritual path. Taking Islamic practices one by one—*ṣalāh, wudū', sawm,* and so on—he tries to show that the Islamic law is incapable of leading a person to an upright, godly life. His conclusion is that God could not possibly have been the author of such an erroneous, misguided book, and that Muhammad has perpetrated a fraud against humanity and, especially, against those who follow him.

His final section discloses the purpose for which the book has been written. It is an exhortation to Christian preachers to undertake public missions to Muslims in the coastal towns of Spain. This is obviously a project close to Gonzales's heart and one to which he had devoted his Lenten and vacation periods over a period of twenty years. Such missions might lead not only to the conversion of Muslims, but also to Jews and non-Catholic Christians being drawn to see the errors of their ways, and Catholics being strengthened in their faith. The section presents much interesting historical information about the efforts at the time in Spanish Catholic circles to convert Muslim slaves, sailors, and merchants through public sermons; and it concludes with practical advice concerning techniques, themes, and Scriptural references.[39]

Reading the work of Gonzales, three hundred years after it was written, one finds elements of perplexity. He followed the exclusivist ecclesial soteriology common to his time, which few Catholic theologians today would want to defend. His emphasis on miracles as proofs of God's confirmation of Christian teachings appears unconvincing to Christians today, as it must have to Muslims in his day.[40] Scripture is used to provide proof texts for scholastic formulations rather than as the central content of the message to be conveyed. The fundamental problem, I feel, however, is the assumption common to polemics of the period that argumentation can lead to certainty, that a Muslim who has listened to a logical presentation of Christian faith must in conscience be led to baptism. The author seems to leave no room for conscientious doubt, sincere objection, the free action of God's grace, or the inadequacy of his own argumentation.

While this criticism of Gonzales needs to be made at the theoretical level, his experiential accounts, particularly that of his above-cited dialogue with Hamid, show that in practice Gonzales was more inclined to accept the limits of rational argumentation, the mysteries of response and refusal, and the ultimate referral of questions of human salvation to divine wisdom than his rational theology could admit.

The *Breve Trattato* of Emmanuele Sanz

Emmanuele Sanz, S.J., *Breve trattato nel quale con ragioni dimostratiue si conuincono manifestamente i Turchi, senza che in guisa veruna possano negarlo, esser falsa la legge di Maometto, e vera solamente quella di Cristo* (Catania: Paolo Sisagni, 1691), 246.[41]

The Spanish Jesuit Sanz,[42] after having taken up his duties in the Jesuit college on Malta, found himself in direct contact, for the first time, with many Muslims. Many Christians had Muslim slaves, and the towns of Malta contained the same type of foreign Muslim business colonies and transient seamen from Muslim lands that Gonzales had encountered in Spanish ports. Although it may be presumed that a large, probably preponderant, number of the Muslims on Malta were Arabs, Sanz uses the term "Turchi" to embrace all. Although he is aware (p. 29) that this is properly indicative of a nation rather than a religion, he, like Gonzales, follows the popular usage of the time in making "turco" synonymous with "Muslim."

The situation he discovered among this heterogeneous population of Malta was that the level of religious discussion was quite low. To the Christian claim "You should become a Christian," the Muslims responded, "No, you should become a Turk." "But our religion is true and yours is false." "No, ours is the true religion. You are in error." To this juxtaposition of contrary claims, another factor disturbed the author. On the one hand, the Muslims were convinced of their religion and content to remain in it, while, on the other hand, Christians were complacent in allowing Muslims to practice their own religion and felt no need to try to convert them to the Christian faith.

He summarizes the arguments proposed for acceptance of the status quo of religious diversity. The Muslims held that God, had He wanted, could have made them Christians, but He has not done so, so they remain in the faith into which God had them born. Moreover, it is a grave sin to renounce one's faith; each person should love his own religion and hold it to be true. They held that God has not touched the hearts of Muslims to become Christians, so they should be allowed to remain in their religious belief. They cited instances of Muslims they knew who had converted to Christianity who, they felt, had not become good Christians. It is better to remain a good Turk than to become a bad Christian. They claimed further that there are already enough Christians in the world; why are the preachers trying to make more?

A pragmatic argument was introduced by those who noted that Muslim slaves will eventually return to their native countries, where they will encounter difficulties if they have in the meantime become Christians. Moreover, it was a fact of history that Christians and Muslims have always contradicted each other; this is the way it has always been and will always be, so why fight it? Finally, the Muslims held that the person who lives properly is saved, while he who lives badly is condemned, whether that person be Christian or Turk. In other words, let Muslims live as good Muslims and Christians as good Christians, and be done with divisive religious controversy.

There is a strong ring of authenticity to the arguments, which seem to find their setting in the public squares of Maltese port towns rather than in theological polemics. The "live and let live" attitude of the author's interlocutors seems to reflect a religious tolerance at the level of common believers, which to the missionary preacher and theologian smacks of indifferentism. However, these arguments may also reflect the stance adopted by Muslim foreign residents in a militant Christian region (the crusading order of the Knights of St. John— renamed the Knights of Malta after their expulsion from Rhodes by Süleyman the Great and reestablishment on the island of Malta—was the governing power on the island at the time) whose well-being depended on deflecting religious controversy by not allowing themselves to be drawn into provocative debates.

To the author, a consultor to the tribunal of the Inquisition in Malta, such arguments prescinded from questions of the truth necessary for salvation, and hence could not be accepted. The basic premise of his work is that all persons, even the worst and most perverse, want to be saved and to avoid eternal punishment. However, the ways are diverse and only one can be correct. "Will someone who follows the wrong path all his life ever arrive at the Fatherland?" he asks. His book claims to be an examination of the various religious paths in an attempt to discover the correct one.

His method is twofold. In the first part, he argues that all the teachings of the Qur'an about Jesus—his birth from a virgin, his sinlessness, his miracles— all point to God's confirmation of everything that Jesus taught and claimed as recorded in the Christian Gospels. Conversely, God never confirmed by genuine miracles the message delivered by Muhammad in the Qur'an. Central to this argumentation is the claim that the Gospels are the original and uncorrupted testimony of the teaching and mission of Jesus.

There is not much originality in this part of Sanz's treatise. He follows arguments well established in the Christian polemical tradition that preceded him. In the central importance that he places on miracles as the confirmation of Gospel claims concerning Jesus, one suspects his reliance on the earlier work of Gonzales, who, as general [superior] of the Society of Jesus in 1689, approved Sanz's work for publication.

In the second part of this work one can sense the preacher offering his own method "for the conversion of the Turks," and it is here that his original contribution to the Christian controversialist literature can be found. He begins with the Christian's first encounter with a hypothetical Muslim, and then guides him, step by step, to a recognition of the falseness of Islam, then to a desire for baptism, and finally through the whole catechetical course. These instructions are in the form of a dialogue in which Sanz attempted to follow the same argumentation that he used in the first part, however, in the simple language of everyday discourse.

The first dialogue begins as follows:

Christian:	God keep you, my friend. What is your name?
Turk:	Sir, my name is Mustafa.
Christian:	What country are you from?
Turk:	I am from Constantinople.
Christian:	Were you born in the same city?
Turk:	Yes, sir.
Christian:	How many years have you lived in this country?
Turk:	I have been here about nine years.
Christian:	Nine years! But how is it that in all that time you have not become a Christian?
Turk:	Sir, I do not want to become a Christian.
Christian:	Why not? Isn't it better to be a Christian than a Turk?
Turk:	No, sir, because I was born a Turk and that is a sign that God wants me to be a Turk. My father and mother were Turks and died Turks, and I also want to die a Turk.
Christian:	My Mustafa, this is not a good answer, since it is a clear matter that just because your father and mother harmed themselves, you should not therefore harm yourself.[43]

And so on. By the end of the first dialogue, Mustafa has decided to become a Christian, and is then referred to as "Catechumen." Eventually, by the third dialogue he is baptized "Giuseppe." In the course of these dialogues, which cover 163 pages of the 240-page work, the Christian uses citations from the Gospels and the Old Testament to convince his interlocutor that the Roman Catholic Church is the sole path that leads to salvation. Once Mustafa has accepted baptism, Islam withdraws from the scene and the intent is more to refute the teachings of Luther and Calvin. This is followed by two long chapters against the Schismatics (Orthodox) and the Jews. The dialogues conclude with the teaching about heaven and hell and "the goal of human life"—that is, the contemplation of God's love.

The author makes no pretence that these dialogues are anything other than a literary form by which to present the Christian faith, as understood by the Catholic Church, in a popular, interesting form. The Muslim convert Mustafa is no more than a foil for the catechist, asking leading questions at the proper moment, and enthusiastically admitting his errors when confronted with the sound teaching of the Christian preacher.

The argumentation being such that would not convince anyone who was not already a believing Catholic Christian, it is difficult to imagine that these dialogues could have been drawn from Sanz's personal experience, but seem, rather, to reflect discussions among Christian theologians concerning the best way to present the Christian faith to Muslims.

Le Moderne Prosperità of Nicolò Pallavicino, 1688

Nicolò Maria Pallavicino, S.J., *Le Moderne prosperità della Chiesa Cattolica contro il Maccomettismo* (Rome: Giacomo Komarek Boemo all'Angelo Custode, 1688).[44]

In contrast to the works of Gonzales, Sanz, and Nau, which relied primarily on theological arguments in their confrontation with Islam, Pallavicino's work is primarily political. As such, and in contrast to the "timeless" nature of the theological polemics, the historical setting of this work is essential to understanding the author's purpose. The work was written in 1687, only four years after the lifting of the Ottoman siege against Vienna. Pope Innocent XI was instrumental in forming the Holy League of the Empire—Poland, Venice, and Russia—which restored Hungary to Christian rule in 1686 and was advancing on Belgrade. Belgrade, seen as the gateway to the Ottoman heartland itself, would fall to the armies of the league only a few months after the publication of Pallavicino's treatise.

Pallavicino has two purposes in writing his work.[45] Firstly, he felt that recent events marked a new stage in history, when God, through the victories granted to the Christian princes against the Muslims, was confirming the truth of the Christian faith against the claims of Islam. Second, he hoped to persuade the members of the league (particularly Leopold of Austria, to whom the work is dedicated) to continue their offensive against the Turks until the Ottoman Empire should be overthrown and Ottoman domains subjected to Christian rule.

The work is thus "triumphalist" in the strict sense of the word. He sees the enemies of the Catholic faith in four categories: heretics (Lutherans and Calvinists), Schismatics (Orthodox and English), Maccomettans (Muslims), and Jews. Islam arose in the Eastern parts of Christendom, "the land of heresies," and is thus seen as "a great sea of all the heresies, greater even than Calvinism, to which, of all the modern sects, it is closely similar."

Beginning from Old Testament examples of God's destruction of the empire inimical to the Chosen People, he celebrates, as signs of God's favor, the victories of Ferdinand I, Charles V, Philip II, Charles II, Peter of Portugal, Ferdinand II, Ferdinand III, and, most of all, Leopold against the enemies of the church, especially Muslims.[46] He holds that God takes special care of popes and gives a historical account of papal campaigns against Muslim armies. The author feels that God's intervention at Vienna and the subsequent victories of the league are all the more miraculous because of the sad state in which Christendom had found itself only a short time before. In 1676, most of the Catholic monarchs were at war, usually among themselves. No help against the Turk could be expected from the powerful British or Dutch. The English had succumbed to Calvinist doctrines and were engaged in a bloody persecution of the true church. The Dutch not only gave shelter to the Calvinist heresy but were engaged in spreading, through their conquests in Sri Lanka, Malacca, and the Moluccas, that doctrine throughout the world.[47]

France, surprisingly, receives only one sentence in Pallavicino's otherwise thorough account of the situation of Western Christianity; moreover, it is the only reference that I have found in this 292-page work that refers to the contemporary existence of that politically and religiously important country. Acknowledging that the French were enjoying peace, the author nevertheless laments that they nourished "millions of Hugenots" at their bosom who like snakes were poised to strike their mother. The reasons for his reticence concerning France were two: first, France had traditionally been in political and military alliance with the Ottoman Empire and had refused to join the Holy League; second, the controversy between Innocent XI and Louis XIV over the Gallican articles was at its peak. In 1687, the pope had rejected Louis' nominee for Archbishop of Cologne and accepted that of Leopold, and in January 1688, he secretly informed Louis that he and his ministers were excommunicate. A strong, almost fanatic, papal supporter, Pallavicino could be expected to side with Innocent; on the other hand, Jesuits were always unwilling to criticize France, their traditional protector. Pallavicino seems to have resolved this dilemma by a discreet silence on the role of France.

In rallying the Christian princes to fight the Ottomans, the author rarely speaks of "the church." Instead, he consistently uses the phrase "mystical body of Christ" in the highly militant sense of the universal body of Christians, who have the responsibility to fight a common cause against their enemies. Citing Urban II's earlier calls for crusade against the Saracens, he claims that the outrages of the Turks are even worse. His main complaints concern the *devshirme*, the Ottoman practice of taking Christian boys and rearing them as Muslims for the janissary corps, and that of forcing Christian girls into the harems.[48] He is not interested in discussing the theological differences between Islam and Christianity, but notes that Turks will not willingly, "save by a miracle of grace," become Christian. The only way to save them from their infidelity is to overcome them with arms and force them to listen to the preaching of the Gospel.

The rhetoric of the book is that typical of wartime propaganda. The Ottoman Empire is a "dragon waiting to devour Christians," and the Christian world has a sufficient number of heretics and rebels who are willing to induce the dragon to strike.[49] The Turks are described with the biblical image of a "roaring lion" who *circuit quaerens quem devoret* ("seeking someone to devour"). Any offensive war against the Turks, he holds, is really defensive (and thus legitimate according to the just war theory), because the Turks will never be satisfied until they overrun all Christendom.

There is more to this treatise, however, than simple warmongering. The author offers astute insights into both the strengths and the weaknesses of the Ottoman Empire. He observes three advantages that the Turks have arising from their "art" or strategy of government. The first is to render many nations eager, or at least willing, to be governed by them. To an extent unthinkable in seventeenth-century Europe, they "have granted wide freedom of conscience to their peoples, embracing Christians, Jews, Muslims, Heretics, and Schismatics within their dominion," with only pagan idolaters outside the limits of their toleration.[50] This makes their governance tolerable to Catholics, to whom they allow free exercise of their religion, and positively desirable to Jews, Heretics, and Schismatics, who "being excluded from the vast part of the Catholic world, find secure exile in regions subject to the Turk." The Turks are like bandit captains who accept all kinds of riff-raff, renegades, and evildoers among their followers. Nevertheless, he admits, "an Empire which offers exile and welcome to all unfaithful persons and those rebellious to their princes, has in itself an extraordinary strength, both for conservation and for propagation."[51] The liberty of conscience promoted by the Turks, he claims, gives them an advantage in warfare, since they are able to intervene in contested regions as helpers and then remain as masters.

The second strategy of the Turks is their manner of undertaking wars.[52] Deriving from their reputation for freedom of conscience is their practice of intervening in wars at the behest of the people of the land. This gives them the advantage of waging a war at the expense of others. A second advantage is that their soldiers fight with more ardor, since they are being enriched not only by the spoils of the conquered land, but with free-will gifts of the host people.[53] Finally, having cast out the enemy, they are in a position to demand and usurp the goods of the ruling class of that land.

However, their third and most successful strategy is to engage themselves only in one war at a time, after which they quickly sue for peace.[54] After conquering a region, they offer advantageous terms to the people of that land, whereby the status quo is largely maintained. Thus nourished by the material gains and the new sources of manpower, they are ready to begin a new war. He advises the Christian princes that they could profit much by learning from the Turkish strategies and imitating them.

He also points out weaknesses of the Ottomans that the Christian rulers should be prompt to exploit. The military discipline in the Ottoman armies is weak, the human resources of the sultanate are diminished, and they lack the natural leaders that had made them so successful. Sultans Ibrahim and Mehmet IV are not of the political or military stature of their predecessors: Beyazit, the Mürats, Mehmet I and II, Selim, and Süleyman. His point is that this is the moment to strike if the Ottoman rule is to be overcome and eliminated.[55]

The author tends to see the history of Europe as a contest between the indigenous Christians and the Muslim invaders. The civilized world, he claims, is divided in two: Christendom and Islam. At present, the Turks are stronger than any single Christian power, but weaker than all if acting together. In spite of this schematic view of European history, Pallavicino is not beyond suggesting that in any Holy League against the Turk, the Persians, bitter enemies of the Ottomans, should be invited to take part.[56] He feels that the real issue is one of Christianity versus Islam. Many think mistakenly that the Turks are interested only in power, but their true intent is to exterminate Christian rule. Europeans point out that Christianity is tolerated in Ottoman lands, but actually there is no greater persecutor of Christians than the Turks. Through their practice of granting freedom of conscience to Christians living in their domains, the Turks are worse than the early Roman emperors who persecuted Christianity. The Turks have not made the mistake of the Neros and Diocletians, who made martyrs of Christians. The Turkish technique is rather to integrate conquered Christian peoples into their religio-political system so that many voluntarily abandon their faith and adopt that of their rulers.[57] The Turks thus make apostates, not martyrs.

He makes an interesting if debatable philosophical parallel. Catholics prefer to teach the philosophy of Aristotle rather than Plato, because Aristotle by his open enmity to religion cannot trick one into betraying the principles of faith. But Plato's philosophy, with its many similarities to religious belief and consequent attractiveness for religious persons, leads to many heresies. For this reason, the Heretics (Protestants) hate Aristotle and are enamored of Plato. Has the Ottoman Empire run its historical course, asks Pallavicino, so that today it is ripe for destruction? He notes that for four centuries, while the Turks have prospered and been permitted by God to establish their rule over Christian regions, as a punishment to Christians for their sins of heresy and rebellion, visionaries, astrologers, and apocalyptic preachers have repeatedly predicted that the time of the demise of the Turks is at hand. He cites as an example the predictions of the Carmelite St. Angelo, who in 1219 predicted that the Christians would be subjected, for their sins, to the rule of the Turks for a time, but, using passages from the Apocalypse, sought to calculate the day of the Christians' liberation. Pallavicino dismisses such predictions of the future as based on invalid interpretations of Scripture. He rejects similar prognostications made by astrologists as trafficking in the dark arts, where humankind is open to diabolical deceptions.

However, in an approach that reminds one of Ibn Khaldun's pioneering sociological studies, the author indicates that there is sound evidence to show that the élan of the Ottoman Empire has been spent and that its days are numbered. The Turks have overreached themselves militarily and financially, while their ruling family has sunk into internecine treachery and debilitating self-indulgence.

In the past, the Turks possessed some important moral virtues, which they translated into political and military strengths: the rigor of military discipline, frugality in personal habits, abstinence from wine, and disapproval of pleasures and luxury. Moreover, unlike the ancient Greeks and Romans, the Turks have never been contaminated by the vices "whose mother is idolatry, to which they are enemies just as much as Christians."[58] Rather, their chief sin is pride, thinking that four centuries of success is an indication that God will preserve them from future calamity. The moral virtues that made their empire strong, the author holds, are today in disarray; as a result, they are vulnerable to attack by Christian forces. His conclusion is that the Christian princes would be derelict in their divinely appointed role if they did not carry the war all the way to Istanbul.

Pallavicino was simultaneously a preacher, assuring the princes that God would sanction and support their cause, and a shrewd master of realpolitik, even presenting reasons why war against the Turks would not be prohibitively expensive.[59] Yet he was ready to grant the Turks their good qualities, even their moral strengths from which the Christian princes could learn. One suspects that, in his praise for the tactical advantages of the Ottoman practice of freedom of conscience and unity within the religious community, he was indirectly offering the Christian princes advice that went beyond mere strategy for waging war against the Turk.

Although Pallavicino was unsuccessful in persuading the Christian princes to act in concert in launching a military drive against Istanbul, modern historians, from a comfortable position of hindsight that was unavailable to Pallavicino, confirm many of his observations. Halil Inalcik marks the very years in which Pallavicino was writing as the end of an era for the Ottomans. "Ottoman statesmen now finally accepted the superiority of the 'Franks' and the weakness of their own state. . . . The belief that the state could be revived by a return to the order imposed on it by Süleyman the Magnificent was abandoned, and the Ottomans turned their eyes to the West."[60]

The eighteenth and nineteenth centuries proved disastrous for the Ottoman state, as the European nations continually gained in strength vis-à-vis the Ottomans. Moreover, the interventions of the Christian nations in Ottoman affairs increased steadily until the "Old Man of Europe" was unable to operate without a continual series of concessions and disadvantageous alliances.

Pallavicino was a shameless Catholic supremacist whose judgments on Orthodox and Reform Christians were often harsher than his condemnation of Muslims. He was a propagandist whose interpretation of history was colored by the course of action he was advocating. His silence concerning the significant role of Orthodox Russia in the Holy League, the earlier Venetian refusal to take part in an anti-Ottoman Holy League that led to the papal interdict of 1605, and the contemporary opposition of Catholic France leads to the conclusion that Pallavicino has been highly selective in his use of history. Nevertheless, Pallavicino's work exemplifies the interweaving of practical politics and religious goals in a manner that would become increasingly rare in Christian Europe. Written in the final century before the American and French revolutions, Pallavicino's treatise, with its evocation of Crusader ideals and the role of the pope as the arbiter of political as well as religious unity of Europe, must already have seemed like a revanchist curiosity to many of his contemporaries.

The *Religio Christiana* of Michel Nau

Michel Nau, S.J., *Religio Christiana contra Alcoranum per Alcoranum pacifice defensa ac probata* (Lutetiae Parisiorum: Gabrielem Martinum, 1680).[61]

This engaging treatise grew out of the author's long stay in Aleppo, Syria, then part of the Ottoman Empire. Nau[62] learned Arabic well, as is attested in the Qur'anic citations in this book; the work was written while he was still in Syria but published in France shortly before his return there in 1682. He begins with a common objection made by Christians. It would seem a worthless task, and even dangerous, to discuss the Christian faith with Muslims. In fact, as has been mentioned, the early Jesuit General Superiors had instructed Jesuits living in Muslim lands to refrain from proselytizing or entering into polemics with Muslims and to direct their attention exclusively toward the pastoral care of local Christians.

Nau defends his interest in discussing Christianity with Muslims by holding that if dialogue is carried out in the context of love and friendship, with respect and humility, without denigration of or hatred for Islam, such discussions need not lead to rancor and division.

> He (the Muslim Interlocutor) will not be able to be offended and aroused against you, since you will not speak injuriously of his religion or bring it under discussion, but when asked, at least you can expound yours, in a moderate and unassuming spirit, so that you will give rise to praise and friendship, not recriminations and wrath.

With this introduction, the author proceeds to the main part of his text, "A Peaceful Dialogue between a Christian and a Muslim concerning the Christian Religion." The interlocutors are a (fictional) Syrian Muslim, well known for his learning and his understanding of the Qur'an, and a European Christian who has done much study in the communication of the Christian faith and is acquainted with the text of the Qur'an.

The Muslim begins the dialogue by stating, "I am amazed at you Christians, who have been taught by a divine Book handed down from heaven, that you profess things which are alien to human common sense," that no rational person, much less a believer who desires to serve God through faith, could believe. Thus, at the beginning the problem that Christian mysteries present to the rationalist bases of Islamic faith is raised.

The Christian replies with citations from the Qur'an concerning *al-ghayb*, that which cannot be known from human reason, but only through revelation. Christians are only following, he holds, what is written in the Gospel. But the Gospel that Christians have, answers the Muslim, is corrupt, and thus the issue of *taḥrīf* is joined.

The Christian defense is that *taḥrīf* is a gratuitous charge made by Muslims for which they have no proof. The Muslims are no more able to produce the hypothetical book that they claim to have been given to Jesus than they can prove that the Qur'an is identical to that given, according to their claim, by God to Muhammad. The Muslim interlocutor is allowed to defend at length the textual integrity of Qur'an, arguing that not the slightest corruption of the Qur'anic text could have taken place subsequent to the edition compiled at the time of the Caliph 'Uthman. The Christian accepts the textual integrity of the Qur'an and uses the same kind of argumentation to show that the Gospel as well as the Old Testament could not have undergone alteration.

Anticipating the later critical principle of *"lectio difficilior verior"* ("the more difficult reading is truer"), the Christian then asks why anyone would want to produce an evangelical teaching so difficult to live.[63] The asceticism of the cross and the difficulty of understanding dogmas like that of the one triune God give evidence of their own authenticity.

The Muslim admits that the arguments for the integrity of the Gospel are convincing, but notes that the Gospel is not in agreement with the legal traditions of the Hebrew Bible.[64] The Christian responds with Qur'anic citations concerning abrogation and gives examples of how neither the Gospel nor the Qu'ran follows the legal prescriptions of the Jews. There follows a long section in which the Christian attempts to show, basing himself mainly on verse 4:171, that the Qur'an itself teaches the triune nature of God.[65] When the Muslim responds that the Christian's interpretation of the Qur'anic passages is a form of "associationism" (*shirk*), the Christian endeavors to show that the Qur'an rejects the application of *shirk* and *kufr* to Christians.[66] The Muslim is finally convinced of the legitimacy of Christianity as a monotheistic religion free from associationism and unbelief. However, he is not convinced that the Christian faith is the *sole* medium of salvation.[67] According to Islam, he holds, each person is called to be a man of faith, to undertake a life of virtue, to act uprightly and in a praiseworthy manner. Such a person will receive his reward and need not fear on the last day. At this point, the Christian takes the offensive and, in the final section of the book, tries to show, with many Qur'anic citations, that following Muhammad is not sufficient for salvation. He holds that the Qur'an attests to the many sins and failings of Muhammad and the Christian dwells on the traditional Christian preoccupations of Muhammad's wives, his harsh treatment of enemies, and the voluptuous descriptions of paradise in the Qur'an. The book ends abruptly with the Muslim interlocutor saying how good God is and affirming how well the Christian has explained all the "moments of religion."[68] It is worth noting that, against the reader's expectations, the Muslim does not finally embrace the Christian religion.

This short work is an intelligent and perceptive discussion of those elements of faith about which Muslims and Christians today are still in dialogue. Nau's argumentation is based on a "Christian reading" of the Qur'an, which the author seems to have studied thoroughly. The precolonial setting of a Christian missionary living in Muslim domains at the permission of the local government, rather than as a representative and collaborator of colonial powers, might help to explain the humble and deferential tone. Clearly this is a work that has grown out of the personal experience of many years of shared life and thoughtful dialogue with Muslims.

Notes

1. The pioneer work in this literature was done by M. Steinschneider and I. Goldziher. At the time of publication of Steinschneider's catalogue (*Polemische und apologetische Literatur in arabischer Sprache* [Leipzig: F. A. Brockhaus, 1877]), fewer than ten of

the works listed were in print. By 1989, when this article was first published, about half had been printed in Arabic, and new works of this genre had been discovered. A year after the publication of Steinschneider's catalogue, Goldziher, one of the main contributors to the catalogue, published the first important study of Islamic polemical literature, "Uber muhammedanische Polemik gegen Ahl al-Kitab," *ZDMG* 32 (1878): 341-87. This was followed by the studies of A. Palmieri and I. di Matteo in *Bessarione* and the later works of C. H. Becker ("Christliche Polemik und islamische Dogmenbildung," *Zeitschrift für Assyriologie und verwandte Gebiete* 12 [1926]: 175-95) and E. Fritsch (*Islam und Christentum in Mittelalter* [Breslau: Verlag Muller, 1930]).

2. See the bibliography in *Islamochristiana* 1:135-76; 2:188-245; 3:255-84; 4:247-65; 5:299-316; 6:259-78; 10:274-90; 13:173-80.

3. G. Levi della Vida, "P. Ludovico Marracci e la sua opera negli studi islamici," Estratto del Tomo VII della Nuova Serie (III) degli, *Aid dell'Accademia Lucchese di Scienze, Lettere ed Arti* (Genova: Biblioteca Universitaria, 1949), 3-4.

4. J. M. Gaudeul, *Encounters and Clashes: Islam and Christianity in History*, vol. 1 (Rome: P.I.S.A.I., 1985), 214.

5. This translation was never published and has never received the benefit of scholarly study; it was apparently made for the use of students in Jesuit colleges. The manuscript remains in the university library in Genoa. See Levi della Vida, "P. Ludovico Marracci e la sua opera negli studi islamici," 20.

6. G. Goyau, "Les Jesuites sur le Bosphore," *En Terre d'Islam* 9 (1934): 7-19, 86-103.

7. Eliano is an interesting figure. Born in Alexandria, the son of a well-known Jewish scholar, he received a traditional Jewish religious education and was fluent in both Hebrew and Arabic. He traveled to Europe, where he was baptized and then accepted into the Society of Jesus by Ignatius. He was later sent on various diplomatic missions by the pope; in Cairo he worked (unsuccessfully) for unity between the Coptic Church and that of Rome. He is later credited with introducing the Arabic Bible to the Maronites of Lebanon.

His work on Islam, "*Hādha muṣāḥabā rūḥānīyah baīna 'l-'ālimaīn*" ("This is a conversation between two scholars"), was written in Arabic and published in Rome (Roman College, 1579). It was subsequently translated into English by W. Bedwell and published in London in 1615 under the provocative title: "Mohammedis imposturae, that is a discovery of the manifold forgeries, falshoods and horrible impieties of the blasphemous seducer Mohammed: with a demonstration of the insufficiency of his law, contained in the accursed Alkoran, delivered in a conference had between two Mohammetans in their return from Mecka." Eliano's name nowhere appears in this English translation, which states only that the work was "written long since in Arabicke."

8. This unpublished work, written in 1605, is contained in a manuscript entitled "De los Moriscos de España," located in the British Library. F. de Borja de Medina, "Legación Pontificia a los Siro-ortodoxos, 1583-1584: las relaciones de Ignacio de las Casas de la Compañia de Jesus," *Orientalia Christiana Periodica* 55 (1989): 127.

9. A. Possevino, *Qua agitur de Ratione Studiorum In Historia, In Disciplinis, In Salute Omnium procuranda* (Rome: Typ. Apostolica Vaticana, 1593), Book IX, Cap. VI. A modern commentator on the work of Possevino sees in his approach to Islam an attitude similar to that adopted in the nineteenth century by Cardinal Lavigerie and in the twentieth century by Charles de Foucauld, that is, of Christians and Muslims meeting on the common terrain of natural morality (S. Lator, "Il P. Antonio Possevino e l'Islam," *Studia Missionalia* 1 [1943]: 224).

10. Arnulf Camps, *Jerome Xavier S. J. and the Muslims of the Mogul Empire* (Schoneck-Beckenried, Switzerland: Nouvelle Revue de Science Missionaire, 1957). A

Spanish manuscript of this work, presumably made by J. Xavier himself, is found in the archives of the Curia Generalizia of the Jesuits in Rome.

11. J. M. Gaudeul traces well the whole controversy in *Encounters and Clashes* I:232-34.

12. Born Stephen Szanto, he used the Latinized surname Arator. A Hungarian Jesuit, one of the founders of the Hungarian College in Rome, he taught classics in Jesuit colleges in regions of modern Hungary, Romania, and Czechoslovakia. His three volume work in Hungarian, dated 1611, has the Latin title, *Confutatio Alcorani*.

13. J. Amieu, a French Jesuit living in Aleppo, in the Syrian vilayet of the Ottoman Empire, was a companion of P. Chézaud who later left the Jesuit house in Aleppo to serve the Armenians in Isfahan. In 1641, Amieu wrote a "Refutation of the Qur'an" in Arabic in response to a Muslim treatise. It is possible that Amieu's work was, like that of Chézaud, in answer to the above-mentioned *risāla* of Ahmad b. Zayn al-'Abidin. See "Extrait d'une lettre du 16e d'août 1641, envoyée d'Alep, par le P. Jean Amieu, de la Compagnie de Jésus, au P. d'Autruy," in A. Carayon, *Documents inédits concernant la Compagnie de Jésus* XI (Poitiers: Henri Oudin, 1864), 152-57. Amieu was also knowledgeable in Turkish and compiled a Turkish-Latin dictionary, but has left no writings in that language.

14. A. Lopez, a Spaniard who spent many years in the southern Philippines, accompanied Spanish troops fighting Muslims in Mindanao and the Sulu archipelago and served as representative of the Spanish governor at the courts of Muslim rulers. Among his writings are a memoir of his cordial reception by the Sultan of Jolo and religious discussions at the court, a grammar and dictionary of Lutuaya, a history of Mindanao, and a refutation of Islam in Cebuano. Together with companions, he was attacked by local pirates near the island of Kawikawi (Tawitawi?) and was killed. See F. Combes, *Historia de Mindanao y Jolo* (Madrid: 1667).

15. F. de Alémán wrote "Explicación de la doctrina cristiana para los moriscos de Granada con la refutación de sus principales errores" (F. de Borja de Medina, "La Compañia de Jesús y la Minoría Morisca," *Archivum Historicum Societatis Iesu* LVII [1988]: 28). Fr. Medina notes that the title is misleading; the contents of the work deal with Islam. At the time of the suppression, his work on Islam was in the library of the Jesuit College in Seville.

16. The work of J. de Almarza is entitled "Método que se debe guardar en la conversión de los moros esclavos a nuestra Santa Fe, con algunas industrias para lograr este fruto." This work was in the library of the Colegio Imperial de Madrid at the time of the suppression of the Jesuits in Spain (1767).

17. B. Christel taught controversial theology in Prague. His work, *Himmel Proviant Christlicher Soldaten wider die Türken* (Prague: Karl Gerzabek, 1688), seems to have been along the lines of the work by N. Pallavicino studied in this article.

18. T. Rutka (d. 1700) taught controversial theology in Poland and spent some years at the Jesuit house in Istanbul. His main writings were against Eastern Orthodox theology, but he also translated the works of Gonzales (pub. Lwów: 1694) and Nau (Poznan: 1697) into Polish and also wrote his own polemic against Islam. Published simultaneously in Latin and Polish, the work carried the title *Gladius contra Turcas a Christo Principe, Rege, Imperatore*; in an indication of the mood of the time, this work is dated "*anno Christi Imperatoris et Bellatoris* 1696."

19. Part II was published in 1688; part I in 1689. The work was published in Madrid in 1687. In the Vatican Library, there is a manuscript of an Arabic translation of part II of Gonzales's work, dated 1724, made by Jaqub Arutin, a Maronite priest of Aleppo. The title of this work may be rendered in English as: "Guide to the conversion of [Mus-

lims]. In two parts. In the first, the truth of the Roman Catholic Christian religion is demonstrated by simple argument. In the second, the falsity of the Mahommetan sect is shown."—Ed.

20. T. Gonzales (d. 1705) was professor of theology at Salamanca and distinguished himself in the field of moral theology as a fervent proponent of probabiliorism. The vast majority of Jesuit moralists at the time held the opposed theory of probabilism. At the behest of the probabiliorist Pope Innocent XI, he was elected superior general of the Jesuits, to widespread dissatisfaction in the Jesuit Order.

21. Ludovico Marracci, *Prodromus ad Refutationem Alcorani* (Rome: Typis Sac. Cong. de Prop. Fide, 1691), 6-7.

22. Particularly in Spain, Jesuits were active in preaching to Muslims and Jews. This took the form of "street missions," public sermons, and catechesis held, usually during Lent and the summer academic recess, in the public squares of the Spanish coastal towns and the ancient Muslim centers in the interior. Gonzales organized and directed these missions in Seville and Malaga in the years 1672-1679. Fr. Madina lists the towns of Spain where such missions were carried out (F. de Borja de Medina, "La Compañia de Jesús y la Minoría Morisca," 25-28).

23. D. Walker, *Unclean Spirits: Possession and Exorcism in France and England in the Late Sixteenth and Early Seventeenth Centuries* (Philadelphia: University of Pennsylvania Press, 1981), 66-67.

24. See the *Islamochristiana* bibliography for references to Ricoldo de Monte Croce (6:275); Peter of Cluny (the Venerable) (5:313); Euthemius (4:261/11:243); St. Peter Paschal (6:271); Juan Andrea (6:270). There have been many studies of Nicholas of Cusa's *Cribratio* and of his approach to Islam. Noteworthy is that of Ludwig Hagemann, *Der Kur'an in Verständnis und Kritik bei Nikolas von Cues: Ein Beitrag zur Erhellung islamisch-christlicher Geschichte* (Frankfurt: 1976). See *Islamochristiana* 5:299.

25. Pedro de Cavalleria, a fifteenth-century Arabist lawyer of Zaragoza, wrote *Zelus Christi contra Judaeos, Sarracenos et infideles* (see *Enciclopedia Universal Ilustrada* XII [Barcelona], 687).

26. The *Tractatus contra principales errores perfidi Machomet* of John of Torquemada was printed in Paris in 1574 and again in Rome in 1606. See U. Monneret de Villard, *Lo Studio del 'Islam in Europa nel XII e nel XIII Secolo* (Vatican City: Biblioteca Apostolica, 1944), 75.

27. Pius II, the famous humanist Pope Enea Silvio Piccolomini, in 1460, wrote to Mehmet II, recent conqueror of Constantinople, with an exposition of both Islam and Christianity and an invitation to Mehmet to become a Christian and the continuer of the Roman Byzantine Empire. Pius's attitude was typical of many Renaissance humanists who saw in Mehmet an exemplification of the Platonic Prince-Philosopher (see F. Babinger, "Maometto il Conquistatore e gli Umanisti d'Italia," in *Venezia e l'Oriente tra tardo Medioevo e Rinascimento*, ed. A. Pertusi (Firenze: 1966), 434.

28. Denis the Carthusian's "Contra perfidiam Mahometi e Disputatio inter Christianum et Sarracenum" is found in vol. 36 of his *Omnia Opera* (Monstroli: 1896).

29. William Postel (d. 1581), an early Jesuit, in 1543 and 1544 wrote two works in which he tried to establish a parallel between Islam and Lutheran doctrines. After having been dismissed from the Jesuits in 1545, he went to the Middle East to collect manuscripts for another treatise aimed at the conversion of Muslims to Christianity (*Dictionnaire de Spiritualité* XII, 2:2007-12 ; and Gaudeul, *Encounters and Clashes*, 219).

30. For Antonio Possevino (P. Possevin), see note 9 above. Gonzales uses his *Biblioieca Selecta*, Book IX.

31. Both Christian and Muslim sources relate stories of a Christian monk, Sergius (or Nestur), with whom Muhammad was in contact. The Christian accounts tend to picture Sergius as the unorthodox (or even renegade) monk who taught Muhammad a distorted view of Christianity. Muslim accounts center on Sergius's recognition of Muhammad as the awaited Messenger. The historical existence of Sergius is highly questionable.

32. Following the practice in Europe at his time, Gonzales uses "Turks" as a general term to refer to all Muslims. When referring specifically to Muslims of Spanish origin, he uses the term "Moors."

33. Gonzalez, *Manuductio*, Part II, 25.

34. Ibid., 35.

35. Born Muhammad al-Tasi in the city of Fez, Morocco, in 1613, at the time of his baptism he took the Christian name Baltasar Diego Loyola de Mandes. Baltasar, who claimed to be the son of 'Abd al-Wahid Mtah Ahmad Sherif, the local ruler of Fez, became a Jesuit in 1657 and died in Madrid ten years later. The fact that local histories of Morocco do not mention anyone with his father's name has given rise to doubts about his claims to royal origins. After his death, he became a well-known figure in Spain and Calderon wrote a drama, "Gran Principe de Fez," about his life. A good study on Baltasar is that of C. Garcia Goldaraz, *Baltasar Loyola Mandes, S.I., Hijo del Rey de Fez* (Burgos: Imprenta Aldecoa, 1944). On pp. 7-8 and n. 4, Garcia reviews the earlier literature on Baltasar.

36. The dialogue device was extremely popular in seventeenth-century polemics (we will see it again in the works of Sanz and Nau). The usual form was a conversation between the Christian writer and an imaginary Muslim *adversarius*, in which the Christian gradually answers all the objections and doubts of the Muslim, who by the end admits his errors and requests baptism. Eliano, as we have seen, produced the novelty of a dialogue between two Muslims. However, in Gonzales's work, one feels that he is recounting a genuine experience of dialogue; evidence for this is that after having heard all Gonzales's arguments, the Muslim is not convinced and remains in Islam.

37. Gonzalez, *Manuductio*, Part II, 128.

38. Ibid., 155.

39. Ibid., 287-307.

40. In their own polemical tradition, Muslims have produced similar accounts of miracles as evidence of God's confirmation of the messengership of Muhammad and the revealed nature of the Qur'an. One example from many that could be given is Ibn Taymiyya's *Al-Jawāb al-ṣaḥīḥ li-man baddala dīn al-Masīh* IV (Cairo: Matba'at al-Madani, 1383/1964), 67-323.

41. The title of this work may be rendered in English as: "Brief tractate in which the Turks are manifestly convinced by demonstrative reason, so that it cannot in any way be refuted, that the law of Muhammad is false and only that of Christ true."—Ed.

42. Emmanuele (or Manuel) Sanz (d. 1719) was a Spanish Jesuit of the Sicilian province, who went to Malta some time after 1666, where he eventually became rector of the Jesuit college. Two years after the Italian original of his *Breve Trattato*, a Spanish translation, probably made by himself, was published in Seville (1693).

43. Sanz, *Breve Trattato*, 67.

44. The title of this work may be rendered in English as: "The modern prosperity of the Catholic Church against [Islam] Mahommetism."—Ed.

45. Nicolò Pallavicino (d. 1692) taught Scripture in Rome, was a theologian of the Sacred Penitentiary and a "qualifier" of the Holy Office. Most of his writings are controversialist, mainly against the Reformers and the Orthodox.

46. Pallavicino, *Le Moderne prosperità*, 52-89.
47. Ibid., 200-203, 24.
48. Ibid., 175-76.
49. Ibid., 186.
50. Ibid., 182.
51. Ibid., 189.
52. Ibid., 183.
53. He is probably referring to the situation of the Protestant stronghold of Transylvania, which accepted Ottoman protection against the Habsburgs during the Thirty Years War.
54. Pallavicino, *Le Moderne prosperità*, 184.
55. Pallavicino's perception of the military and political weakness of the Ottoman state is confirmed by secular historians. In 1687-1688, when this treatise was written and published, the state was in civil crisis and verging on anarchy. A local military adventurer, Yeghen Osman Pasha, rose to become "the most powerful personality in the empire," and was appointed commander-in-chief of the army. Sultan Mehmet IV, as Pallavicino notes, was weak, and real power was in the hands of the Janissaries and his mother. They had Yeghen Osman Pasha assassinated, and private militias stepped into the power vacuum, gaining effective control of most of Anatolia. As a result of the costly and expensive campaign for Crete, the state was near bankruptcy; the army was demoralized by the assassination of Osman Pasha (H. Inalcik, "The Heyday and Decline of the Ottoman Empire," in *The Cambridge History of Islam*, vol. 1A, ed. P. M. Holt, Ann K. S. Lambton, and Bernard Lewis (Cambridge: Cambridge University Press, 1970), 350-52.
56. Pallavicino, *Le Moderne prosperità*, 194.
57. Ibid., 198.
58. Ibid., 236.
59. Ibid., 219.
60. Inalcik, "Heyday and Decline of the Ottoman Empire," 353.
61. The title of this work may be rendered in English as: "The Christian religion against the Alcoran."—Ed.
62. Michel Nau, born in Tours, was assigned in 1665 to the Jesuit house in Mardin and later to that of Aleppo. It was in this latter city that he penned the work studied here. In 1682, he returned to Paris, where he died a year later. A late (nineteenth century) manuscript in Arabic of his *Religio Christiana*, entitled *Ithbāt al-Qur'ān li-ṣiḥḥat al-dīn al-Masīḥī*, is found in Beirut. Georg Graf believes that the Arabic version is original and that Nau translated his own work into Latin, but offers no evidence for this view (*Geschichte der christlichen arabischen Literatur* IV [Vatican City: Biblioteca Apostolica Vaticana, 1951], 219).

In addition to the *Religio Christiana*, Nau also wrote an analysis of contemporary Islam entitled *L'état présent de la religion mahométane, contenant les choses les plus curieuses qui regardent Mahomet et l'établissement de sa secte*, published posthumously in Paris in 1684 (P. Bouillerot). It must have been widely received, judging from the fact of its having been reprinted in 1685 and again in 1687.
63. Nau, *Religio Christiana*, 16.
64. Ibid., 20.
65. Ibid., 22-28.
66. Ibid., 29-32, 33-34.
67. Ibid., 41-42.
68. Ibid., 54.

11

Islam and Terrorism

Are We Missing the Real Story?

Linking Islam with Terrorism

Some years ago on Italian television, the daily news report was much concerned with the Muslim world. One story noted the closure of the American Embassy in Riyadh, Saudi Arabia, after the terrorist attack on the foreign compound. A second story related the terrorist attacks in Casablanca, Morocco, that occurred three days later. A third story recounted how in Ankara, Turkey, a would-be suicide bomber belonging to a radical leftist group was killed when her bomb exploded prematurely in a restaurant restroom. As the news commentators speculated how more "Islamic terrorist attacks" might be expected in reaction to the American-English war on Iraq, the television images showed long rows of men in oriental dress at prayer in an outdoor mosque.

The message (intended or unintended, I can't say) conveyed to the viewers was that Islam is a violent religion (talk of terrorism superimposed on images of men at prayer), and the flowing robes and turbans of the worshipers reinforced the impression of many that Islam is both culturally alien and opposed to modern life. Islam and its followers were clearly depicted as a dangerous threat both to Europeans as well as to all who cherish modern values.

While the facts presented in this typical newscast cannot be denied—the terrorist attacks did occur, and many Muslims do gather for prayer in traditional dress—the presumed connection between these facts can and needs to be questioned. For example, since the Ankara terrorist was a member of an antireligious Maoist political movement, in what way could her actions be construed as Islamic? More broadly, did any of the men seen at prayer engage in or approve of violence, and if so, how many? Did most of the worshipers support violent political activity? Only the occasional exception, or perhaps none of them? In short, should violence and terrorism be seen as an inherent characteristic of

Previously published as "Christian Muslim Relations: Are We Missing the Real Story?" in *East Asian Pastoral Review* (Manila) 41, no. 3 (2004): 240-47. Reprinted by permission.

Islamic faith, a typical response of Muslims to modernity, or rather as an aberration from the teachings of Islam engaged in by very few Muslims?

I wonder whether in our—by which I mean non-Muslim, modern—preoccupation with terrorism we are perhaps missing the real story of what is going on in the Muslim world. I should explain the basis from which I will present my views. For more than thirty years, I have been living and teaching in Muslim countries: in Indonesia as a member of the Indonesian province of the Society of Jesus, in Lebanon and Egypt where I did Arabic and Islamic studies, and most recently in Turkey where I regularly teach courses on Christian theology in Islamic theology faculties. As director of the Islamic Office of the Vatican Council for Interreligious Dialogue for thirteen years, I have spent some time in almost every Muslim-majority nation and spent hours in long discussions with many Muslim scholars, religious leaders, politicians, students, and countless ordinary Muslim believers.

Celebrating the Birthday of Muhammad

My conclusion after all this time is that what Muslims are really concerned about is very different from anything to do with terrorism or violence, both of which are strongly rejected and opposed by the vast majority of Muslim believers. Let me begin with a recent personal experience. A few years ago, I was in Turkey to lecture at the university theological faculty in Urfa in eastern Anatolia and to deliver public talks in the nearby cities of Birecik and Gaziantep. I was asked to give an additional talk in Istanbul on my return trip to Rome. Thus, on Easter Monday I found myself talking to over four thousand Muslim youths gathered in a large auditorium. The occasion was the celebration of the birthday of Muhammad, the prophet of Islam. It is significant that this year they had invited a Catholic priest to speak on the prophets as a blessing of God to humankind.

I was enthusiastically greeted with rousing applause before and after my talk. After I finished speaking, the program continued with a young Turkish poet reading his own poetic compositions in honor of Muhammad, and then a folk singer who, accompanied by an electric guitar, sang hymns in praise of God in the soft-rock style we associate with contemporary Gospel music.

What was going on here? The cheerful young men and women, mainly dressed in jeans, t-shirts, and running shoes, were obviously modern young people who share many elements of contemporary youth culture with people their age in Italy, Brazil, or the United States. The only visible mark of their Islamic faith was the headscarf worn by the young women. In talking with the youths before the celebration, I discovered that the students were not primarily engaged in religious studies, but were following courses in secular fields, such as computer science, medicine, and mechanical engineering. Others were not students, but workers—clerks and secretaries, travel agents, and those engaged in driving delivery trucks and in construction work.

In short, they represented a cross section of the modern urban youth of Istanbul whose common bond was their Islamic faith. Their delight and enthusiasm in welcoming a Christian speaker was undeniably sincere, as was their appreciation for the contemporary styles of praising God and honoring their prophet Muhammad in song and poetry. War had been recently raging in neighboring Iraq, but the talk that evening was not about geopolitics. The celebration featured no harangues or protests, but rather a desire to thank God for all that they had received as Muslims through the message of the prophets.

My question is, who is more representative of the Muslim world today, these young people in Istanbul for whom Islam is fundamentally a religious faith, a path to approach God in worship and a project for doing God's will in daily life, or those who want to kill and destroy in the name of God? I am convinced that the vast majority of Muslims around the world would agree that these deeply committed, open-minded, modern believers, and those like them in other countries, are the true hope of the future rather than the terrorists, whom they openly condemn. My experiences in Indonesia, Egypt, Malaysia, Iran, and Bosnia lead me to believe also that the young Muslims themselves in those countries would find far greater affinity with their Turkish contemporaries than they would with violent extremists.

Problems in Muslim Societies

All of this does not deny that problems, ideological conflicts, hypocrisy, and manipulation of religious identity abound in the modern Muslim world, although one might well ask whether such human vices and weaknesses are more prevalent among Muslims than in predominantly Christian societies. Issues of justice and good governance are central today in Muslim nations, as they are elsewhere. The need for effective, representative, democratic government is felt everywhere. The preponderance of corrupt regimes that appear to serve mainly the interests of the ruling elite, who too often have attained power through dynastic succession or military coups d'état and who remain in power by sophisticated security systems and alliances with the Great Powers, have created a lack of confidence in political systems and leadership.

The economic effects on ordinary citizens of neoliberal market policies, for which globalization has become the code word, are a cause of anger and unrest. Unequal distribution of wealth and opportunities for advancement have produced angry and frustrated masses who see no hope of betterment in structures of the status quo. There is a broadly based perception that at the root of these societal ills lies a neocolonial American hegemony in which small groups of money managers in New York and London make, on the sole basis of profit, financial decisions that affect adversely the lives of millions of people elsewhere. There is a belief that the American government supports monarchies and dictatorships so long as they allow market freedom to foreign businesses and vote correctly in the United Nations, but is ready to wage war to destroy those who stand in the way of America's economic and military aims. In this perception, the Muslim world is no different from other parts of Asia, Africa, and Latin America. Muslims often see themselves primarily as victims, rather than per-petrators, of violence, whether the oppressors be the local Muslim elites or, as in the case of Palestine, Chechnya, Kashmir, Kosovo, and the Philippines, non-Muslim governments and armies.

No increase in international security systems will be able to put an end to terrorism so long as the root causes of anger and frustration are not faced and resolved. The availability of destructive weapons today is such that any group with a cause can either purchase them or make their own. Focusing almost exclusively on Muslims, as politicians and the news media seem to be doing, fails to recognize the disquieting fact that acts of mass violence have become an inescapable reality in modern life. The necessary technology is well known and waiting to be used. Today it may be Al-Qa'ida, but tomorrow it will be some other group of another region, of another religion or of no religion, that will undertake terrorist acts in support of their political cause. So long as the peoples of a few highly industrialized nations continue to control and utilize for their own benefit an outrageously disproportionate share of the world's resources, the world will not be safe from terrorism.

Islamic Values

Many Muslims, including the great majority who do not approve of violence and terrorism, have religiously based objections to the dominant ideology promoted by the West and particularly by the United States. They regard modernist ideol-ogy as materialist, relegating God and God's will to the margins—at best—of social, economic, and political life. They see modernism as profit-oriented and consumerist, implying that a person's worth is measured by his economic status, social prestige, and power to achieve one's goals. They see the dominant ideol-ogy as dividing the world into winners and losers. The winners drive good cars, carry gold bank cards, eat well, and vacation in exotic places, while the losers are expected to work hard in difficult or insecure jobs in order to survive and to accept their lot peacefully. Their views are discounted or ignored and their voices are not heard in the councils of the mighty.

To Muslims, these are not the values by which God intends people to live. Islam, like the Christian faith, teaches that the purpose of human life is to know, worship, and obey God, to love and serve others, and to hope for the day when those who remain faithful to God will be rewarded with eternal life in God's presence. Thus, the values that should characterize human societies are solidar-ity, mutual assistance, concern for the poor, and constant recollection of God's greatness, gentleness, and compassion. The God-centered society should be one of peace (*salām*): peace with God by living in accord with God's will, peace in fellowship among the various sectors of society, and peace among nations.

In articles, speeches, and the private discussions I have had with Muslims since the tragic events of September 11, 2001, I see a great emphasis placed on Islam as a religion of peace and the duty of Muslims to work with others to build world peace. How is this to be explained? I think that many Muslims had regarded the nature of Islam as a religion of peace as a fact so evident that it did not require explanation or defense. The attacks on the World Trade Center and the subsequent war on terrorism convinced many Muslims of two things: that Islam's reputation among non-Muslims was not that of a religion of peace but rather one of violence, and that Muslims needed to work together with like-thinking believers of other religions if they were to counter the generally negative impression others have of Islam and to actually build peace in this world. In short, Muslims could no longer assume Islam's peace-oriented nature as self-evident, and Muslims could no longer try to "go it alone" in today's world.

Has God Desired Enmity between Christians and Muslims?

When Muslims look around to identify their natural allies in affirming divine values in the modern world, it is often sincere, believing Christians who come to the fore. Already at the beginning of the twentieth century, some forward-looking Muslims such as the Turkish scholar Said Nursi saw "real Christians" as the natural co-workers of Muslims in upholding the prerogatives of God in modern life. The roots of this natural affinity that should exist between Muslims and Christians go back to the very scriptural origins of Islam, where the Qur'an states: "The closest in affection to [Muslims] are those who say: 'We are Christians,' for among them are priests and monks and they are not arrogant" (5:82).

This perception of divinely willed friendship and cooperation between Muslims and Christians was expressed on the Christian side when the Catholic Church, in the Second Vatican Council decree *Nostra Aetate*, pleaded with Christians and Muslims to move beyond the suspicions and conflicts of the past in order to work together to carry out a common mandate from the one God whom both groups worship. "For the benefit of all," the decree states, "Let them together preserve and promote peace, liberty, social justice, and moral values" (§3).

In this perspective, the long history of conflict, oppression, violence, and war between Christians and Muslims must be understood as acts perpetrated by Muslims and Christians who failed to live according to the genuine teaching of their respective faiths or else as the misguided actions of those whose theological vision was too narrow to recognize God's work of grace within the other community. In other words, the history of conflict and war has not been prescribed by either religion, but is a deviation, due to human weakness, from the mutual love and support desired by God.

Muslim-Christian Cooperation "For the Benefit of All"

What can be said today is that many Muslims and Christians throughout the world have become involved in working together "for the benefit of all." This cooperation takes many forms. To take one region, the southern Philippines, as an example, we could mention the human development and antipoverty work of MuCARD (Muslim-Christian Agency of Rural Development), an umbrella group of people's organizations in 120 villages; the work for justice of Zamboanga's Islamic-Christian Urban Poor Association; the work for peace of PAZ (Peace Associates of Zamboanga); that of reconciliation carried out by the Muslim-Christian Interfaith Conference and the Moro-Christian People's Alliance; and the efforts of the Silsilah group at mutual understanding and education for dialogue.[1]

Said Nursi's early teaching on the need for Muslim-Christian cooperation in faith values has been taken up by many movements formed by his thought, especially in the educational efforts inspired by the charismatic Turkish leader Fethullah Gülen. Gülen's movement runs almost three hundred schools in almost thirty countries, mainly those of the former Soviet Union, dedicated to offering education of high quality with particular attention to character building and moral values. Through its *Zaman* newspaper, its Samanyolu television station, and its dialogue organization, the movement has undertaken many initiatives to promote mutual respect and esteem.[2]

In the United States, the American Society of Muslims and the Catholic Focolare Movement cooperate in organizing seminars on "the art of loving," seeking together to instill spiritual values in a modern, secularized society. In Washington, D.C., the Center for Muslim-Christian Understanding of the Jesuits' Georgetown University has a first-class faculty composed of Muslim and Christian scholars that offers exemplary academic training in the issues that have long divided the Christian and Muslim worlds.[3]

In the Middle East, two of Lebanon's Christian universities train both Muslims and Christians in an understanding of each other's faiths. In Tripoli, the University of Balamand, established by the Orthodox Church, at its Center for Christian-Muslim Studies, and in Beirut, the Jesuits' University of St. Joseph, at its Institute of Islamic-Christian Studies, offer academic preparation for those who seek to promote Muslim-Christian dialogue and understanding.[4] In the Gulf region, Bahrain's Tenth Islamic-Christian Dialogue Conference, which brings together Muslim and Christian scholars from many Arab-speaking nations, was held in October 2002, to explore ways that Christian-Muslim cooperation might be fostered in the region.

In Asia, the Asian Muslim Action Network, a progressive Muslim movement in more than twelve Asian countries, is jointly organizing peace seminars and workshops together with the offices of the Catholic Federation of Asian Bishops' Conferences and the Christian Conference of Asia.[5] They are working together to build a common "peace curriculum" that can be offered to *imāms*, religion teachers, seminarians, and catechists.

The sad turn of events since September 11, rather than dividing the Islamic and Christian communities from each other, has in many cases spawned new initiatives for peace. The consistent message of Pope John Paul II during his twenty-seven years in office showed Muslims that recent political and military conflicts are not instances of "Christian against Muslim." Joint statements against the Iraq War were issued by National Councils of Churches, bishops' conferences, and Islamic organizations, including those of Great Britain and the United States. In March of this year, an interreligious delegation of Indonesian religious leaders, led by the Cardinal Archbishop of Jakarta with the heads of Indonesia's major Islamic organizations, traveled to Rome and Brussels to meet with the pope and the European Union in a common appeal for peace.

I could go on and on, but these few examples will have to suffice to show that throughout the world many Christians and Muslims are refusing to accept that history's sad record of conflict between the two communities is what God desires. They are putting their convictions into concrete programs and reaching broad constituencies. One might say that Muslim-Christian dialogue is both the need of our day and an idea whose time has come.

This shared vision is not utopian. Christians and Muslims in dialogue must recognize that the problems of our world are of such complexity that the two communities are often pitted one against the other and, moreover, that many of the troubles arise not from external factors but rather from those who identify themselves as Muslims or Christians. What has become clear is that Christian-Muslim dialogue is not something that can wait until easy relationships characterize the two communities around the world, but a need that must be pursued in the midst of and despite the tensions and conflicts of our time.

Notes

1. For more information, see http://mucaard-uk.org/Whoweare.aspx (accessed August 15, 2009).—Ed.

2. Comprehensive information on educational and outreach activities of the movement is available at http://www.fethullahgulen.org/ (accessed August 15, 2009).—Ed.

3. For a description of Imam Muhammad's activities in recent decades, visit http://www.ar-razzaq.org/MosqueCares/ (accessed August 15, 2009). To access the official Web site of the Catholic Focolare Movement, visit http://www.focolare.us/ (accessed August 15, 2009). For information on the Prince Al-Waleed Bin Talal Center for Muslim-Christian Understanding, visit its Web site at http://cmcu.georgetown.edu/ (accessed August 15, 2009).—Ed.

4. More information on these institutions of higher learning is available at http://www.balamand.edu.lb/english/index.asp, and at http://www.usj.edu.lb/en/index.html (accessed August 15, 2009).—Ed.

5. The Web sites of these organizations are: http://www.arf-asia.org/aman.php, and http://www.fabc.org/ (accessed August 15, 2009).—Ed.

12

Abdul Ghaffar Khan and
the Servants of God

Islamic Nonviolence as an Instrument of Social Change

On January 20, 1988, Abdul Ghaffar Khan, one of the twentieth century's great proponents of nonviolent change, died at the age of ninety-eight and was buried in Jalalabad, Afghanistan. His funeral was the occasion of the first visit of an Indian prime minister to Pakistan in three decades and also occasioned a temporary cease-fire observed by both Soviet and *mujāhidīn* forces in Afghanistan, in order to allow free access to his burial. Three years before his death, Abdul Ghaffar told an interviewer, "For today's children and the world, my thoughts are that only if they accept nonviolence can they escape destruction, and live a life of peace. If this doesn't happen, then the world will be in ruins."

Early Years and Training

Abdul Ghaffar, called "Badshah Khan" (Khan of Khans) and "Fakhr-e-Afghan" (Pride of the Afghans) by his people, was a Pathan, born in 1890 in the village of Utmanzai, in the North-West Frontier Province of British India. Son of Behram Khan, a wealthy landowner and Mohamadzai chieftain, Abdul Ghaffar Khan began his education at a local *madrasa*, but left dissatisfied with the quality of education. He continued his studies at the Edwards Mission High School in Peshawar and then at the Mohammedan Anglo-Oriental College, as it was then called, in Aligarh.[1] His opposition to British rule led him to reject

---

Previously published in Leslie Tramontini and Chibli Mallat, *From Baghdad to Beirut: Arab and Islamic Studies in Honor of John J. Donahue, S.J.* (Beirut: Beiruter Texte und Studien, 2007), 371-82.

an opportunity offered to study in England as well as a coveted commission in an elite British Indian army unit.

Abdul Ghaffar's conscientization to the realities of colonial rule began early when, at the age of seven, he witnessed the bloody repression of a local uprising by the British forces. He saw moreover that not all the destruction of human life was due to the colonial rulers; throughout his youth he also witnessed the recurrent cycles of vendettas caused by blood feuds among the tribes. From these early experiences emerged the twin goals of his life: the need to struggle for Pathan independence—first from the British and later from Pakistan, where his region was assigned in the division of British India—and second, to establish the principles of nonviolence through popular education.

His first involvement in public life was as a schoolteacher in his home village. Together with the well-known Pashtun spiritual leader Haji Sahib Turangzai, Abdul Ghaffar founded thirty to forty village schools in the years 1912-1919. Haji Sahib, whose real name was Haji Fazl-e-Wahid, is a colorful figure in the history of the Frontier Province. A *dacoit* (bandit) in his youth, Turangzai underwent a conversion and eventually became a Sufi *pir* of the Qadiriyya Tariqa. In addition to waging jihad against colonial rule, Haji Sahib led a populist social reform aimed at ameliorating the situation of marginal sectors of society. He is remembered particularly for providing dowries for poor girls to marry and for his efforts at education. He is credited with founding a total of 120 schools in the North-West Frontier, including laying the foundation in 1911 for what is today the Islamia College of Peshawar. Haji Sahib's contributions to Pathan history were recently commemorated in a seminar held in Charsadda in April 2002.[2]

The schools set up by Haji Sahib and Abdul Ghaffar Khan, since they operated independently of the colonial administration, were viewed with suspicion by the British authorities. When the pair announced the explicitly anticolonial intentions of their schools, Abdul Ghaffar and Haji Sahib were forced to flee for their lives to tribal areas.

Like Gandhi and many others in British India, Abdul Ghaffar's opposition to colonial rule turned to public protest with the promulgation of the Rowlett Acts of 1919, which curtailed the rights of freedom of the press and assembly, suspended popular participation in the appointment of local officials, and permitted the imprisonment of dissenters without charge. When in Amritsar protesters against the acts were fired on by colonial troops, 379 were killed and many more injured, and Gandhi announced his policy of noncooperation. Abdul Ghaffar was among those arrested and imprisoned in the Frontier Province and spent the first of almost forty years he would pass in prison during his lifetime for nonviolent activities.

The Khilafat Movement (1919-1924)

Abdul Ghaffar's earliest political involvement was with the Khilafat movement, founded in 1919 by two brothers, Muhammad Ali and Shaukat Ali. The Khilafat Conference grew out of the repercussions resulting from the decision of the Ottoman state to enter World War I on the side of Germany. During the war, several leading Muslims in British India, including Muhammad Ali, were imprisoned for their support of the Ottomans, who were fighting against the British forces. After the war, there was widespread fear among Muslims in India that the Ottoman Empire would meet dismemberment in a fate similar to that accorded to the Austro-Hungarian Empire and that, in the process, the Holy Cities of Mecca and Medina would be placed under non-Muslim colonial rule.

Unlike the Muslim League, the heretofore leading Muslim nationalist organization in India, the Khilafat movement was pan-Islamic in orientation, with the Ottoman caliphate as its political symbol. The movement brought together Muslims of various religious backgrounds and political vision. Mahmud al-Hasan, leader of the conservative Deoband-based Jam'iyat-i Ulama-i Hind (Indian [Muslim Religious] Scholars Organization), was in contact with Ismail Enver Efendi and the Turkish leaders and acted as an Ottoman agent in Mecca. He was arrested by the Sharif Husayn and handed over to the British, who imprisoned him for the duration of the war in Malta.

The Sharif was hated by the followers of the Khilafat movement, who saw him as a rebel against the legitimate Sultan, an ambitious upstart who wanted to use his alliance with the British to pursue his rival claim to the caliphate. To Indian Muslims engaged in agitating for the expulsion of the British from India, the fear was that the Sharif's plan would open the door to British control over the Hijaz.

The Khilafat Conference rejected the 1920 Treaty of Sèvres, which humiliated the Ottomans by reducing Turkish sovereignty to approximately two-thirds of Anatolian territory, with Italian, Greek, French, and Armenian control over the rest and with Greek sovereignty in Thrace extending to the Black Sea. A particularly bitter article of the treaty stipulated shared Greek-Turkish authority over the Bosphorus, Marmara, and Dardanelles. England, France, Italy, and Greece were the principal guarantors to ensure that Turkey complied with the provisions, opening the possibility of further intervention if Turkey was not seen to be implementing the treaty.

It is noteworthy that among the Allied Powers who were signatories to the treaty was "The Hedjaz," an inclusion, obviously dictated by the British, which seemed to confirm the worst fears of those involved in the Khilafat Conference. The treaty was an affront to Muslims around the world, and in British India it was a key factor in mobilizing Muslim public opinion against colonial rule.

The leading Khilafat theorist was Abu'l Kalam Azad, a progressive thinker much influenced by the ideas of Jamal al-Din Afghani. According to Azad, the Islamic *ummah* formed a cohesive social organism opposed to *jāhilīyah*, a situation of political chaos and confusion. It was meant to be presided over by a *khalīfah*, who governed through consultation. The model of government was the period of the four Rightly Guided Califs. Although the caliphate became monarchical in form under the Umayyads and Abbasids, and subsequently reduced to figurehead status in Mamluk and Ottoman times, the institution of the caliphate was, in the view of the Khilafat Conference, essential to the nature of the *ummah* and owed allegiance by all Muslims.

Muhammad Ali succeeded in spreading these ideals to the Muslim masses of India, and in 1919-1922, the Khilafat Conference and the Indian National Congress worked as twin organizations with a joint leadership. In this period, Gandhi espoused the Khilafat cause, while Muhammad Ali and Shaukat Ali committed the Khilafat Conference to the noncooperation movement.

Unforeseen historical developments in the Middle East and events in the Indian subcontinent worked against the central concerns of the Khilafat movement and rendered its religious and political agenda irrelevant. In Turkey, with the emergence of Mustafa Kemal Atatürk and his expulsion of the foreign armies from Anatolia in 1921, the Treaty of Sèvres was set aside and replaced by that of Lausanne, which Bernard Lewis describes as "an international recognition of the demands formulated in the Turkish National Pact."[3] In India, fears of European occupation and mutilation of the Ottoman sultanate dissolved. When in the following year the sultanate was abolished, followed by the caliphate in 1924, by the same Muslim hero who defied and defeated the European powers, reactions among Indian Muslims were ambivalent and confused.

Moreover, the conquest of the holy cities by the Saudis in 1924 resolved the fears of Indian Muslims that the Hijaz would fall prey to British occupation. In India, during the same period, Muslim-Hindu relations deteriorated with local incidents of communal violence, and Muslims began to see their political agenda as different from that of Hindus.

However, the Khilafat movement was instrumental in providing a platform for Muslims such as Abdul Ghaffar Khan to involve themselves in the independence movement and develop the techniques of nonviolent resistance. Abdul Ghaffar made his first contact with Gandhi and other leaders at the Khilafat Conference in Delhi and then at the congress session at Nagpur in December 1920. Through his association with Gandhi, Abdul Ghaffar became the leading exponent of the noncooperation movement in the Frontier Province, advocating a boycott of colonial schools and courts, returning colonial academic degrees and military commissions, and the introduction of homespun cloth against British economic domination.

The Servants of God

In the 1920s, Abdul Ghaffar spent five years in prison for his protest activities. There his ideas continued to develop and led to an unshakeable commitment to nonviolence as a viable social and political option. In 1927, he founded a Pashto journal, *Pukhtoon*, to further his goals. However, Abdul Ghaffar's most profound contribution to Pathan history lay in his ability to instill in others the ideals by which he lived. In 1929, he founded a nonviolent movement called the *Khuda-i Khidmatgar*, the "Servants of God." The movement, which eventually enrolled over one hundred thousand Pashtun/Pathan followers, was dedicated to social reform, poverty alleviation, conscientization of the peasantry, and bringing to an end by nonviolent means British rule in the still-undivided India. Abdul Ghaffar became a close associate of Gandhi and remained so until the latter's assassination. He is still remembered today in the subcontinent as "Frontier Gandhi." His calls for social change, equitable land distribution, and religious harmony were seen as a threat by the British *raj* as well as by some local politicians, religious leaders, and landlords; and Abdul Ghaffar survived two assassination attempts and almost forty years of imprisonment.

In Gandhi, he found a fellow spirit, and Abdul Ghaffar traveled extensively through the rural areas of the North-West Frontier Province, preaching hard work, discipline, and forgiveness rather than vengeance, and set up hundreds of schools for tribal children. His charismatic personality attracted followers to his cause and the Khidmatgar movement. One historian describes Abdul Ghaffar's movement as follows:

> The fullest practical expression of Gandhism anywhere in India appeared among the Afghan tribes along the northwest frontier, under the leadership of Abdulghaffar Khan. Noted for their feuding and raiding, these tribesmen were won to an active and almost universal program of social self-reform. Feuding was stopped, discipline was imposed under the name of Service of God (*Khudā-i-khidmat*). . . . When nationalist campaigns for independence were launched, the Khudai-khidmatgars gave effective and faithful support. At all times they remained firmly nonviolent. Qur'anic encouragement of forgiveness as better than revenge became the foundation of a highly Muslim interpretation of Gandhi's ideas.[4]

Abdul Ghaffar applied the principles of Gandhi's civil disobedience movement to the demands of the semitribal Afghan frontier region. He urged his people to return the medals won in the British military, encouraged parents to withdraw their children from British universities, and advocated that Pathan lawyers cease practicing in British courts. In the 1930s and 1940s, the British army tried to crush the Khidmatgar movement with extreme brutality, employing mass killings, torture, and destruction of members' homes and fields.

The "Surkh Posh" (Red Shirts), as they were called from their practice of dying the homespun cloth in tanning dye, coupled social service and education with nonviolent protest, a practice that both won the hearts of the Pathan people and conscientized the tribal peoples to the Quit India movement. The Khidmatgars were early practitioners of techniques of conflict transformation, which they applied to the recurrent internecine feuds among the Afghan tribesmen. The British simply could not believe that a widespread nonviolent movement could arise in Pathan culture and responded with harsh repression. A historian notes: "The British treated Ghaffar Khan and his movement with a barbarity that they did not often inflict on other adherents of nonviolence in India. 'The brutes must be ruled brutally and by brutes,' stated a 1930 British report on the Pashtuns."[5]

Abdul Ghaffar spent fifteen of those years in prison, often in solitary confinement, but the Pathans refused to give up their disciplined nonviolence even in the face of severe repression. In the worst incident of the long struggle, the British killed over two hundred Khidmatgar members at the Kissa Khani (Qissakhwani) Bazaar in the heart of Peshawar on April 23, 1930. The arrest of Abdul Ghaffar's lieutenants prompted the Khidmatgar to declare a general strike, and a huge crowd assembled in the bazaar. The British confronted the assembly with armed troops and ordered the people to disperse. When the unarmed crowd refused to leave the bazaar, the troops opened fire. A historian has described the day:

> When those in front fell down wounded by the shots, those behind came forward with breasts bared and exposed themselves to the fire. The people stood their ground without getting into a panic. This continued from 11.00 until 5.00 P.M. The carnage stopped only because a regiment of Indian soldiers finally refused to continue firing on unarmed protesters, an impertinence for which they were severely punished.[6]

Another scholar notes that Abdul Ghaffar's commitment to nonviolence was even more sweeping than that of Gandhi's Indian National Congress. It also differed from the congress because the movement had "first of all, a religious basis. . . . It took as its objective both local socioeconomic reform and political independence. . . . Its adoption of nonviolence was more thorough than that of the Indian National Congress inasmuch as the Khudai Khidmatgar pledged themselves to nonviolence not only as a policy, but as a creed, a way of life."[7]

Nonviolence as an Islamic Principle

Abdul Ghaffar's nonviolent activism was firmly rooted in his understanding of Islam, which he summarized in the key words *maḥabba* (love), *'amal* (service), and *yakīn* (certitude, faith). He interpreted Islam as a moral code with pacifism at its center. He once related to Gandhi a discussion he had with a Punjabi Muslim who did not see the nonviolent core of Islam: "I cited chapter and verse from the [Qur'an] to show the great emphasis that Islam had laid on peace," which is its cornerstone. "I also showed to him how the greatest figures in Islamic history were known more for their forbearance and self-restraint than for their fierceness."[8] He viewed his struggle as a jihad in which only the enemy was holding swords.

Abdul Ghaffar's daughter-in-law, Begum Nasim Wali Khan, was interviewed shortly after his death. "He told people that Islam operates on a simple principle—never hurt anyone by tongue, by gun, or by hand. Not to lie, steal, and harm is true Islam," she said. Although firmly based on the principles of Islam, the movement was nonsectarian. When Hindus and Sikhs were attacked in Peshawar, ten thousand Khidmatgar members actively helped protect their lives and property. When communal riots broke out in Bihar in 1946-1947, Khan toured with Gandhi to bring about peace.

"Although the character of the movement was intensely Islamic . . . one of the objectives of the organization was the promotion of Hindu-Muslim unity,"[9] Joan Bondurant observes. A strong proponent of a united India with Hindus and Muslims living in peace, Abdul Ghaffar was deeply disappointed by the carnage that followed partition. Although the Khidmatgars were an Islamic movement, non-Muslims were accepted if they were willing to accept the movement's ideals and discipline. Abdul Ghaffar maintained close bonds with Hindus even after partition, which led to his being imprisoned in Pakistan on accusations of being "pro-India."

During the early years of the noncooperation program, Abdul Ghaffar Khan sent his children to the village schools that he founded, although he could have afforded better education. He felt that only if his own children were educated in the primitive facilities of the village schools could he counter criticism of the schools' material poverty. After partition, he sent his daughters and granddaughters to the Jesus and Mary Convent School in Murree. In a 1995 interview on Pakistani television, his eldest son, Abdul Ghani Khan, a leading Pashto poet, commented: "Whenever Father went to the convent to see them, he used to sit and talk to the Mother Superior and all the sisters. He had great love and admiration for them. He used to say they are wonderful people; they will not get married, they have no ambitions, they just want to serve."[10]

"Something Larger Than Oneself"

In the 1990s, Mukulika Banerjee, a lecturer in anthropology at University College London, spent months with Khan's family and interviewed seventy Khidmatgar members. She reports that while people initially joined the organization due to Abdul Ghaffar's charisma, later on it happened out of excitement of becoming part of something larger than themselves. Their commitment to nonviolence was stronger than their allegiance to Khan. In 1938, Gandhi asked some members of the movement if they would take up violence if Ghaffar Khan ordered them to, they replied emphatically "No!"

The principles of the *Khuda-i Khidmat* are well-expressed in the oath taken by new members:

1. I am a Servant of God: as God needs no service, serving his creation is serving Him.
2. I promise to serve humanity in the name of God.
3. I promise to refrain from violence and from taking revenge.
4. I promise to forgive those who oppress me or treat me with cruelty. I promise to refrain from taking part in feuds and quarrels and from creating enmity.

5. I promise to treat every Pathan as my brother and friend. I promise to refrain from antisocial customs and practices.

6. I promise to live a simple life, to practice virtue, and to refrain from evil.

7. I promise to practice good manners and good behavior and not to lead a life of idleness.

8. I promise to devote at least two hours a day to social work.

A Pathan Nationalist in Pakistan

Abdul Ghaffar was nominated a member of the Congress Party working committee in 1931, but his commitment to nonviolence led him to resign from the party in 1940 when the congress extended conditional support to England during World War II. He was once again imprisoned in 1944 for his continued opposition to the war. In defending his decision to withdraw from the congress, Abdul Ghaffar reaffirmed absolute nonviolence as a way of life:

> Some recent resolutions of the working Committee indicate that they are restricting the use of non-violence to the fight for India's freedom against constituted authority. . . . I should like to make it clear that the non-violence I have believed in and preached to my brethren of the Khudai-Khidmatgars is much wider. It affects all our life, and only that has permanent value. . . . The Khudai-Khidmatgars must, therefore, be what our name implies, servants of God and humanity by laying down our own lives and never taking any life.[11]

In the final years of the *raj*, the Khidmatgars opposed partition. When communal riots broke out following the announcement of the Partition Plan in 1946, Abdul Ghaffar visited riot-torn Bihar as part of a delegation to seek peace. Refusing to have anything to do with partition, the Khidmatgars boycotted the July 1947 referendum held to seek the opinion of the people of the North-West Frontier Province about whether or not they should join Pakistan.

The carnage that followed partition and the assassination of Gandhi were events that deeply troubled Abdul Ghaffar. To the end of his life, he continued to believe that partition was a mistake that could have been avoided. He refused to break his ties with India or to take part in the ongoing enmity between India and Pakistan. This led him to be considered pro-Indian by Pakistani authorities and he was repeatedly imprisoned for his outspoken criticism of successive governments.

A second cause of conflict between Abdul Ghaffar and the Pakistani authorities was the status of the Pathan homeland within the state of Pakistan. Taking advantage of the weak Afghan King Abdur Rahman Khan, the British in 1895 had forced a new border between Afghanistan and British India. Known as the Durand Line, the border cut the Pathan homeland in two, ignoring traditional tribal regions and bringing Peshawar and the Peshawar valley under British sovereignty. After partition and the establishment of the state of Pakistan, Afghanistan demanded a return to pre-1895 borders and the inclusion of Peshawar within Afghan borders. Abdul Ghaffar supported the Afghan proposal on the grounds of reunification of the Pathan homeland, a position that was viewed as treasonous by Pakistan. The issue, which remained a bone of contention between Pakistan and Afghanistan for over thirty years, led not only to Abdul Ghaffar's frequent imprisonment but to a concerted effort by Pakistani authorities to erase all memory of the Pathan nationalist Khuda-i Khidmat movement. The history and achievements of the movement were not permitted to be taught in schools or spoken of on television.

Although Abdul Ghaffar's journal *Pukhtoon* was suppressed by the Pakistani regime in 1947, a year later he founded and became first president of the opposition Pakistan People's Party. In 1956, together with other nationalist leaders, he founded the National Awami Party, which was banned in 1958. Once again arrested, in 1962, he was declared Prisoner of the Year by Amnesty International. Still refusing to recognize the validity of the Durand Line, which cut the Pathan homeland in two, he settled in the Pathan region of Afghanistan between 1964-1971. After returning to Pakistan, he was jailed again in 1975 and once again, at the age of ninety-three, in 1983.

The Significance of Abdul Ghaffar

Evaluating the achievements of someone who has had such significant impact on the history of a nation and his people, extending over a period of so many years, is not an easy task. Yet the life of Abdul Ghaffar demands such an evaluation. Several elements of such an evaluation seem particularly important.

1. Neither the habit of violent response to conflict nor that of peacemaking and forgiveness is an innate and unalterable feature of human nature. Both ways of acting can be built and taught, and both can be changed or fall into disuse. Abdul Ghaffar was successful in overcoming a longstanding tendency to settle tribal feuds by local warfare through educating people and providing them with the tools and motivation to find viable alternatives to violent resolution. By calling on the Islamic invitation to forgiveness and reconciliation and appealing to ethnic pride and solidarity, he was able to convince his fellow Pathans that violence was not the only, or even the most effective, solution to human conflict. Like Gandhi, he was able to teach that even political goals could be better achieved through a comprehensive adherence to concerted effort and nonviolent discipline. In this, he showed that no nation is a slave to its past and that time-honored attitudes and habits of violence can be changed.

On the other hand, subsequent history of the Pathan peoples in the North-West Frontier Province and Afghanistan shows that the lessons taught by Abdul Ghaffar and accepted for a time by his people had no lasting effect. Perhaps no nation in Asia in the past forty years has suffered more than Afghanistan from the recourse of a series of armed conflicts. Extreme positions of left and right, secular and religious, have dominated the political, social, and military scene and left the country divided and in ruins. Reliance on questionable influence from foreign interests, whether from the Soviet Union, Saudi Arabia, Pakistan, or the United States, has served to eradicate from public life the principles of solidarity, self-reliance, and pacifist discipline that were instilled by Abdul Ghaffar. It would seem that nonviolence is an ideal that must be taught anew to each generation if it is to be sustained over a period of time.

2. Abdul Ghaffar was neither the first nor the last to interpret Islam as a religion that espouses and teaches the principles of nonviolence, but he was one of the few who succeeded in translating this conviction into a mass movement. His understanding of jihad as the struggle to work in nonviolent ways for justice, freedom, and human dignity on Islamic principles is one that inspires individual Muslims, but is still awaiting committed, charismatic personalities like Abdul Ghaffar to shape the thinking and actions of popular movements that can affect history. The Islamic principles of "love, service, and faith," self-restraint, and forgiveness enunciated by Abdul Ghaffar are much needed if the Islamic *ummah* is to fulfill its destiny to be *raḥmat li'l-'ālamīn*, "a mercy for the universe."

3. The significance of Abdul Ghaffar Khan in the recent history of peace activism is his conviction of the importance of discipline in peacemakers. Working for peace and building peace runs counter to many natural impulses. When one is a victim of oppression, the normal human instinct is to fight back, to respond to violence with more of the same. Forgiveness does not come easily, nor does patience or the kind of forbearance that places long-term goals ahead of immediate, spontaneous reactions. Abdul Ghaffar and the Khidmatgars were able to counter these natural impulses only by a comprehensive and consistent commitment to nonviolence that adopted self-discipline as the communal bond, enabling them to be strong, patient, and forbearing even in the face of brutal violence.

4. Finally, the story of Abdul Ghaffar shows that hope can arise in surprising places. Courageous individuals with a vision can make an impact and transform history. At the present moment in history when polarization and the recourse to war and terrorism seem to dominate the policies of world leaders and opposition movements, the example of Abdul Ghaffar offers a way out of the destructive and self-destructive cycle of violence and counterviolence. I close, as I began, with a reference to Abdul Ghaffar's funeral in Jalalabad. It has been described as "the world's longest funeral procession," with over twenty kilometers of bumper-to-bumper traffic—cars, buses, and truckloads of villagers, tribesmen on horseback, thousands of mourners on foot—all paying final homage to this man who offered a genuine alternative to a violent world.

Notes

1. Later named Aligarh Muslim University.—Ed.
2. "Charsadda: Independence Heroes Remembered," *Dawn*, April 15, 2002, 2.

3. Bernard Lewis, *The Emergence of Modern Turkey* (London: Oxford University Press, 2001), 254-55.

4. Marshall G. S. Hodgson, *The Venture of Islam*, vol. 3, *The Gunpowder Empires and Modern Times* (Chicago: University of Chicago Press, 1977), 344.

5. Amitabh Pal, "A Pacifist Uncovered," *The Progressive,* February 2002.

6. Gene Sharp, *The Politics of Nonviolent Action* (Boston: Porter Sargent, 1973).

7. Joan Bondurant, *Conquest of Violence: The Gandhian Philosophy of Conflict* (Princeton, N.J.: Princeton University Press, 1988), 134.

8. Ibid., 139.

9. Ibid., 135.

10. Abdul Ghani Khan, television interview, available at www.harappa.com/sounds/ghani0.html (accessed August 15, 2009).

11. Abdul Ghaffar, cited by Fazal-ur-Rahim Marwat in *The Frontier Post*, available at www.theamericanmuslim.org/tam.php/features/print/khan_abdul_ghaffar_remembering_a_non_violent_soldier/ (accessed August 15, 2009).

13

Christian Reflections on a Qur'anic Approach to Ecology

When a Christian reads the Qur'an or the sacred scriptures of another religion, our primary goal must be to *understand*. We approach such a study to be enriched by the wisdom that God has generously planted, at all times and places, in all religions and cultures. The early Fathers of the Christian community were well aware that the divine wisdom that God had so bountifully distributed among men and women should be understood as the effect of the work of God's own Spirit. In a beautiful observation attributed to St. Ambrose, it is said: "Every truth, by whomever it is expressed, comes from the Holy Spirit" [*omne verum, a quocumque dicatur, a Spiritu Sancto est*].[1]

During his papacy, Pope John Paul II encouraged Christians to study and learn from the wisdom that has been granted to others. Already in 1979, in the first year after he became pope, he said, "The Christian ought to have great interest to observe truly religious peoples and to read and learn the testimonies of their wisdom, to confront the direct proofs of their faith, to the point of recalling the words of Jesus, 'Not even in Israel have I found such faith'" (Luke 7:9; Matt. 8:10). If this principle is valid in general, how much more is it applicable to the followers of Islam, our fellow believers who trace their origins in faith to Abraham, who like us adore the one God, and whose commitment to conform themselves to God's supreme will is so similar to our own.

For this reason, when Christians encounter passages of the Qur'an that speak of the relationship of humans to the natural world, we must ask ourselves: What is the truth that God can teach to me and to my Christian community through these passages? Sometimes the answer will be a reaffirmation of what we have already learned by way of our own Christian tradition. At other times, we will find expressions that, while not denied by our own Scriptures, have not been so explicitly stated or so thoroughly developed as they have been in the Qur'an. On still other occasions, we will discover new visions and approaches

A previous version of this essay was published as "The Teaching of the Qur'an about Nature," in *Bulletin of the Pontifical Council for Interreligious Dialogue* 79 (1992): 90-96. Reprinted by permission.

to the natural world in which we can discern the movement of the Spirit of Truth and that we can profitably integrate into our own ways of thinking and acting. In this brief article, I would like to offer insights from the Qur'an that can serve as theological bases for an Islamic approach to questions of ecology.

Purpose of Creation and Human Responsibility

The fundamental principle that underlies the approach of the Qur'an to the natural world is the serious nature of the divine project. The Qur'an states: "We have not created the heaven and the earth and all that is in them in jest. If we had wanted to look for a pastime, we would have been able to find it in Ourself" (21:16-17). Similarly, "And we have not created the heavens and the earth and all that is in them as a game. We have created them for no other purpose but the truth; but most people do not know this" (44:38-39).

The earth, sea, atmosphere, and all the creatures that they contain are not the result of some divine sport, nor are they the casual result of processes begun and left to follow their own destiny by an irresponsible creator. The approach of the Qur'an to nature is always theological. God has carried out all this creative activity and continues to act in this world for a reason. God's way of acting in nature is purposeful, part of a great, eternal design. Therefore, nature must never be treated lightly, for it possesses a seriousness that derives from the end to which God has destined it at the beginning and that will continue on until the Day of Judgment.

This purpose can be expressed as "to give glory to God," an attitude well known by the psalmist. As the Qur'an puts it: "The seven heavens and the earth and all that is in them praise Him and nothing exists which does not celebrate His glory. But you do not understand their praise" (17:44). And again, "Haven't you seen that God is glorified by everything that is in the heavens and on earth, and by the birds in their flight? He knows the prayer of each and their glorification, and God is aware of all that they do" (24:41; see also 57:1; 59:1; 61:1).

Nature is "*muslim*"[2] because it carries out the will of God, it submits to God's commands, it acts within the limits that God has set for it. The birds, for example, give glory to God simply by being what they are; in this way they fulfill the purpose for which they were created. In the whole universe, it is only humankind that can choose freely either to obey and submit itself to the commands of God or to refuse to believe, to be ungrateful, and to act corruptly.

In an enigmatic verse, the Qur'an states: "Look, We offered the *trust* to the heavens and the earth and the mountains, but they refused to carry it and were afraid of it. But man accepted [the challenge]. He has indeed been unjust and ignorant" (33:72). The Qur'anic scholars offer various interpretations concerning the "trust" that the heavens, earth, and mountains were afraid to bear, but that humankind accepted. Some say that the trust refused by the natural world consisted in accepting the challenge to give a free response of submission and service to God. Others hold that the trust was the responsibility to establish a moral social order on earth. Still others claim that the trust implies a commitment to guide and administer the universe in the manner of a responsible steward. The Qur'an recognizes that even if humankind has often failed to perform properly this difficult task, the commitment to respond freely to the challenge of obeying God's commands constitutes the true greatness of humanity.

Whatever the proper interpretation of the above-mentioned verse, the relation between humanity and nature is clearly stated. The natural world must perforce be *muslim*. It must submit to God's designs. It must give glory to the Creator. Only humankind is able to accept or to refuse the commands of God, to care for or to destroy nature, to act in a responsible and moral manner or else to "pollute the earth." In this way, humans give glory to God not because they are forced to do so, but through wisdom and by the use of free will to show their privileged place in nature by taking up the trust that has been granted them by God. This very freedom of response also means that man is also capable of misusing this trust, of dissipating his primacy through greed and injustice.

It is clear from the Qur'an that humankind will one day have to answer for its sins against the natural world. In a powerful poetic passage the Qur'an invokes the Day of Judgment and presents the image of the natural universe rising up to accuse humankind of its crimes: "When the earth shall quake violently, and the earth shall bring forth its burdens, and man shall say: 'What is happening to it?' on that day, it shall tell its stories" (99:1-4).

How many tales, how many complaints covering so many centuries, will the earth be able to tell, of contaminated seas, of polluted air, of lands made desolate through overproduction and wartime destruction, of forests stripped, of animals killed unnecessarily for sport or for their furs, hides, and tusks, of whole races of animals and plants wiped out through the indiscriminate use of pesticides and the dumping of industrial wastes, of its beauties disfigured and its treasures sacked, all in the name of greed masquerading as progress? The point is that humans will not go unpunished for the sins and misdeeds that they have committed against the earth. The Qur'an views nature as a creature of God, and as such it has an inalienable dignity that should be respected. Nature is not a neutral field for those who possess the greatest power, capabilities, and resources to exploit it according to the principle of "first come, first served." It is a possession entrusted by God to be used, as a good administrator ought to do, for the good of all.

While the Qur'an affirms the duty of humans to treat nature with care and respect, it does not propose a romantic nostalgia that would prohibit the proper use and development of natural resources. Nature is seen as a blessing of God for humankind, and as such ought to be utilized for the needs and happiness of the human family. In the Surat al-Nahl, the Chapter of the Bee (16), which could be called the Surah of Nature, humankind is taught that nature is a gift that the loving Creator has given to us for our benefit and pleasure:

And God has created domestic animals *for you*. From them you get warm clothes, you can find many uses for them, and you can eat them.

And what a beautiful thing it is to bring them home in the evening and to drive them out to pasture in the morning. They carry your merchandise to lands which otherwise you could not reach except with great difficulty. Your Lord is really Gentle and Merciful. And God has made *for you* horses, mules, and donkeys so that you can ride them and decorate them, and God is creating other things you don't know about. (16:5-8)

It is God who sends down rain from heaven, which you can drink and which causes the plants to grow, where your animals can pasture. With rain, God causes grain, olives, date palms, and grapes to grow, and all kinds of fruits *for you*. There are truly signs in this for those who think about them. (16:10-11)

And God has subjected to you the night and the day. The sun and the moon and the stars are also subject to you by God's command. In this there are signs for those who can use their minds. Think of the various colors that God has spread over the earth *for you*. Here too are signs for those who remember to think about them. And God has subjected the sea to you, so that you can eat fresh fish, and gather shells and other ornaments to wear. You can see ships plowing across its waves, so that you can go seek God's bounties and so that you give thanks. And God has set up firm mountains on earth so that it does not slip away underneath you, and rivers, paths, and landmarks so you do not get lost; also by the stars you can find your way. (16:12-16)

These Qur'anic passages outline some of the many blessings that God bestows on humankind in the natural world: animals; rain; night and day; the sun, moon, and stars; the sea and all it contains; mountains; rivers; and landmarks. The passage emphasizes repeatedly that God has created all these things *for you* (16:5, 8, 11, 13). They are gifts of the beneficent God intended not only for humankind's survival (food, drink, shelter, clothing) and convenience (ships and landmarks for travel and commerce), but also simply to give humans aesthetic pleasure and admiration of God's greatness. "What a beautiful thing it is to bring them [cattle and flocks] home in the evening and to drive them out to pasture in the morning." Or, "Think of the various colors that God has spread over the earth for you." In nature, God has provided much of what makes life good and pleasurable and beautiful, something to be truly grateful for.

Moreover, there is a message for humans in all God's gifts. The passage constantly underlines that nature's gifts all contain "signs" for those who are willing to take the time to think about them, for those who are ready to reflect on what this magnificent world is for. Nature is not simply something "given," raw material to be selfishly used any way one wants. Nature is rather a textbook by which men and women can come to know God better and to know their own relationship to the Creator of all things.

Nature as Our Teacher

The theme of nature as teacher runs through the Qur'an. Humans are taught not to take for granted the wonders of the natural universe, but rather to become aware of them, to reflect upon them, and to come to know God through them. The Qur'an states:

> Have you thought about your agriculture? Do you produce it yourselves, or are We the sower? Had We wished, We could have reduced it all to rubble, and then you would have been wondering. (56:63-65)

> Have you seen the water you drink? Were you the ones who brought it down from the clouds, or did We send it down? Had We wished, We could have made it bitter. If only you would give thanks. (56:68-70)

Elsewhere the Qur'an invites humans to reflect on fire, trees, on the alternation of day and night, on the stability of river beds, on landmarks in the desert, on the fixed stars, on bees and the mystery of honey, on the rebirth of the earth after rains and on the movement of winds. The list could be extended indefinitely, but these few examples must suffice to show that nature is full of lessons for those who are ready to learn from it.

The first lesson we can learn from nature is the unlimited creative power and the Lordship of God, who can accomplish wonders impossible for humans. The progress of scientific knowledge in modern times merely underlines the insignificance and weakness of humans before the great processes of nature. In an assertion reminiscent of God's message to Job in the Bible, the Qur'an states that "God is creating other things you don't know about" (16:8).

A second lesson is the mercy and love of God for humankind. The good things brought by nature ought to bring people to an awareness of the goodness and generosity of God. The proper response to God for the things revealed in nature is faith and gratitude.

A third lesson sought by nature to those who reflect on it is that the recurrent cycle of nature and its order should lead us to be conscious of God as a proficient governor who "measures" the capacities and the limits of everything and governs the universe in an orderly fashion. The order of nature is not haphazard, but an order that reflects the wise reliability of its Creator. The Qur'an explains this as follows:

> The sun moves to its proper place—this is the decree of the Almighty, the All-Knowing. And the moon, We have determined its phases, until it returns like a curved staff. The sun is not going to overtake the moon, nor the night outstrip the day, for each is floating in its own orbit. (36:38-40)

According to the Qur'an, nature indicates a wise, good, powerful, stable God, and these indications are evident to anyone who seeks to understand them. However, many people, because of a short-sighted preoccupation with immediate causes and temporary phenomena, ignore the message of nature and live as if they themselves were the ultimate goal, or as if there were no ultimate purpose in life. So long as life proceeds smoothly and nature acts as an obedient servant, they lose interest in seeking the Lord of nature and His will. In times of crisis they return to God, but when the crisis situation is resolved, they fall back into their egocentric indifference. The Qur'an describes this human phenomenon as follows:

> It is He who enables your journey on land and on sea. When you are in ships which sail forward driven by a fair wind, they rejoice, but when a stormy wind comes upon them and waves surge over them from every side, they think that they are being overwhelmed. At that time, they call upon God, sincerely professing submission to Him: "If you save us from this, we shall be truly thankful." But when He saves them, they resort to acting rebelliously on earth. (10:22-23)

For humans, true wisdom is awareness and gratitude to the Lord of nature in times of safety and prosperity, *before* calamity occurs.

The Qur'an teaches that nature is itself one of the great miracles of God. Some people tend to define a miracle as "that which goes beyond the bonds of nature." The Qur'an teaches that God is well capable of breaking the bonds of nature and states that God's suspensions of natural laws are a proof of God's power. However, the real miracle of nature is found not in the interruption of the natural order but rather in the regularity that God has imposed on it. The predictability of natural laws (sunrise and sunset; the movements of the stars; the recurrence of rainy seasons; the birth of animals; the very fact that the earth does not explode, sink, or go spinning off into space; or that the whole universe does not self-destruct) are all miracles that point to a continual sovereign order established by God. The progress of natural sciences such as geology, meteorology, astronomy, physics, oceanography, agriculture, zoology, and botany ought to lead humanity to a deeper awareness of the miraculous regularity and logic of nature.

Rather than guiding people to a delusion of self-sufficiency, science ought to lead the believer to think about how much of the miraculous is surrounding him. This demands that people study the natural sciences not only to learn about quantitative and spatial relationships, but to strive for true discernment and understanding for a profound perception that it is the divine hand that guides the processes of nature in accord with the purposes that God has established for it.

It is only God, the source and governor of the marvelous regularity of nature, who is able to suppress or suspend natural laws. In fact, it is God's subversion of the natural order that will be the dramatic sign of the imminent Day of Judgment. The Qur'an foresees the eschatological Day of Chaos, when the laws of nature will be suspended and humankind will be called upon to answer for how they have lived. The Qur'an announces:

> When the sun will be overturned, and when the stars fall, and when the mountains will be set in motion, and when the great camels with their young will be abandoned, and when the wild animals will all take refuge together, and when the sea rises . . . and when heaven will be torn away, and when the Fire will be lit and when the Garden will be brought near, at that time, every soul will know what has been prepared for it. (81:1-6, 11-14)

This and similar descriptions of the final chaos serve as an important warning concerning the way in which we live on this earth. A day is coming when we will all have to give an account of our stewardship over the natural world. We can return with profit to the telling passage in the Qur'an:

> On that day, [the earth] will tell its stories, because your Lord will inspire it. On that day, mankind will come forth in small groups to show its deeds. Whoever has committed even a gram of goodness will see it then, and whoever has done even a gram of evil will see it at that time. (99:4-8)

These elements of a Qur'anic approach to ecology arouse many echoes in the Christian reader. When a Christian reads the Qur'anic teaching on nature, it is like going to one's storehouse and finding things old and new. Some images are new and vivid and invite the reader to a renewed examination of our indifference or irreverence toward the divine message found in nature. Other emphases can awaken in the heart of the Christian reader a sense of respect for God's creation and a greater awareness of the seriousness of our sins against the natural world.

The Qur'anic message reinforces the awareness that, in many important aspects, Christians and Muslims are united in the conviction that only God ought to be worshiped and that God's will ought to reign sovereign in our lives. The central element of the teaching of Jesus in the Gospel, the Reign of God— that God reigns and is the supreme ruler of the universe—is not a concept foreign to the spirit and the teaching of the Qur'an.

Notes

1. Quoted in Thomas Aquinas, *ST* II, q. 109, a. 1 ad 1.
2. *Muslim, islam,* and *aslama* are related concepts in the Qur'an referring to the notion of "self-surrender" to God, which results in inner and outer peace.—Ed.

14

The Idea of Holiness in Islam

Islamic spirituality is a path to holiness by which a Muslim, by internalizing the spiritual riches found in Islamic life and practice, is gradually transformed into a person who desires to respond to God's grace with faith and love and to do God's will in all things. In this paper, I will try to present the main characteristics of Islamic spirituality and to note points where Islamic and Christian concepts of holiness coincide, as well as areas where the outlooks of the two religions would tend to diverge. In this way, I hope that some areas will emerge where the particular characteristics of Islamic and Christian holiness might open doors for discussion and growth between Christians and Muslims in dialogue. I will conclude with brief personal reflections on the encounter between Christian and Muslim spirituality.

A Qur'an-Centered Spirituality

Islamic spirituality is a Qur'an-centered spirituality. Reading, reciting, listening to, studying, and reflecting on the Qur'an make up a great part of the devotional life of Muslims. As Muslims believe the Qur'an to be the literal word of God, God's own speech, their encounters with the Qur'an are for them meetings with God who reveals, teaches, and forms believers in holiness. The centrality of the Qur'an in the spiritual life of Muslims is evident in many ways. Islamic education of children begins by learning to read the Qur'an. Religious training begins not with simple catechisms or summaries of faith, but by coming to know the Arabic text of the Qur'an. This approach might seem surprising given the fact that for over 80 percent of Muslims Arabic is a foreign language, one that few Muslims will ever master during their lifetimes. At the young age at which they begin to memorize portions of the Qur'an, it is not only non-Arab Muslims who understand little of the text. Because of its archaic language and the Qur'an's allusive, associative style, even modern Arab children can understand little of what they are memorizing.

Previously published in *Pro Dialogo* 92, no. 2 (1996): 220-40. Reprinted by permission.

Thus, content, at the earliest stages of Islamic education, is secondary to the immediate encounter with the Speech of God, the Holy One. Understanding is expected to come with time, training, and exposure. For those who practice Islam seriously, there are countless occasions to come to understand the meaning of the message. In the Islamic world, educational programs at the mosques, Qur'an study groups, sermons, newspaper columns, and magazine articles center on Qur'anic teaching and its applications.

The focus on the Qur'anic text, even before and beyond its meaning, points to a central Islamic element of Qur'an-based spirituality. The Qur'an is not simply a book to be read, understood, and followed. It is God's own message for humankind, the very encounter with which is for believers an act of faith, reverence, and piety, a personal encounter with the God who speaks. When Muslims listen to a recitation of the Qur'an, their ears glorify God; when they recite the Qur'an, their vocal chords recite a speech that is God's own; in memorizing Qur'anic verses, Muslims take God's own revelation and make it a part of their mind, brain, and person.

The first encounter of Muslim children with the Qur'anic text is by memorization, achieved through oral recitation in common and then through private study. While every Muslim is expected to memorize portions of the Qur'an, the Islamic community grants a special place of honor to those who have memorized the entire Qur'an. Such a person is called *ḥāfiẓ* (m.) or *ḥāfiẓa* (f.) It is considered sinful for a *ḥāfiẓ* to allow this competence to lapse through negligence, and thus the *ḥāfiẓ* is taking on a lifetime responsibility or trust. A Christian scholar has underlined the importance of memorizing the Qur'an for Muslims by likening it to a Christian's reception of the Eucharist, by which Christ himself physically enters the believer and, as food to bring about health, growth, and sustenance, becomes a transforming part of the believer's very self. So also are the brain and memory of the Muslim fed and sustained by God's own speech.

Communal listening to the recited Qur'an forms Muslims into a community of those who "hear the Word of God and keep it." In predominantly Muslim countries, Qur'an recitation can be heard continually on radio and television. Evenings of Qur'an recitation are relaxed but serious occasions of religious socializing. National and international Qur'an recitation competitions are an Islamic equivalent of Eucharistic Congresses among Catholics.

Reciting the Qur'an is a sacred act, demanding careful attention and preparation. It begins, like all Islamic duties, with an act of intention (*nīyah*), by which the Muslim consecrates the time and his/her efforts to God's service. The spiritual implications attached to the act of recitation, in that the Muslim is not simply reading a book aloud but voicing divine speech, can be seen in Al-Ghazali's ten-step instructions for one who is preparing to recite the Qur'an:

1. *Reflect on the importance* of what you are about to do; remember God's kindness in delivering His speech to humankind;

2. *Consider the greatness of the Speaker*, that it is God's own words you will speak;

3. *Enter fully into the world of the Qur'an*, abandoning your own thoughts;

4. *Ponder the words*, do not simply hear them passively;

5. *Try to understand* the meanings [the levels of meaning] contained in the passage;

6. *Get rid of all obstacles* (personal preferences, pride, preconceived ideas) that prevent you from hearing the message in its purity;

7. Be aware that this is *a message first for you*, not simply for others;

8. *Respond emotionally* (e.g., grief, fear, hope, gratitude) to the message;

9. Reach a state where you realize that *the message is from God, not from you*;

10. *Hand over the act completely to God*; get rid of any sense of your own ability.

Recitation of Qur'anic verses is an essential part of the *ṣalāh*, the daily ritual prayer, which means that Muslims who perform *ṣalāh* conscientiously will recite (or listen to) the Qur'an five times a day. Every Friday's sermon begins with Qur'anic verses, and the recitation of the Qur'an begins ceremonies such as marriage, circumcision, and burial, as well as the opening of various occasions such as meetings, academic congresses, festivals, and parliamentary sessions.

Public recitation of the Qur'an is paralleled by the reading of the Qur'an in private, the primary devotional act of Muslims. The Qur'an has been divided into thirty approximately equal parts so that the Muslim can read one section every day in a month. Particularly during the month of Ramadan, many Muslims try to read the entire Qur'an. The sections of the Qur'an are further subdivided into small portions of three to four pages for daily reading and reflection.

The Path to Holiness in the Pillars of Islam

Well known are the five pillars of Islam: the profession of faith (*shahādah*), the daily prayers (*ṣalāh*), the tithe for the poor (*zakāh*), the fast of Ramadan (*sawm*) and, for those who are able, the pilgrimage (*ḥajj*) to Mecca. These are basic obligations for every Muslim which, if one were to omit without sufficient cause, that person would be considered culpable. Since the pillars of Islam are essential to the obedient practice of Islam, it might be worth exploring the implications for spirituality contained in these acts.

The Profession of Faith (al-shahādah)

The profession of faith in the Oneness of God and the prophethood of Muhammad is that which constitutes a person a member of the Islamic community (*ummah*). The first part of the profession "There is no god but The God" expresses the universal dimension of Islam, that which Muslims share with other monotheists, while the second part, "Muhammad is the messenger of God" expresses that which is unique, particular to Islam, and distinguishes Muslims from other religious communities.

The profession of faith, preceded by the personalizing words "I bear witness that," is proclaimed from the minarets five times a day in the *adhān*, the call to prayer. It is significant that after every line of the call to prayer, a period of silence is inserted so that Muslims have time to repeat the phrase silently in their hearts. The point is that Muslims should not remain passive listeners to the call; by repeating it inwardly, they make it their own.

The *shahādah* has many functions in Islamic life. When a baby is born, the parents immediately whisper the profession of faith into its ears, so that the first human words heard will be those that make the child a Muslim. In Islam there is no rite of initiation comparable to baptism. A new convert to Islam professes the *shahādah* in the presence of witnesses and is thereby considered a Muslim.

As the *shahādah* marks the entry of a person into the Islamic community, so is it also the passport to the next world. Dying persons are encouraged to recite the profession of faith so long as they are conscious, and if they are not conscious or in a coma, the bystanders are to whisper the prayer in their ears. A common Egyptian Prayer for a Happy Death is as follows: "O God, enlighten my heart with the light of faith at the end of my life when my death throes are upon me, that I may say: 'I bear witness that there is no god but God, and Muhammad is the messenger of God.'"

Finally, the *shahādah* is the most proper form of *dhikr*, repetitive prayer, which Muslims are encouraged to repeat over and over, whether in informal prayer gatherings or as ejaculatory prayer to accompany the ordinary tasks of daily life. Mystically oriented Muslims hold that the *shahādah* is the eternal speech of paradise. As one of the best beloved Turkish hymns puts it: "The rivers of heaven sing, 'There is no god but God.'"

Ritual Daily Prayer (al-ṣalāh)

Best-known among the pillars of Islam is the daily ritual prayer. This might be called "liturgical" prayer in the sense that the form and content have been handed down by the community since the time of Muhammad and Muslims are not free to make personal variations. How to perform *ṣalāh* is the first prayer taught to Muslim children; it is preeminently "prayer" for Muslims, to the extent that another term (*du'ā'*) is used for all other forms of prayer.

Although the *ṣalāh* is not a lengthy prayer and can be accomplished in less than ten minutes, the timing of the prayer is significant. The prayer is a reaffirmation of submission to God at the key moments of the day: at *dawn*, the start of a new day; at high *noon*, at the moment of intense daily business; *mid-afternoon*, when the day begins anew in those parts of the world that have an afternoon repose; after *sunset*, at the close of the daylight hours; in the *evening* before retiring. As such, the prayer may be compared to Christian monastic practice of consecrating the day to God by structuring work, rest, study, eating, and recreation within the rhythm of the recitation of the Divine Office.

Before undertaking such a momentous and august activity, Muslims must purify themselves with water. The ritual of physically washing the hands, feet, and face, with special attention to the organs of the senses—nose, ears, mouth—symbolizes the inner purification that is the proper disposition for prayer. When they have defiled themselves through a ritually impure action, they must perform a full bath before entering into the state of prayer.

Similar to the prayers of Christian liturgy, the *ṣalāh* is actually made up of many separate parts, each of which speak to various elements of Islamic spirituality. Like all devotional acts in Islam, the *ṣalāh* begins with a prayer of *intention*. This is an entering into a sacred state, a dedication of the act totally to God. After performing the prayer of intention until the conclusion of the prayer, Muslims may not look right or left nor may they depart from the content of the prayer. If one should do so, the act is void and must be performed again.

A characteristic of *ṣalāh* is that it is accompanied by fixed bodily postures. These positions distinguish this prayer from mental or vocal prayer in that the body, mind, and senses (speech and hearing) are coordinated in the act. "Islam" means the submission of one's life totally to God, and the positions of the body, culminating in the full prostration with forehead, hands, and knees touching the ground, symbolically represent this submission. The series of prostrations is generally repeated two to four times, according to the particular prayer time. The full prostration, a position that expresses simultaneously surrender, humility, and trust (in that position, one is defenseless against any aggressive action), so perfectly expresses the relationship of the dependent creature in front of the Almighty Creator that Muslims are forbidden to prostrate themselves before any living or dead person.

Within the ritual, there are various other forms of prayer. The ritual opens with the phrase: "Glory to God and sing His praise." By proclaiming the glory of God (*subhan'Allah*) in praising Him (*bi-ḥamdihi*), the Muslim believes that he or she is joining the heavenly chorus of angels who continually proclaim God's glory. Outside the ritual *ṣalāh*, glorifying God with the "*subhān*" is one of the most common forms of private devotional prayer. Praising God (*al-ḥamdu li'llah*) is a common expression that Muslims (and Christian Arabs) make at times of joy, good fortune, and, more surprisingly, tragedy. The idea is that all things that happen, both good and bad, come from God, and God should be praised in them all.

The heart of the ritual prayer is the recitation of the *Fatihah*, the opening chapter of the Qur'an, followed by an "Amen" in loud voice, and the recitation of Qur'anic verses. The *Fatihah*, sometimes regarded as the equivalent of the "Our Father" among Christians, plays an important role in Islamic spirituality. It combines praise of the God of the universe and acknowledgment of God's tender, motherly compassion (the Qur'anic terms for "compassionate" or "merciful" derive from the Arabic word for "womb") together with a profession of

God's unique worthiness to be worshiped and sought for help, and a petition to keep Muslims on the Straight Path of an upright, holy life.

This is always followed by "Amen" spoken in a loud voice. It is the great communitarian affirmation that Muslims share with Jews and Christians. Their pronouncing of the ancient affirmation, boldly and with great confidence after the *Fatihah*, may be compared to the Great Amen that concludes the communitarian response to the Christian Eucharistic prayer.

Closely connected with the idea of praise is that of *thanksgiving*. The Qur'anic verse "Give thanks to the gracious God, if you are His worshipers" (16:114) establishes the place of thanksgiving in the daily prayer. Failing to thank God is an omission for which the Muslim should repent. A prayer of the Sufi Qadiriyya Order states: "I take refuge with You from my failure to thank You."

The notion of "taking refuge in God" is less familiar to Christians but plays an important role in Islamic spirituality. It is an act of throwing oneself upon God's boundless mercy. In the *ṣalāh*, as at every recitation of the Qur'an, Muslims take refuge in God from the temptations of Satan. As in the aforementioned prayer, *a'ūdhu b'illāh* is an act of repentance, taking refuge in God's mercy when one has sinned. On many other occasions of daily life, Muslims take refuge in God (e.g., on receiving a compliment, they seek God's mercy that they not be tempted by pride; on hearing slander or obscenity, they seek God's refuge that they not give in to illicit enjoyment).

The prayer of *silence* finds its place in the *ṣalāh*. At each of the moments of the prayer there is an obligatory pause, a brief time of silence and composure. This is meant to prevent the prayer from becoming a relentless, rote, headlong rush from start to conclusion. Though brief, these moments of silence in the *ṣalāh* form an essential part of Islamic spirituality. Prayer is a privileged moment of contact with the Creator, the Lord of Life, and must never be allowed to become hurried, routine, mindless, heedless of its sacred and august function.

There is no prayer of repentance in the prayer rite itself, but it is recommended that Muslims insert a prayer to seek *forgiveness* immediately before the greeting of peace. This is usually performed at the morning and evening prayer. The importance of repentance (*tawbah*) in Islamic spirituality cannot be underestimated. Absolutely essential for forgiveness of sin and implying a commitment to reorient one's life according to God's will, sincere repentance brings about the immediate and full forgiveness of all sins through God's gracious action. No further rite of reconciliation is needed, nor in fact exists in Islam, except in some Sufi circles.

Before the conclusion of the prayer, there is a moment for personal prayers of *petition*. Sitting, with palms upraised, Muslims express silently their daily needs, hopes, and desires. Thus, while the *ṣalāh* is mainly a prayer of praise and expression of submission, the needs of the believers also find a place. Muslims are further encouraged to express their needs in private prayer (*du'ā'*). Finally, the prayer concludes with a Greeting of Peace toward the community. Having earlier in the rite greeted the prophet Muhammad, the Muslim at the conclusion of the prayer turns to the fellow worshiper on the right and on the left and says "Peace be with you and the mercy of God" (*al-salāmu 'alaykum wa-raḥmatul-lah*) and receives the response "And with you peace." This offer of peace is the same as that by which Muslims are encouraged to greet members of the community in daily life. In this way, the relationship of believers who come before the Lord together in prayer is seen as the norm and model for their relations in everyday affairs.

The Tithe for the Poor (zakāh)

Every Muslim is required to give a fixed percentage of income for the poor of the community. It differs from almsgiving (*sadaqah*), which is highly encouraged, in that the *zakāh* is obligatory and fixed according to precise rules and calculations. One of the manifestations of Islamic revival is the emergence of "*zakāh* lawyers" in Muslim countries, who are specialized in assisting pious Muslims to determine how much they are to pay in tithe. In several countries, such as Pakistan, the tithe is collected from Muslims by the state and used to finance charitable works for the poor.

This practice is opposed by others (e.g., the Muslim Brotherhood), who see the collection and distribution of the *zakāh* as something outside the competence of the state. The tithe should be a personal offering, they hold, given by the Muslim directly to those in need. Their point is that each Muslim must realize that the poor of the community are his or her responsibility, a sacred obligation that is not to be simply written off on a tax form.

In fact, the manner of collecting and distributing *zakāh* varies widely in the Islamic world. It is a common sight in Cairo and Damascus, especially during Ramadan, to see a bread truck pull up at a mosque in a poor neighborhood, and loaves of Arabic bread distributed to all who ask. In Indonesian and Malaysian villages, *zakāh* is paid in rice. A woman preparing the staple food for her family sets aside every tenth handful. The uncooked rice is collected on Thursday afternoons, brought to the mosque, and deposited in a large wooden bin. This is available, with no questions asked, to those who need it. Elsewhere, well-to-do families conscientiously prepare extra food at midday on Fridays so that they can feed the needy after Friday prayers.

I have already intimated the spiritual implications of the *zakāh*. Caring for the poor of the community is not a matter of choice, mood, or feelings of sympathy. It is a required duty for every obedient Muslim, one that may not be ignored without incurring God's anger. Any relationship to God or a life of prayer, fasting, and other acts of worship that does not include the element of concrete assistance to the poor of the community is not a fully Islamic response to the Qur'anic message. This teaching is repeated over and over in mosques, newspaper articles, and study groups throughout the Muslim world, especially during Ramadan, and marks responsibility to the poor as a key element in the Islamic understanding of holiness.

Fasting During Ramadan (sawm)

The key elements for Islamic spirituality in the month of the Ramadan fast are remembrance, celebration, communal solidarity, spiritual renewal, forgiveness, and exposure to the experience of hunger. Ramadan is a time of grateful *remembrance* in that Muslims believe that the Qur'an was first revealed during this month. In addition to the special prayers thanking God for the gracious revelation of His message to humankind, Ramadan is a time for Qur'an study groups organized among various sectors of society, such as students, housewives, civil servants, and factory workers, and for academic congresses and public Qur'an recitations. During the last week of Ramadan, on the Night of Destiny when the Qur'an is believed to have been sent down from heaven, and when the Day of Judgment is popularly expected to arrive, Muslims are encouraged to spend the entire night in the mosque, reading the Qur'an, listening to its recitation, and performing recommended prayers. It is during this week that the eschatological element of Islamic spirituality, so strong in the early surahs of the Qur'an but usually muted in modern Islam, comes to the fore. With the expectation that the Last Judgment might arrive on the Night of Destiny, they hope to be found in prayer when the time comes.

A second element is *celebration and social solidarity*. Far from being a sad or gloomy period in the Muslim calendar, Ramadan is the happiest month, eagerly awaited by Muslims. The ordinary rhythm of daily life is disrupted and, in fact, completely replaced by a "sacred" schedule, with families rising in the early hours of the day, often as early as 2:30-3:00 in the morning, to prepare a light meal to be consumed before dawn. The work day is frequently shortened. In some places schoolchildren are released in their annual vacation. The mosques are more crowded than usual with worshipers, not only during the obligatory prayer times, but with visitors and private worshipers attending lectures on the Qur'an and recitations of the Sacred Book. At the popular level, many Muslims visit shrines and tombs of holy persons during Ramadan, and Sufis hold sessions of *dhikr* in the mosques. As sunset approaches, an air of anticipation is in the air, with food being prepared but not yet consumed, with much movement in the streets, with workers rushing to get home before sunset, and with families invited out to break the fast hurrying to arrive in time.

Sunset is announced by the call to prayer from the minarets, and in many places by cannons, gunshots, or fireworks. While the more pious perform the sunset prayer before eating, the masses break their fast immediately, in the name of God the Merciful the Compassionate, with traditional and recommended fare—plain water, olives, fruits. The *iftār*, or breaking of the fast, is one of the most loved and enjoyed social functions in Islam. Families, neighbors, friends, and colleagues gather at one another's homes or, in modern cities, restaurants, to break the fast, with the result that Ramadan is a period of intense socializing. After the meal, many return to the mosque for night prayer and the long *tarāwiḥ* prayers that are particular to Ramadan. At the conclusion of the *tarāwiḥ*, shops and markets are again open, social calls are made, and special musical programs are aired on television. The socializing goes on until the early hours.

The spiritual significance of Ramadan cannot be underestimated. Communal performance of a long and difficult fast, with many periods of prayer, followed by communal celebration, creates a strong sense of social solidarity. The disruption of the normal daily schedule, with ordinary activities—rising, eating, praying, shopping—performed at extraordinary hours, results in the creation of a sacred time. Business affairs and work schedules are held to a minimum so that the main "business" of Ramadan is the celebration of all that it means to be Muslim.[1]

Important aspects of the Ramadan fast are spiritual *renewal and forgiveness*. Like other religious believers, Muslims tend to get slack in performing religious obligations. Perhaps in the matter of skipping prayers, perhaps in harsh treatment of their wives and neglect of the children, or in gossiping, tale-bearing, or dubious commercial practices, Muslims fail to live up to the ritual and ethical standards set by their faith. Ramadan is a time for repentance and starting anew, a characteristic it shares with the Christian Lent. The evening *tarāwiḥ* prayers are especially directed toward asking forgiveness for the wrongs committed during the previous year. Muslims believe that God's mercy is boundless and immediate toward one who repents, but during Ramadan God's forgiving grace is superabundant. Muslims believe that through the faithful practice of Ramadan, all their sins are forgiven.

This accounts for the joy with which the *ʿĪd al-Fiṭr*, the Feast of Breaking the Fast, is celebrated. Although not the first day of the Islamic calendar, the *ʿĪd* is the spiritual New Year of Islam, the new beginning and starting over. Having been forgiven by God, Muslims are taught to *forgive one another*. Thus, the vertical and horizontal dimensions of forgiveness are joined. Muslims visit parents, relatives, friends, and co-workers during the feast to beg forgiveness for any wrongs they might have committed toward the others during the previous year. In Southeast Asia, this universal practice is called *halal bi-halal*, which might be translated as "setting things aright." The purpose is to prevent grievances, resentments, and estrangements from persisting from year to year, thereby poisoning human relations.

Finally, an aspect of the Ramadan fast often raised in sermons and articles in the Islamic press is the *experience of hunger*. Muslims who suffer from hunger pangs during the daylight hours are asked to recall the fate of millions of persons in this world who lack sufficient food. Theirs is not a voluntary hunger, like that of fasting Muslims, but a condition enforced by circumstances. Ramadan is thus an experience of conscientization toward the plight of the hungry. Through free-will offerings to the local poor or by influencing government policies, Muslims are urged to address concretely the problems of hunger and starvation.

The *ḥajj*, the Pilgrimage to Mecca

The opportunity to make the pilgrimage to Mecca sometime during one's life is the longing of every pious Muslim, but in fact, due to factors of health, responsibilities (e.g., raising children), expense, and simple logistics, most Muslims are never able to fulfill this desire. Because of the ease and speed of travel and economic capability of many Muslims, the annual applications to make the pilgrimage today exceed those of any previous era, far beyond what can be accommodated by the extensive but still limited facilities in Arabia. The norm laid down by the Saudi authorities is one pilgrim for every thousand Muslims of each nation. Indonesia, with the world's largest Muslim population, this year received 180,000 visas for the *ḥajj*, and the numbers decrease from there. Even though for most Muslims the *ḥajj* remains a dream that will never be fulfilled, the pilgrimage has an important place in the Islamic understanding of holiness. Like the other pillars of Islam, the form and content of the pilgrimage are fixed. The pilgrimage must be made at the proper time and prescribed actions must be performed on the proper days.

The pilgrimage is a reliving of the spiritual roots of their faith. Mecca is not only the scene of Muhammad's birth and early prophetic mission but is the site of the Ka'bah, the direction toward which all Muslims pray daily. For Muslims, the Ka'bah symbolizes both the unity of the Islamic *ummah* and also the ancient, God-given nature of Islam. Muslims believe that the Ka'bah was built by the prophet Abraham, the first structure on earth dedicated to the worship of the One God. The daily act of praying in the direction of one location is a constant reminder of the oneness of the Islamic community. On the wall of the simplest mosque, in homes and hotel rooms, the direction of Mecca is indicated.

Upon arriving in Mecca for the pilgrimage, Muslims enter a sacred state, a time dedicated totally to God. Normal clothing is replaced by two white sheets. It is forbidden to cut the hair or nails. Sexual abstinence is required until the conclusion of the pilgrimage. The preliminary rites of the pilgrimage revolve around Mecca, particularly the circumambulation of the Ka'bah, as Muhammad and his early companions had done, and commemorative reenactment of events from the life of Abraham, Hagar, and the baby Isma'il.

The central and indispensable act of the pilgrimage, however, takes place some thirty kilometers outside Mecca, on the slopes of Mount Arafat. It is here that Abraham was ordered to sacrifice his son Isma'il, and it is also the site of Muhammad's final sermon. The Day of Arafat is the pilgrimage per se. If it is omitted, one has not performed the pilgrimage and the obligation to do so remains.

Muslims ascend the mountain from their tent city at Muzdalifa in time for noon prayers and remain there until after the sunset prayer. During the time on Arafat, Muslims might pray informally, read or recite the Qur'an, or rest.

To understand the deep spiritual implications of a rite that might seem anticlimactic, one must recall the geography of the place. Arafat, in the midst of the Arabian desert, is one of the world's most arid, hot, and inhospitable locations, and has been since the time of Muhammad. There is no earthly reason why anyone would go there. The only conceivable motivation is spiritual; God has commanded it. Obedient to God's command, "even to the end of the earth," the Muslim professes that the human person finds true fulfillment and identity in obedience to God. Standing in the blazing sun under the hot blue sky of Arafat, the pilgrims, by their very presence, affirm that the ultimate purpose and reason for human existence is found in accepting willingly and joyfully one's creature-hood before God and living accordingly. One might say that a whole lifetime of Islamic experience, as incarnated in the individual Muslim, is symbolically represented in this one act.

The "standing" in the sun on Arafat is always physically uncomfortable and, especially when the pilgrimage falls in one of the summer months, can be even injurious to one's health. An account of the experience of a female Muslim underlines both these aspects:

> For six hours, my family and I, with the other pilgrims, stood in the heat of the desert. We prayed and read from the Qur'an. My daughters, like many other pilgrims, held an umbrella over their heads for shade, but I felt the need to suffer the effects of a baking sun, as a testimony of my faith. Many men and women were fainting all around me, and they were carried off on stretchers to the sunstroke vans, manned by hospital attendants.[2]

Upon the return from Arafat, a further moment of the pilgrimage remains to be noted. Halfway back to Mecca, in the village of Mina, Muslims sacrifice a goat or sheep to commemorate the faith of Abraham, who was prepared to sacrifice in obedience his own son, Isma'il. At this point, the pilgrims become united with the whole Islamic community around the world who celebrate the second great Islamic feast, *'Īd al-Aḍḥā*, the Feast of the Sacrifice. Just as the Day of Arafat sums up in one act the Islamic understanding of the meaning and purpose of human life, so the sacrifice expresses their continuity with the faith of Abraham. It is a moment at which Muslims around the world can vicariously participate in the pilgrimage, performing at their own homes or mosques the same rite performed in Mina.

Islamic Spirituality as Imitation of Muhammad

The pillars of Islam, as important as they are, express the obligatory minimum of the Islamic way of life. Each obligatory pillar is complemented by recommended actions whose performance is considered praiseworthy and meritorious, but whose omission is not considered sinful. The profession of faith (*shahādah*) in the Oneness of God and prophethood of Muhammad is amplified in the *aqīdah*, the creed, which centers on the pillars of Islamic faith: belief in God, all His prophets, the Sacred Books, the angels, and the Day of Final Judgment.

In addition to the obligatory *ṣalāh* five times a day, there are recommended times of *ṣalāh*, such as during the night and on special occasions, supererogatory series of prostrations that may be added on to those required, and a vast array of informal prayer, *du'ā'*, which are encouraged but not required. In addition to the prescribed *zakāh*, Muslims are urged to give alms (*sadaqah*) spontaneously to the poor. To the fast of Ramadan, many pious Muslims add other recommended fasts, for example, on every Monday and Thursday, or they extend the Ramadan fast by beginning two months early, making it a ninety-day fast. In addition to the *ḥajj*, Muslims believe that performing the *umrah*, an informal pilgrimage to Mecca outside the season of the *ḥajj*, is a highly meritorious act. Today, almost two hundred thousand Muslims every month arrive in Mecca to perform the *umrah*.

The range of recommended actions, which includes both ritual acts such as prayer and instructions on mundane affairs such as receiving guests, eating, traveling, carrying on business, family relations, even the performance of bodily functions, compose the *sunnah*. It is *sunnah*, for example, to eat everything on one's plate (i.e., not to waste food). It is *sunnah* to offer cologne to guests. It is *sunnah* to say at the conclusion of a journey, "Praise God for a safe arrival" (*al-ḥamdu li'llah 'ala salāmah*), a phrase regularly heard among airline passengers when the plane lands safely.

The *sunnah* is derived from the practice of Muhammad and found in the collections of hadith reports of his sayings, deeds, and decisions. As such, an important aspect of Islamic spirituality is the imitation of Muhammad. Muhammad is understood in the Qur'an not only as the messenger who brought the Qur'an, but also as its first hearer. He is seen as the model Muslim whose life was shaped to the smallest detail by the Qur'anic message. He is their friend and mentor who will intercede for them on Judgment Day.

The role that Muhammad plays for the Islamic community today is well summed up by the recommended prayers at his tomb in Madinah. The Sunni prayer reads:

I bear witness that you are the Messenger of God. You have conveyed the message. You have fulfilled the trust. You have counseled the community, enlightened the gloom, shed glory on the darkness, and uttered words of wisdom.

The prayer of the Shi'a is even more invocative:

I bear witness that you have conveyed the Lord's messages and declared His command. You have borne hardship in His cause and summoned people with wisdom and proper exhortation to His way. You have carried out that which was entrusted to you. You have been compassionate to believers and harsh to stubborn unbelievers. You have worshiped with a single-heartedness that brought you total certitude. To me you are as [as beloved as] father, mother, my own self, property, as my own child.

The place of Muhammad in the hearts of Muslims thus goes far beyond that of being simply the messenger who brought the Qur'an. He is the exemplary model and is regarded with affection as toward a family member. On this basis, one can understand the anger and sense of personal insult with which Muslims react to any slander or slur on the character of Muhammad.

Information about the life and deeds of Muhammad is found in the early biographies, but much more in the collections of hadith reports that are traced from him. There are over a hundred thousand hadiths, but only about two thousand are considered soundly authenticated, and hence the basis for Islamic faith and practice. Many of the most characteristic elements of Islamic spirituality, from the form of the daily prayer to the rites of pilgrimage, while not found explicitly in the Qur'an, are recorded in the hadith.

The case of the pilgrimage exemplifies the function of the hadith. When, near the end of his life, after his victory over the pagans of Mecca, Muhammad made the pilgrimage from Madinah to Mecca, every detail was meticulously recorded and preserved, so that, until today, hajjis imitate in detail the example of Muhammad's own performance of the pilgrimage.

Not only do the hadith reports elaborate on the teachings of the Qur'an, but they also counsel Muslims on the interior attitude that should accompany Islamic practices. For example, a hadith regarding almsgiving recalls to Christians Jesus' Sermon on the Mount: "If you give alms openly, that is good, but if you give them to the needy in secret, it is even better, and will atone for some of your bad deeds. God is aware of all you do."

Muhammad is not only a model of behavior, but a much loved exemplar. The deep affectionate love that Christians have toward Jesus expressed, for example, in Sacred Heart devotions, or toward Mary and the saints finds its parallel in the human affection that Muslims feel toward Muhammad. One writer on Islamic spirituality has put it like this:

> No one can estimate the power of Islam as a religion who does not take into account the love at the heart of it for [Muhammad]. It is here that human emotion, repressed at some points by the austerity of the doctrine of God as developed in theology, has its full outlet—a warm human emotion which the peasant can share with the mystic. The love of this figure is perhaps the strongest binding force in a religion which has so marked a binding power.[3]

The Qur'an and *sunnah* form the principal bases of the *sharī'ah*, the Islamic way of life. Containing elements of law, but going far beyond the notion of law, the *sharī'ah* indicates the totality of actions and attitudes that characterize Islamic life and society and distinguish them from that of others. Elaborated in the course of time by a subtle art of jurisprudence, the *sharī'ah* covers every aspect of human life, from family relations, to the social, economic, and political organization of the community.

The community itself has a role in the determination of the *sharī'ah*; when there is consensus of the community regarding an action or element of faith, that is to be considered Islamic. Much stressed in recent decades is the personal contribution (*ijtihād*) of the individual Muslim, who has a responsibility to apply the *sharī'ah* according to the needs of every culture and place and at every period in history. One cannot understand Islamic spirituality if one does not recognize that Muslims, far from being embarrassed by having a religion of law, are convinced that the comprehensive *sharī'ah* is one of God's greatest gifts to them. It is an approach to religious life that has more in common with the Jewish attitude to the Torah and its elaboration in the *halakah* than one that finds any immediate parallel with the Christian tradition.

The Sufi Path to Holiness

Observers of Islam have at times identified Islamic spirituality with the phenomenon of Sufism, and some observers have gone so far as to set up a dichotomy between the "spiritual, interiorized" Islam of Sufis and a dry, legalistic formalism that is said to characterize "official Islam." I hope that all that has preceded has shown the inaccuracy of this judgment. If normative Islam did not itself offer its followers deep spiritual elements, symbols, and emotions, an immediate response of the human person to the Divine in our midst, the message of Islam would appeal to few, and its hold on believers would remain superficial and ephemeral.

The Sufis were not out to set up a parallel Islam in opposition to the *sharī'ah*. They wanted to mine the riches of spirituality already found in Islamic practices and to draw out the implications for personal growth in holiness. As one writer puts it:

> One should not forget that the *sharī'ah*, as proclaimed in the Koran and exemplified by the Prophet, together with a firm belief in the Day of Judgment, was the soil out of which their [the Sufis'] piety grew. They did not abolish the rites but rather interiorized them. . . . The performance of ritual prayer, fasting, and pilgrimage to Mecca constituted, for the majority of the early Sufis, the minimal religious obligation without which all possible mystical training would be useless and meaningless.[4]

From the earliest centuries, some Muslims stressed the potential of the Qur'anic message to effect an inner transformation of the believer. In one sense, theirs were voices of protest against the worldly power and wealth that entered the community in the generation after the death of Muhammad. They stressed the need for a simple, prayer-centered life and adopted many of the harsh ascetical practices of the Christian monks of the desert. Basing their teaching on Qur'anic passages, they stressed the transforming power of God's love in human hearts and understood Islam as a path to attain union of love and will with God.

Spiritual teachers began to attract disciples, and some began to write down instructions for their students and for posterity. Chains of initiation began to develop, so that a student on the path identified, through his spiritual teacher and his teacher's teacher, with one of the great spiritual masters of the past. Already by the second century of Islam, these people came to be called "Sufis," although scholars still dispute about the origins of the term.

By the thirteenth century, most Sufis were inscribed as members of one or another order or brotherhood (*ṭarīqah*), each with its own forms of prayer and patterns of spiritual exercises, often with its own distinctive dress, lodges, and methods of initiation. Having many elements in common with Christian lay confraternities and religious orders, the brotherhoods often attracted a specific clientele, one drawing mainly from the cultured intelligentsia, another from members of a specific craft guild, yet others from soldiers or from the urban or rural masses. While some were very international and missionary-minded, others identified with certain localities and ethnic groups.

The Sufis saw Islam as a path leading progressively to a union of love and will. Through a prescribed set of spiritual exercises, under the guidance of a spiritual director, the spiritual seeker passed through a series of stations (*maqāmāt*) in which he or she strove to overcome the human obstacles to the action of God's grace. The Sufi would have to learn humility, obedience, poverty, patience, diligence, temperance in matters of food and sex, and the like. At some point, the Sufi would be blessed with special states (*ḥāl*, pl. *aḥwāl*), when God would enlighten the seeker's heart with strong experiences of love, trust, joy, fear of the Lord, and so on, when God would intervene directly by grace to carry the believer farther along the Path. These states were not always uplifting. The Sufis knew the "dark nights" described by the Christian mystics of the Carmelite tradition, when they had to trust in God despite the lack of sensible or emotional evidence.

The final state before reaching the Goal was that of *fanāʿ* when everything worldly would pass away and all that would remain (*baqā*) was God's loving presence. The Sufi had arrived at the Truth, the ultimate goal of human life, a union of life with God where the believer no longer had an independent will of his own, but desired nothing but the will of God. Students of Christian spirituality will find surprising parallels between the stages of the Sufi path and the purgative, illuminative, and unitive ways described by Christian writers.

One of the most distinctive characteristics of Sufi spirituality is their development of the Qur'anic injunction to "Remember God often" (33:40). The word *dhikr* means "remembrance" and can refer to a wide variety of short, repeated prayers whose purpose is to center one's concentration on the immediate presence of God. This is similar to the *théomnémie* of the Christian Byzantine tradition and the Russian "Jesus prayer." According to the particular tradition followed, *dhikr* may be done alone and silently, or it can be recited aloud in common, often accompanied by bodily movements, musical chanting, and instruments. As noted above, the most widespread prayer formula of the *dhikr* is the *shahādah*.

A form of *dhikr* practiced by both Sufis and non-Sufis is the rosary (*tasbīḥ*), with which the Muslim recites on each bead one of the Beautiful Names of

God. Ninety-nine of these names are mentioned in the Qur'an, hence Muslim rosary beads usually have 99, 66, or 33 beads. As each name corresponds to one of God's qualities, the Muslim prayer becomes a meditative reflection on the nature and characteristics of God.

Some mystical traditions have tended toward a type of pantheism, where God is seen as the only true reality, and the transient beings of this universe are no more than epiphanies or shadows of the One Reality. Their view may be regarded as an interpretation of the *shahādah* to mean: "There is no reality but God." This view was not accepted by other Muslims, who felt that it made God wholly immanent and destroyed God's essential differentness and transcendence. The resulting controversy marked many periods of the "middle centuries" of Islamic history.

In this century, the influence of Sufism has declined in the Islamic community, partly due to the criticism of reformers who felt that the preoccupation with personal perfection was a deviation from the original purpose of Islam, and partly due to modernizing and secularizing forces within the Islamic community itself. However, in many parts of the Islamic world Sufism is still very much alive and active. West Africa, the Maghrib, Egypt, Sudan, and South Asia are outstanding examples. In Central Asia, the Sufi orders formed the backbone of resistance to communism, the one societal structure that the Communist regime was unable to infiltrate and control. A resurgent interest in Sufism can be seen in modem Muslim publications in Egypt, Turkey, Pakistan, and Indonesia. The Sufi understanding of holiness, while at the moment in eclipse in the Islamic world, must not be discounted as an element of the spiritual life of Muslims.

Christian Reflections

What can the Christian learn from a reflection on Islamic spirituality? What lessons can we draw that might enrich our encounters with Muslims? Where might we find ourselves challenged by seeing Islamic spirituality as lived by Muslims today? These questions I would like to address briefly in these concluding paragraphs.

1. The encounter with Islamic spirituality is a corrective to the current trend of our secular age, which is to view Islam not as a religion, an approach to God, and a locus of divine activity in human lives, but primarily as a geopolitical force. Politicians, journalists, and scholars are preoccupied, some might say obsessed, with Islamic revival, fundamentalism, and political movements, but this is not the way that the Second Vatican Council documents and the teachings of recent popes have taught Catholics to approach Islam. Our approach as Christians is to seek "the seeds of the Word" and to "discover the treasures of human spirituality." For us, first and foremost, Muslims are fellow believers who claim, like us, spiritual descent from the faith of Abraham in the One God.

No doubt there are Muslims who understand Islam to be an all-embracing sociopolitical movement, and Christians who live among Muslims are rightly concerned about the implications this can have for their own lives. On the other hand, for all Muslims, whether or not they have any interest in politics, Islam is primarily an encounter, in faith and obedience, with God. If we hope to have any meaningful communication with Muslims, it must be on the grounds of our sometimes intersecting and sometimes divergent spiritualities. If this is true for the vast majority of Muslims who are not involved in sociopolitical movements, it is also true for revivalist Muslims. If we are not ready to talk about how God is at work in our lives in the modem world, we will have nothing of importance to say to Muslims.

2. If we ask why Islam seems to be so successful in today's world in retaining the allegiance and active commitment of Muslims despite the secularizing forces rampant in every corner of the globe, much of the reason would seem to lie in its effectiveness in instilling a sense of belonging and direct contact with God. The symbolism of prostration, the Ka'bah, going on pilgrimage, fasting, the Greeting of Peace, washing the body, and standing on Arafat are still meaningful and effective ways of expressing spiritual realities that can only inadequately be put into words. These realities challenge Christians to ask whether the decline of symbolic representation of deep spiritual truths does not sometimes make our approach to religious practice too rationalistic and hence unable to engage the whole person, body and soul.

It is too easy to dismiss the fact that Muslims but rarely leave Islam to join another religion as simply due to fear of ostracism or even persecution by family, social milieu, or state. This is undoubtedly sometimes the case, but the deeper reason is that Islamic spirituality has been successful in creating a strong sense of belonging to a community of faith. This is often achieved precisely through those communal actions that involve the most difficulty and physical inconvenience: the Ramadan fast, rising before dawn to pray, standing in the blazing sun on Arafat. It would seem to respond to a very human conviction: something that is too easy is not worth doing.

3. When Christians observe the Islamic *shariʿah* (and the parallel development in Judaism), there is a tendency to dismiss these as religions of law. It is as though we remember Jesus' criticism of the legalism of the Pharisees without recalling his words that "not one jot or tittle will be lost until all has been fulfilled." Islamic spirituality should be a reminder that it is *legalism* that Jesus condemns, an attitude that one is saved by performance, with corresponding judgment passed on those who do not perform. Islam, as it has been taught by the great spiritual masters like Al-Ghazali in the past and is still taught by many Muslims today, knows that nothing is possible except through God's grace. All the norms and regulations of the *shariʿah* must be internalized and understood in the context of the believer's relationship to the Creator. Nothing is automatic or magical; there is no forgiveness without repentance, no prayer without a "movement of the heart," no true holiness without concrete service to the neighbor in need. Obviously, many Muslims have a legalistic mentality, and many are intolerant of others. Hypocritical Muslims perform actions to be seen by others or to gain the prestige accorded to hajjis, for example, or to Sufi

shaykhs. Others rationalize and compromise, faithful in prayer but corrupt in business practices. Some overemphasize certain elements of the Islamic tradition while conveniently forgetting others. Self-critical Christians, who are not blind to similar occurrences in themselves and in the Christian community, must admit that abuses of religiosity do not negate the real depths of holiness found in an Islamic life when it is followed sincerely and humbly.

4. A real encounter of spiritualities can take place if we perceive its value and are willing to devote time to it. In this paper, I have mentioned some of the elements of spirituality that are of particular concern to Muslims because of the nature of their religion. They are often genuinely interested to know if these elements are found also in the religious life of Christians. But they often have a prejudice, not totally unfounded, that many Christians today are so secularized that their spirituality is shallow and perfunctory. Many Muslims think we pray only once a week. Christians, on the other hand, are not accustomed to talking about matters of inner piety and our lives before God. We might rationalize and tell ourselves that Muslims are not interested in such matters or that they would feel insulted or that we were proselytizing should we speak about the deeper truths of our faith. Christians must be confident of the riches of faith in God, sacramental life, love of neighbor, service to and defense of the poor, Christian fellowship, popular devotion, mysticism, the vast variety of forms and times of prayer, the action of the Spirit, programs of growth in holiness, lay movements old and new, vows, orders and monastic life, feasts and the liturgical year—all gifts with which God has blessed the Christian community over the centuries. The Christian who rejoices in the spiritual riches we possess knows that there is literally a world of things to discuss with Muslims. The encounter between Christian and Muslim brings together two spiritual universes that demand to be explored together.

From personal experience I can attest that Muslims, for whom God is the most "real" of all realities, show a genuine interest in the inner dimensions of the Christian's life with God. How, when, and to whom do we pray? Where is Christ, in heaven or on earth? Why do we say Jesus had to die—could God have not found a more humane way to save us? What is the purpose of committed celibacy? Why do we confess our sins when God is able and eager to forgive directly? What role does the Virgin Mary play in our relation to God? If we claim to be freed from the law, what is canon law? Who can be saved: all Christians, only some Christians, or others as well?

These questions, and hundreds more, that have been raised to me personally by Muslims touch on issues of Christian spirituality. The questions are often poorly phrased, as are our questions to Muslims, but the interest they imply is no less genuine for that. The only satisfying manner of response is to draw on the depths of our tradition and to explain how the topic of the question fits into our Christian life with God. In the encounter of spiritualities, the Christian and the Muslim are not out to convince each other that their way is superior. They are fellow travelers on the path, sharing from their riches what makes sense to them and what gives direction to their lives. They are fellow believers in a modern world where it is not always easy to believe in God. For both, the crucial question is: How does God act in human lives and in society? How does God act in my life?

In dialogue, they find that many of the same concepts are expressed in different ways, but also that the same terms often refer to very different understandings of reality. They find that there are points of contact and points of divergence. In the encounter, it is God who is most active of all, enlightening both with His abundant grace. Are we enriched by the encounter with Islamic holiness? My answer, after all these years, is yes. Are Muslims enriched by encountering Christian spirituality? I hope and pray that their answer also will be yes.

Notes

1. I have occasionally asked Muslim converts to Christianity if they ever feel nostalgia for leaving the Islamic community, and consistently they speak of Ramadan. To them, modern Lenten practice seems bland and perfunctory by comparison.

2. Jean Sasson, *Daughters of Arabia* (New York: Doubleday Books, 1994), 124.

3. Constance E. Padwick, *Muslim Devotions: A Study of Prayer-Manuals in Common Use* (London: SPCK, 1961), 145.

4. Annemarie Schimmel, *Mystical Dimensions of Islam* (Chapel Hill: University of North Carolina Press, 1975), 106.

15

Islamic Ethical Vision

The essence of the Islamic approach to ethics is contained in the very name of the religion, *Islam*. Faith is a submission of the human will to that of God, performing those deeds that God has commanded and avoiding everything that He has forbidden. Thus, the source and basis of ethical vision for Muslims is what God has taught and commanded, in other words, God's moral will for humankind as it is to be lived in the personal, familial, social, economic, and political spheres.

The Foundations of the Islamic Ethical Vision

Muslims discover the ethical directives by which they should live, above all, in the Qur'an. They believe the Qur'an to be God's direct revelation. His eternal Word in final and definitive form, the very speech of God in that the Qur'an is accepted to have been revealed literally. As such, the Qur'an is the primary source of the Islamic way of life, the *sharī'ah*.

In addition to this divine source of ethical vision, there is also the prophetic source: the *sunnah* of Muhammad. Muhammad is regarded by Muslims not only as the messenger who brought the final and perfect revelation from God but also as the model Muslim, the first hearer and practitioner of Qur'anic revelation. For Muslims, therefore, it is extremely important to know what Muhammad taught, how he acted, and what decisions he gave on questions proposed to him. These words, deeds, and decisions of Muhammad have been reported by his companions and the first generations of Muslims.

In the early centuries of Islam, there were many oral reports of Muhammad's sayings and deeds (hadith), most of which were spurious. If Muslims were to take Muhammad's behavior and teaching as the basis for religious and ethical life, it became essential to distinguish between the sound (*ṣaḥīḥ*) reports and those that were false. Muslim scholars developed a science for determining which of the many reports about Muhammad were trustworthy, and these sound hadiths were codified in books that are still carefully studied by Muslims.

Previously published in *Journal of Dharma* (Bangalore) 16, no. 4 (December 1991): 398-409. Reprinted by permission.

The sound hadiths from Muhammad form the *sunnah* of the prophet, which complements and completes the divine message found in the Qur'an. The vast majority of Muslims in the world today identify themselves as Sunni Muslims, that is, those who follow the *sunnah* of Muhammad. A minority of Muslims, called Shi'ah, accept yet another definitive font for religious and ethical practice: the writings of the Imams, who as infallible teachers provided inerrant and normative commentaries on the teaching of the Qur'an and prophetic *sunnah*. While most Shi'ah accept twelve Imams in direct descent from Muhammad, a minority, called Isma'ilis, accept a line of seven infallible teachers.

As time went on, it became clear that new situations were arising that had not been explicitly discussed in the Qur'an and *sunnah*. Thus, a third source came to be accepted as a basis for religious practice and ethical values, the communitarian basis called *ijmā'*. *Ijmā'* indicates the consensus of the Islamic community and holds that whenever the community is in agreement on a certain question, it cannot be in error.

In time, a fourth source of Islamic behavior was seen to be necessary, the individual effort of the well-informed Muslim scholar, called *ijtihād*. This principle holds that when confronted by a question for which no clear indication is given in the Qur'an and *sunnah*, and on which there is no consensus among the scholars, an individual who is well-versed in the Islamic tradition can study the matter, weigh the various arguments, and arrive at his own conclusion. The *mujtahid* (one who does *ijtihād*) can thus propose his interpretation to the community and is free to follow his own opinion on the matter.

It is clear that the principle of *ijtihād* makes the *sharī'ah* an open-ended and flexible basis for arriving at ethical judgments in accord with Islamic faith. *Ijtihād* gives no assurance of correctness; it remains always the well-informed, considered opinion of a scholar.

The Classical Formulation of Moral Norms

Because of the possibility of error, most Muslim scholars in medieval times held that "the door of *ijtihād* was closed"—that is, that the *sharī'ah* had been exhaustively studied, the principles of jurisprudence laid down, and the Islamic way of life had been defined and codified into a fixed body to be followed by Muslims. Discussion was permissible only on details of the law, which was elaborated in four mutually acceptable *madhhabs* or legal traditions. Ordinary Muslims should accept and obey what was taught by the scholars without questioning; this blind following of tradition was called *taqlīd*.

The legal scholars attempted to categorize all human actions within a five-fold pattern, *al-ahkām al-khamsah*, "the five categories."[1]

1. Some actions are *obligatory*, and their omission is sinful (e.g., caring for aged parents, paying the *zakāh*—a tax on possessions and income to be used for the poor—fulfilling the terms of contracts).

2. Other acts are *recommended*, but their omission is not sinful (a wide range of devotional and moral practices ranging from the duty of hospitality to strangers, giving alms to beggars, freeing slaves, modesty in dress and ornamentation, and so on).

3. Many human acts are *indifferent*, bearing neither reward nor punishment (e.g., eating permitted foods, sleeping).

4. Some acts are *reprehensible* and hence to be avoided, although not absolutely prohibited (e.g., divorce, smoking).

5. Some deeds are absolutely *forbidden*, such as adultery, theft, homicide, rebellion, interest-taking.

It is to be noted that these five categories apply to all human acts, not only those that ethicists would classify as having a moral basis. They also apply to ritual activities (e.g., the five daily prayers, the Ramadan fast, and the pilgrimage to Mecca are obligatory; many other devotions and fasts are recommended but not obligatory; eating unwashed food is indifferent; performing one's ritual prayer late is reprehensible; eating pork and drinking alcoholic beverages are forbidden).

These categories admit of extenuating circumstances. A person in poor health or engaged in heavy manual labor has no obligation to fast. Someone whose economic or familial situation does not permit it is not obliged to make the pilgrimage. If one has sufficient reason, such as job requirements, one may perform the prayers late. The basic principle is that no one is to be burdened with duties that would cause them or those dependent on them harm (e.g., an expectant mother should not fast, since the unborn child needs the regular nourishment).

This principle the Muslim scholars call the rule of "resoluteness and relaxation" (*'azīmah* and *rukhṣah*).[2] Depending on the circumstances, a Muslim might have to consider permitted or indifferent acts impermissible or obligatory. For example, free-will almsgiving is always recommended, but when others are in danger of death, it becomes obligatory. Conversely, for one who, for health reasons, has been warned by his doctor to avoid certain foods, eating those foods, which would ordinarily be an indifferent act, becomes reprehensible or even forbidden.

The Development of Islamic Jurisprudence

In order to arrive at judgments on the moral status of human acts, the science of Islamic jurisprudence (*fiqh*) was developed. The purpose of this religious science was to examine the fonts of the *sharī'ah* and to produce techniques for applying them. Which teachings are to be plied broadly and which in a narrow sense? Which teachings are abrogated by others? How does one decide in cases of apparently conflicting obligations? The jurists proposed a wide range of legal principles and techniques, such as analogy, duress, and the welfare of the community, by which the scholars could arrive at a sound judgment on the nature of any given human act.

One can see that this understanding of the *sharī'ah* could easily develop into an external, formalistic ethic, a "pharisaic" preoccupation with conformity to legal details of the type condemned in the Gospels. It is noteworthy that throughout history Muslim scholars have themselves been aware of this danger and have rejected this as a false understanding of *sharī'ah*. Although the *sharī'ah* contains elements of a legal code, it is rather to be understood in the sense of an elaboration of the moral ideals by which Muslims hope to structure Islamic societies in accord with God's will.

With this background, one can more easily understand the difference between the *sharī'ah* and the law codes drawn up by civil societies. With the exception of a few serious crimes against society, no punishments are laid down for infringement of *sharī'ah* regulations. Moreover, a Muslim does not need the permission of anyone else to exempt himself from a requirement, if he judges that circumstances demand that he not fulfill that duty. Moreover, no other Muslim may question his judgment on the matter. For example, a person who, because of his occupation or state of health, judges that keeping the Ramadan fast would be detrimental to him, may and should exempt himself, and no other person is entitled to accuse him of wrongdoing.

In the twelfth century, the famous theologian Abu Hamid Al-Ghazali inveighed against the practice of *taqlīd*. He stressed that the Islamic ethical vision was not that of blind obedience, but rather the active effort to internalize Islamic teaching, to understand the interior, spiritual reasons for ethical and ritual precepts, and to conform one's life to God's will not solely in externals but also in the depths of one's religious experience. In this way, Al-Ghazali brought together the ethical ideal with the mystical quest for union of will with God, the Highest Good.[3] He is aware that by his unaided efforts, the human person cannot attain this goal; it is only possible through the grace-filled intervention (*tawfīq*) of God.

In the fourteenth century, the great Hanbali scholar, Ibn Taymiyya, argued forcefully that "the door of *ijtihād*" was not closed and that it was incumbent on Muslims to extend, by the conscientious and consistent practice of *ijtihād*, the *sharī'ah* to every aspect of human life. Ibn Taymiyya understood the Qur'an as having revealed God in two principle roles: Creator of the universe, and Commander of the *sharī'ah*. Just as God was ontologically supreme as Creator, so in the ethical sphere He was supreme as Commander.[4] As at the metaphysical level no being was outside God's creative activity, also in ethical matters no conceivable human action could be considered independently of God's commanding will.

Ethical Ideals in Early Islam

From the beginning, the Islamic community was exposed to other ethics than that founded in the Qur'an. Muhammad and his companions were heirs to a pre-Islamic Arabian ethic, with its emphasis on a this-worldly "manliness" (*muruwwah*), encompassing the virtues of courage, loyalty, personal honor, patient endurance, generosity, self-control, and hospitality.[5]

Another aspect of the "tribal ethic" that would have great influence on later developments in the Islamic community was the "horizontal," communitarian nature of authority. Decisions were to be made through consultation (*shūrā*), and the power to govern derived less from inherited rank than from leadership qualities rising naturally to the fore. Conformity to community standards was strictly enforced and deviations from the norm severely punished.

The Qur'an, in what today would be called "a dialogue with culture," affirms and reinforces some of these values at the same time that it reorients and redefines others, while explicitly rejecting some qualities of the pre-Islamic ethic. However, the horizontal rather than vertical or hierarchical orientation of religious society remains until today one of the distinguishing characteristics of the Islamic community. One becomes a member of the *'ulamā'*, for example, by community acceptance rather than through ordination, appointment, or academic degree.

Moral standards continue to be transmitted and imposed primarily by community agreement and pressure. As sociologists and Muslim preachers have often noted, this can cause problems when Muslims emigrate out of Muslim societies, where moral values and imperatives find strong social reinforcement, to regions such as Western Europe or North America, where ethical values are mainly regarded as individual choices.

The conquest of Iran in the first Islamic century and the eventual conversion of Iranians to Islam introduced Muslims to an ancient and living Persian ethical tradition.[6] After entering Islam, Iranian *litterateurs* continued to produce writings in the same tradition, which was slowly Islamized, with a consequent de-emphasis of opportunistic elements and the strategic value of polite manners in favor of moral uprightness (*ṣalaḥ*) and goodness (*iḥsān*).

Very early on, an entirely different ethic came to be proposed by Muslims of the Sufi tradition. Sharply distinguishable from both the pre-Islamic ethical ideal as well as that of Iran, the Sufi ethical ideal emphasized ascetical qualities of abstinence, self-denial, simplicity of life, humility, and fear of God, as well as the virtues of piety such as trust in God, awe, thirst for God, and brotherly love. One of the ninth-century Persian ascetics put it: "Who wants to attain to highest honor should prefer seven to seven: poverty to wealth, hunger to satiety, lowliness to prestige, humiliation to honor, modesty to pride, sadness to joy, death to life."[7] It is significant that the ethical model in the Sufi tradition was very often the Islamic prophet Jesus, whose evangelical and extra-evangelical sayings were handed down for centuries in Sufi circles.

Rationalist Ethics and Muslim Theology

As the Islamic tradition came into contact very early with Hellenist thought, the question arose of the agreement of the Islamic way of life with natural ethics. Already by the eighth century (third century of the *hijrah*), Greek ethical treatises, including those by Plato and Aristotle, were translated into Arabic and commented on by Muslim scholars. These works presented serious challenges to Muslim thinkers, who undertook to answer or integrate the problems raised.

Greek ethics, based on a presumption of human free will and the power to choose freely between various differing alternatives, seemed to contradict Qur'anic teaching concerning God's omnipotence. If the human person has the power to freely choose and thereby determine his destiny, human actions would seem to be outside the creative activity of God. Muslim theologians tended to favor the view, therefore, that human actions, like everything else that happens in the universe, are determined by God.

Moreover, Greek thought held that the moral nature of a human act was determined by its conformity to nature. There is a consistency and order to the universe with which human actions must conform. Through the study of first principles, it was possible to arrive at a knowledge of this natural law by use of reason and to construct accordingly an ethical system whose validity could be checked, not by recourse to divine revelation, but by its being a faithful reflection of the nature of the cosmos.

For Muslims, this raised the question of whether the moral teachings of the Qur'an and *sunnah* simply confirmed what could be known through ethical philosophy or whether Islamic teaching revealed the divine will in a way that transcended the possibilities of human effort.

On this question, the theological school of the Mu'tazila sought to show that Islamic teaching affirmed perfectly what could be known by natural ethics. Acts were not good or evil *because* God had determined them to be so, but God in His wisdom knows perfectly the natural order and taught humankind to act in those ways that were in conformity with it. Thus, the moral injunctions of the Qur'an describe rather than determine the ethical qualities of human actions. Furthermore, God, who is infinitely good, must desire what is best for humankind and could thus only teach what is proper and just.

This view, to other Muslim theologians, seemed to place limits on God's revelatory powers. In asserting unlimited divine freedom, they held that acts were good or evil by God's having commanded some and having forbidden others: homicide or adultery were not evil per se, but rather because God had prohibited them. Piety, faithfulness, distributive justice, and charity were good because God had commanded them. Had God wished, it was well within His power to have commanded adultery and forbidden justice, but He did not will to do so.

This view, which is intended to preserve God's prerogatives, was proposed with some modifications by the Ash'ari school of theology (*kalām*). To the Mu'tazila, this view seemed to reduce God's will to a set of random, arbitrary commands and to cut off morality from its rational bases, turning it into a simple obedience to the divine will. The internal ethic of an informed, religiously committed person would be replaced by a set of externally imposed moral imperatives. Moreover, they claimed, the Ash'arites left no room for the "rightness," the justice, of God's ordering all things for good in His wisdom.[8]

Their position on the question of natural morality directed the response they proposed to a related problem, that of reconciling human freedom with divine omnipotence. The Mu'tazila held that any genuine ethics demanded an agent who was free to choose between alternative actions. If human actions were predetermined by God, human freedom was merely illusory. Furthermore, if the divine will predetermined human acts, such as the decision to do good or to do evil, humans were not really responsible for their actions, so that God would not be just if He were to reward some with heaven and condemn others to hell on the basis of their deeds.

Al-Ash'ari and those who followed him countered with the argument that even though in reality there existed no independent human power to choose, in the very act of performing a good work, a person acquired (*kasb* or *iktisāb*) responsibility for that deed. God, who judged according to the acts performed, was therefore just in rewarding good deeds and sentencing to punishment those who were responsible for evil actions.

The weakness of the Mu'tazili argument from an Islamic point of view consisted in the limits that it placed on God's prerogatives as creator. The Mu'tazila were accused by Ash'arites and others of being dualists, of positing a divine creator as well as a human creator of human acts. In their desire to defend and preserve the justice of divine judgments, the Mu'tazila were considered to have compromised God's omnipotence. Many Muslim scholars were further convinced by Al-Ash'ari's accusation that the ethical position of the Mu'tazila did not even save the just nature of God's judgments.

To Al-Ash'ari is attributed the famous story of the three brothers, oft repeated with many elaborations and variations. There were three brothers, one who died as a child, a second who lived longer and did good deeds, and a third who did evil. The second brother was given a higher place in heaven than the first. The one who died as a child complained that his brother had a higher place. God explained that his brother had done many good deeds and God had rewarded him justly. The "child" then asked why he had not been allowed to live longer so that he also could have done good deeds. God answered that He foresaw the child would grow to be a sinner and so, doing the best for the child, took his life before he had done acts worthy of eternal punishment. At this point, the third brother cried out from the depths of hell, "Then why didn't you allow me to die as a child before I became a sinner ?"[9]

Later Developments

Unfortunately, over the centuries the position of the dominant Ash'arite school moved increasingly toward a complete denial of the link between cause and effect, an "ethical atomism" whereby each instant of time, and hence every human act, was created anew directly by God. Human responsibility for one's deeds was defended through complex formulations of the concept of acquisition (*iktisāb*), an explanation no more convincing despite its ever-increasing subtlety.

Al-Ghazali's response to the malaise that affects religious life when human responsibility is effectively denied was to retain the theological formulations and to imbue them with new life through the infusion of virtues derived from the Sufi ethic. The *sharī'ah* regulated external behavior, but needed to be interiorized in order to affect a spiritual transformation of the person. He thus recalled Muslims to a Sufi ideal of union of love and will with God, which was to be attained through the personal appropriation of the ethical qualities inherent in the practices of the Islamic way of life (*sharī'ah*).

Ibn Taymiyya's subsequent response to the ethical dilemma posed by the theologians of the Mu'tazili and Ash'ari traditions was more radical. Dismissing the Mu'tazila as ethical dualists, he maintained that the determinism of the Ash'arites drained religious conviction of its dynamic, active quality. What was needed were not new formulas to define human ownership of divinely caused human acts, but rather a return to a pretheological Qur'anic élan. The Qur'an teaches clearly that God is the Creator of all things, but the Holy Book affirms just as strongly that human beings are truly responsible for how they live on this earth. Central to Islamic faith is an activist commitment to build a human society according to God's will, with the *sharī'ah* forming and informing every aspect of human life.

The Mu'tazila were widely rejected in the Islamic world as unorthodox. Ibn Taymiyya's view found some support during his lifetime and in the next generations after his death (1328), but his critique of *kalām* ethics could not supplant the Ash'arite theological position. A third theological tradition, that of Al-Maturidi, which allowed more room for human ethical responsibility, was limited in its influence to Turkish-speaking regions of the Muslim community. Sufism continued to spread and, due to the strong missionary efforts of the Sufis, Islam was brought to new regions of Asia and Africa. However, on the question of divine omnipotence and human acts, the Sufis tended to preach and teach an Ash'arite determinism.

As the Islamic community approached the modern age, the malaise that gripped theology and ethics was symbolized by the loss of independence of one Muslim region after another to the previously discounted European powers. Jurisprudence was reduced to discussions of minute details of differences among the four *madhhabs*. Sufism was widely diffused but was all too often in a state of decadence that differed little from popular magic, fortune-telling, and preoccupation with preternatural wonders.

In this situation, from a remote part of the Islamic world, came a call for reform. Muhammad ibn 'Abd al-Wahhab, living in the Najd in central Arabia, discovered in the writings of Ibn Taymiyya a way out of the impasse, a return to what he saw to be the activist ethic of the early generations of Islam. The Muslim world was reduced to a backward and subservient state, he claimed, because of its abandonment of the pristine values of the original community. Over the centuries, many "innovations," departures from the spirit and practice of the early generations (*salaf*), had crept into the Muslim community. These innovated practices, he held, had weakened the community by turning it away from the original goals that God had set for Islam in the Qur'an and *sunnah*.

Muslims had to return to the original spirit of the religion by eliminating even time-honored practices if they were judged inconsistent with the original message. Ibn 'Abd al-Wahhab's program for reform thus carried with it a strong critique of the Islamic tradition as it had developed over the centuries. The Wahhabis, as those who took up the reformist ideas of Ibn 'Abd al-Wahhab were called, were equally critical of popular Sufism, classical *kalām* theology, and the dry formulations of the legal scholars.

One might say that the great "internal debate" going on within the Muslim community for over a century and a half has been between proponents of classical "traditional" Islam and those who advocate a more or less radical reform. On the one hand, the solutions proposed by the reformers have been considered by many Muslims to be too disruptive of Islamic life as it has developed over the centuries. On the other hand, the reformers criticize traditional leaders for allowing Muslims to fall into patterns of religiosity, which they judge passively complacent, fatalistic, and syncretistic.

The rapid changes that have swept the Muslim world since the end of World War II, with the rise of independent nation-states, the clash of conflicting political and economic ideologies, the introduction of alien moral values and behavior patterns through increasing mobility and the pervasiveness of communications media, and the varying degrees of participation in the benefits of modern society, have all offered challenges to both traditional and reformist understandings of Islam; Muslim thinkers have produced a wide variety of responses to the new challenges.

In all this there are ethical implications. There is the question of the human rights and responsibilities of individuals and the relation of these rights to those of society. An important issue concerns the role of the state in regard to the obligation of Muslims to live according to the *sharī'ah*. Should the state consider this an exclusively religious duty whose fulfillment is the personal responsibility of the believer, or does the state have the role of encouraging adherence to the *sharī'ah* through civil enforcement of its regulations? How are Muslims to live in societies of a pluralistic nature, whether they be in the majority or a minority group, with those whose moral standards and religious commitment are not those of Islam? How can moral values, historically transmitted in the context of strong extended-family relationships, be communicated through national school systems in traditionally Islamic regions, as well as in areas where educational and social practices are determined by non-Muslim beliefs and values? It is within the framework of such questions that the "internal" ethical debate in the Islamic community is today being carried out.

Notes

1. Joseph Schacht, *An Introduction to Islamic Law* (Oxford: Clarendon Press, 1975), 121.

2. Ignaz Goldziher, "'Azima," *Encyclopaedia of Islam*, 2nd ed. (Leiden: Brill, 1997), 1:846.

3. Abdul Khaliq, "The Ethics of Al-Ghazali," *A History of Muslim Philosophy* (Wiesbaden: Otto Harrassowitz, 1963), 1:626.

4. Thomas Michel, *A Muslim Theologian's Response to Christianity* (Delmar, N.Y.: Caravan Books, 1984), 64-66.

5. The best treatment of the pre-Islamic Arab ethic of *muruwwah* is still the early work of Goldziher [1889], "Muruwwa and Din," in *Muslim Studies* (Chicago: Aldine, 1967), 11-44.

6. R. Walzer, "Akhlak," *Encyclopaedia of Islam*, 1:326.

7. Annemarie Schimmel, *Mystical Dimensions of Islam* (Chapel Hill: University of North Carolina Press, 1975), 35.

8. For more information on these early theological schools of thought, see the excellent online resource http://www.muslimphilosophy.com/ip/rep/H052 (accessed August 15, 2009).—Ed.

9. This story has been repeated often. A useful analysis is found in W. M. Watt, *The Formative Period of Islamic Thought* (Edinburgh: Edinburgh University Press, 1973), 305.

Selected Bibliography of the Works of Father Thomas F. Michel, S.J.

Books

1984.   *A Muslim Theologian's Response to Christianity: Ibn Taymiyya's al-Jawab al-Sahih.* Edited and translated by Thomas F. Michel. Delmar, N.Y.: Caravan Books.

1994.   Fitzgerald, Michael, and Thomas Michel. *Recognize the Spiritual Bonds Which Unite Us: Sixteen Years of Christian-Muslim Dialogue.* Vatican City: Pontifical Council for Interreligious Dialogue.

1997.   *A Christian Looks at Islamic Spirituality.* Zamboanga City, Philippines: Silsilah Publications.

2003.   *What Muslims Should Know about Christianity.* Nairobi: Paulines Publications.

2004.   *Alla Confluenza dei Due Mari: Un Cristiano incontra l'Islam.* Rome: Icone.

2004.   *Christian Faith Explained.* Kota Kinabalu, Malaysia: Daughters of St. Paul, 2002; Nairobi: Paulines Publishers.

2004.   *Christlich-Islamischer Dialog und die Zusammenarbeit nach Bediüzzaman Said Nursi.* Istanbul: Nesil.

2005.   *Said Nursi's Views on Muslim-Christian Understanding: Eight Papers.* Istanbul: Söz Basim Yayin.

2006.   *Bediüzzaman'a Göre Müslümanlik-Hıristiyanlik Münasebetleri.* Istanbul: Etkileğim Yayinlari.

2007.   *Friends on the Way: Jesuits Encounter Contemporary Judaism.* New York: Fordham University Press.

Journal Articles and Chapters in Books

1979.   "Teaching about Islam in Christian Theological Schools." *South East Asia Journal of Theology* (Manila) 20: 29-34.

1980.   "Christianity among the Arabs in Pre-Islamic Times." *Proche Orient Chrétien* (Jerusalem) 30: 364-65.

1981.   "Ibn Taymiyya's Sharh on the *Futuh al-Ghayb* of Abd al-Qadir al-Jilani." *Hamdard Islamicus* (Karachi) 4, no. 2: 3-12.

1982.   "Wirbel um das Tagebuch eines jungen indonesischen Muslim." *KM: Themen, Dokumente, Informationen* 6: 189-92.

1983.   "Ibn Taymiyya's Critique of Falsafa." *Hamdard Islamicus* (Karachi) 6: 3-14.

1983.   "Proceedings of the International Congress for the Study of the Qur'ān." *Hamdard Islamicus* (Karachi) 6: 97-101.

1984.   "The Rights of Non-Muslims in Islam: An Opening Statement." *Journal of Muslim Minority Affairs* (London) (1984): 7-20.

1985.   "Colloquium on 'Holiness in Islam and Christianity.'" *Journal of Ecumenical Studies* (Philadelphia) 22: 678-79.

1985.   "Ibn Taymiyya: Islamic Reformer." *Studia Missionalia* (Vatican City) 34: 213-32.

1985.   "Mary of the Koran: A Meeting Point between Christianity and Islam." *Theological Studies* (Milwaukee, Wis.) 46: 387-88.

1987.   "Pope John Paul II's Teaching about Islam in Addresses to Muslims." *Islam and the Modern Age* (New Delhi) (February): 67-76.

1987.   "The Role of Mary in Popular Islamic Devotion in Southeast Asia." In *Maria nell'ebraismo e nell'islam oggi*, 167-75. Rome: Edizioni Marianum.

1988.   "Christian-Muslim Dialogue since Vatican II." *The Month* (May): 671-76.

1988.   "La sainteté dans le monde moderne." *La spiritualité: une exigence de notre temps*. Tunis: Centre des Etudes et Recherches Economiques et Sociales.

1989.   "Sufi Experience of Self." In *Self and Consciousness: Indian Interpretations*, edited by Augustine Thottakara, 193-205. Bangalore: Dharmaram Publications.

1990.   "The Turkish Minority in Bulgaria." *Islam and Christian-Muslim Relations* (Birmingham, UK) 1: 269-79.

1991.   "Historical Background and Religious Aspects of the Gulf War." *SEDOS Bulletin* (Rome) 23: 79-84.

1991.   "Il mondo arabo musulmano di fronte ai problemi della crisi del Golfo Persico." *La Civiltà Cattolica* (Rome) (March 16): 584-92.

1991.   Michel, Thomas, and Bettina Halbe. "Zwischen Tradition und Reform: Der Islam in Asien." *Internationale katholische Zeitschrift 'Communio'* (Freiburg) 20: 500-513.

1992.   "Christian-Muslim Dialogue in a Changing World." *Theology Digest* (St. Louis, Mo.) 39, 4 (Winter): 303-20.

1992.   "Islamic Fundamentalism." *SEDOS Bulletin* (Rome) 24: 141-50.

1993.   "Católicos y musulmanes ante al problema de los derechos humanos." *Boletin Informativo* (Madrid) (January-April).

1993.   "Economic Questions and Interreligious Dialogue." In *Rerum Novarum: New Conditions of Life in a Changing World*. Ankara: Ankara Üniversitesi Basımevi, 165-73.

1995.   "A Christian Encounter with Islamic Spirituality." *Religiosa: Indonesian Journal on Religious Harmony* (Yogyakarta) (August): 52-72.

1995.   "Presenting One's Faith to Another: A Witness." *Islamochristiana* (Vatican City) 21: 15-21.

1996.   "Post-Migranti: I musulmani europei alla ricerca di una nuova sintesi." *L'occidente di fronte all'islam* (Milan): 202-21.

1998.   "Accommodation or Confrontation: Indonesian Muslims and Politics in the New Order." In *Faith, Power, and Violence: Muslims and Christians in a Plural Society, Past and Present*, edited by John J. Donahue and Christian W. Troll, 207-22. Rome: Pontificio Instituto Orientale.

1999.   "Muslim-Christian Dialogue and Cooperation in the Thought of Bediuzzaman Said Nursi." *The Muslim World* (Hartford, Conn.) 89: 325-35.

2000.   "The Roots of Muslim Anger and Its Challenge for Christians." *SEDOS Bulletin* (Rome) 32: 40-44.

2003.   "Fethullah Gülen as Educator." In *Turkish Islam and the Secular State*, edited by M. Hakan Yavuz and John L. Esposito, 69-84. Syracuse, N.Y.: Syracuse University Press.

2004.   "Islamic Revival and Its Implications for Christian-Muslim Dialogue." In *Ethical Approaches to Population, Poverty and Conflict*, edited by Stan D'Souza, 304-12. Delhi: Indian Social Institute.

2005.   "Sufism and Modernity in the Thought of Fethullah Gülen." *The Muslim World* (Hartford, Conn.) 95, no. 3 (July): 341-58.

2005.   "Turkish Islam in Dialogue with Modern Society: The Neo-Sufi Spirituality of the Gülen Movement." In *Islam and Enlightenment*, edited by Erik Borgman and Pim Valkenberg, 71-80. London: SCM Press.

2005.   "Der türkische Islam im Dialog mit der modernen Gesellschaft. Die neo-sufistische Spiritualität der Gülen-Bewegung." *Concilium* (December): 526-34.

2007.   "The Challenge of Interfaith Dialogue." *Asian Christian Review* (Kanagawa, Japan) (Winter): 24-30.

2007.   "Fethullah Gülen: Following in the Footsteps of Rumi." In *Peaceful Coexistence: Fethullah Gülen's Initiatives in the Contemporary World*, edited by Ihsan Yilmaz, 183-91. Leeds: Leeds Metropolitan University Press.

2009.   "Der Flügel des Vogels: Gülen über Aufrichtigkeit." *CIBEDO-Beiträge zum Gespräch zwischen Christen und Muslimen* (Frankfurt) 3: 99-108.

2010.   (forthcoming). "Catholic Approaches to Interreligious Peacebuilding: Lessons from Indonesia's 'Sad Years.'" In *Peacebuilding: Theology, Ethics and Praxis*, edited by Robert S. Schreiter, Scott Appleby, and Gerard Powers.

Index

Other Titles in the Faith Meets Faith Series